Pro Office 365 Development

Second Edition

Mark J. Collins

Michael Mayberry

Apress®

Pro Office 365 Development

ISBN-13 (pbk): 978-1-4842-0245-6

ISBN-13 (electronic): 978-1-4842-0244-9

Trademarked names, logos, and images may appear in this book. Rather than use a trademark symbol with every occurrence of a trademarked name, logo, or image we use the names, logos, and images only in an editorial fashion and to the benefit of the trademark owner, with no intention of infringement of the trademark.

The use in this publication of trade names, trademarks, service marks, and similar terms, even if they are not identified as such, is not to be taken as an expression of opinion as to whether or not they are subject to proprietary rights.

While the advice and information in this book are believed to be true and accurate at the date of publication, neither the authors nor the editors nor the publisher can accept any legal responsibility for any errors or omissions that may be made. The publisher makes no warranty, express or implied, with respect to the material contained herein.

Managing Director: Welmoed Spahr
Lead Editor: Gwenan Spearing
Development Editor: Douglas Pundick
Technical Reviewer: Sahil Malik
Editorial Board: Steve Anglin, Mark Beckner, Ewan Buckingham, Gary Cornell, Louise Corrigan, Jim DeWolf, Jonathan Gennick, Jonathan Hassell, Robert Hutchinson, Michelle Lowman, James Markham, Matthew Moodie, Jeff Olson, Jeffrey Pepper, Douglas Pundick, Ben Renow-Clarke, Dominic Shakeshaft, Gwenan Spearing, Matt Wade, Steve Weiss
Coordinating Editor: Melissa Maldonado
Copy Editor: Lori Cavanaugh
Compositor: SPi Global
Indexer: SPi Global
Artist: SPi Global
Cover Designer: Anna Ishchenko

Distributed to the book trade worldwide by Springer Science+Business Media New York, 233 Spring Street, 6th Floor, New York, NY 10013. Phone 1-800-SPRINGER, fax (201) 348-4505, e-mail orders-ny@springer-sbm.com, or visit www.springeronline.com. Apress Media, LLC is a California LLC and the sole member (owner) is Springer Science + Business Media Finance Inc (SSBM Finance Inc). SSBM Finance Inc is a Delaware corporation.

For information on translations, please e-mail rights@apress.com, or visit www.apress.com.

Apress and friends of ED books may be purchased in bulk for academic, corporate, or promotional use. eBook versions and licenses are also available for most titles. For more information, reference our Special Bulk Sales–eBook Licensing web page at www.apress.com/bulk-sales.

Any source code or other supplementary material referenced by the author in this text is available to readers at www.apress.com. For detailed information about how to locate your book's source code, go to www.apress.com/source-code/.

To my precious wife, Donna—Every day with you is a treasured gift!

—Mark J. Collins

To Camille—yesterday brings happiness, today excites, and tomorrow stirs anticipation.

—Michael Mayberry

Contents at a Glance

Contents

About the Authors

Mark J. Collins has been developing software solutions for over 30 years. Some of the key technology areas of his career include .NET, SQL Server, and SharePoint. He currently serves as a senior architect for multiple high-tech organizations. He has authored numerous books on .NET and SharePoint. You can see more info on his web site, www.TheCreativePeople.com. For questions and comments, contact Mark at markc@thecreativepeople.com.

Michael Mayberry has been developing software with Microsoft technologies for over 14 years. Over those years he has consistently adopted new solutions and tools to solve increasingly larger problems. Michael has always valued team building and sharing his knowledge with others. Recently, he expanded his focus to include writing and reviewing. He has written or coauthored other books and has been a technical reviewer for many projects. When he is not working, Michael enjoys spending time with his beautiful wife and five children. For questions and comments, contact Michael at michael.mayberry@outlook.com.

About the Technical Reviewer

Sahil Malik, the founder and principal of `Winsmarts.com`, has been a Microsoft MVP and INETA Speaker for the past 10 years, author and reviewer of many books and numerous articles in both the .NET and SharePoint space, consultant and trainer who delivers training and talks at conferences internationally. Sahil has trained for the best names in the Microsoft technology space, and has architected and delivered SharePoint based solutions for extremely high-profile clients. Sahil has worked in 16 countries, 5 continents, and has authored 15 books on topics ranging from .NET, SQL Server, and SharePoint 2007, 2010, and 2013.

Acknowledgments

First and foremost, I acknowledge my Lord and Savior, Jesus Christ. The divine and eternal perspective on life, which can only be found in Him, is an anchor, steadfast and sure. I humbly conclude that His hand has guided me, often carrying me, through every endeavor, great and small.

I want to say a very big thank you to my beautiful wife, Donna. I can honestly say that I would not be who I am if it were not for what you have sown into my life. I am truly blessed to be able to share my life with you. Thank you for your loving support and for making life fun!

Also, I want to thank Michael Mayberry for his tremendous help on this project. As with every project that we have done together, I believe the result is always greater than the sum or our efforts.

Next, I'd like to thank all the people at Apress who made this book possible and for all their hard work that turned it into the finished product you see now. Everyone at Apress has made writing this book a pleasure.

—Mark J. Collins

I first bow my head in thanks to Jesus Christ for giving meaning to life. In a world that so desperately needs love, you showed us how much God loves us all.

I thank my wife Camille. You make our home a great place to work, write and play. Thank you for your encouragement and support.

Mark Collins, working with you is always a joy. You always raise the bar and then help me to reach it.

With so many books published, one might think that books just happen. The truth is, even the writing is just one of the many moving parts of the process. Thank you to everyone at Apress who worked so hard to make this project happen. I truly appreciate your effort in making this book possible.

—Michael Mayberry

Introduction

Office 365 brings together a fully integrated suite of office automation tools including the key server components – SharePoint, Exchange, and Lync. Volumes have been written on each of these products. In addition, there is an impressive list of client applications that can be leveraged including:

- Access
- Excel
- Visio
- SharePoint Designer
- Visual Studio

There is so much that you can do with this platform that it's not possible to cover every aspect in a single book. However, we have tried to pack in as much as possible and demonstrate the features that will be most useful. The topics cover a wide range of subjects, including web databases, declarative workflows, custom Lync and Exchange applications, and public-facing web sites.

How This Book Is Structured

Each chapter presents a solution that leverages one or more features of the Office 365 platform using one of the various development tools that are available to you. These were carefully chosen to demonstrate a good cross-section of the platform capabilities as well as presenting a broad overview of the toolset.

Chapter 1 provides an overview of the Office 365 platform, explaining the various server and client components. In Chapter 2 you'll use the site designer to create a public-facing web site.

Chapters 3, 6, and 7, use Visual Studio 2013 to build custom applications. In Chapter 3 you'll create a SharePoint app using HTML, CSS, and JavaScript. Chapters 6 and 7 each create a WPF app that show you how to build custom Exchange and Lync applications, respectively.

Chapter 4 takes you through the process of creating a workflow application using Visio and SharePoint Designer. This also demonstrates some of the key SharePoint concepts such as content types. In Chapter 5, you'll use Access 2013 to create a web-enabled database application.

In the final three chapters, we'll explain how to use the new REST APIs to integrate the data in your Office 365 site with a wide-range of client applications. This API provides a uniform developer experience when accessing cloud-based SharePoint, Exchange, and Lync servers.

Each chapter invites you to work through the exercise yourself with step-by-step instructions. You can simply read the chapter and learn a great deal. But following along yourself will be even more beneficial. During this process we'll explain some of the hows and whys.

Prerequisites

To work through the exercises in this book you will need an Office 365 account. A few of the solutions will require one of the Enterprise plans but most can be implemented on any plan. Some of the chapters will require additional Office products such as Access or Excel. These are included with some of the Office 365 plans and can be added to others for a monthly fee.

■ **Tip**   You can get a free 30-day trial subscription for either the Small Business or Enterprise plan. If you need more time you can generally get a 30-day extension. Also, the Small Business plan is a monthly subscription and you can cancel it at any time.

You will also need Visual Studio 2013 to work through the coded solutions. Some of the exercises require other free products and these will be explained in the appropriate chapters.

CHAPTER 1

Introducing Office 365 for Developers

Office 365 provides lots of opportunities for developers to build custom applications. In this book, we've selected some of the most useful development technologies such as Visual Studio, SharePoint Designer, and Access. We've also chosen some of the more common customization scenarios including workflows, SharePoint lists, Exchange and Lync integration, and web databases. Each chapter then pairs these together to demonstrate how to build a working application. Our goal is to present a fairly broad spectrum of both tool sets and applications so you'll have a good sense of what you can accomplish in an Office 365 environment.

Before you dive into developing some nifty applications on Office 365, we want to first explain what Office 365 is and how it works.

Office 365 Architecture

Office 365 is an interesting collection of both server and client applications that allows you to experience a fully integrated Office solution. This is provided as a hosted solution, which requires little or no IT infrastructure.

Traditional Office Server Environment

To fully explain Office 365, I need to start by describing the traditional on-premise Office server environment. If you had an unlimited budget and installed all of the Office server products, your network might look something like Figure 1-1.

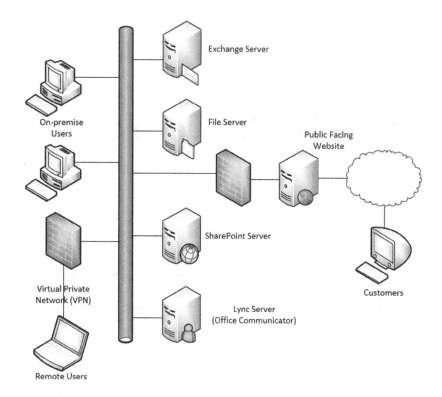

Figure 1-1. *The traditional Office server environment*

You would have

- An Exchange server to handle incoming and outgoing e-mails.

- One or more file servers for storing documents.

- A SharePoint server for collaboration features such as shared documents and task lists.

- A Lync server to support instant messaging and online meetings.

For larger organizations you would likely cluster these servers to provide redundancy as well as increased capacity. So instead of a single Exchange server, for example, you might have two or more. You may also need to support geographically distributed scenarios. You can see that the number of servers you would need could become extensive.

You would also have a public-facing web site for your online presence. This would provide basic content for your customers such as details provided on the Contact Us page; your company's mission statement, core values, products, or services offered; company history; and so on.

On each of the client workstations you would install the Office client applications such as Outlook, Word, Excel, and One Note. To support remote users, you would need to provide a virtual private network (VPN), which would allow them to connect into your network and work just like the local users. You would also need to allow for the growing use of mobile devices.

The Office 365 Environment

All of the functionality described in Figure 1-1 can be easily provisioned on Office 365. The same feature set implemented on Office 365 would look like Figure 1-2.

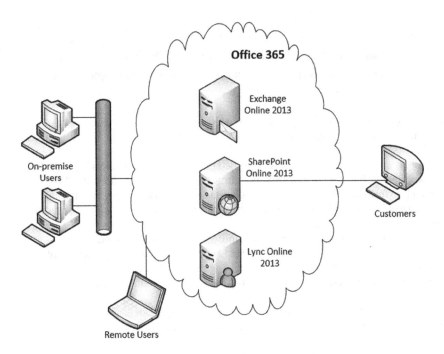

Figure 1-2. *The Office 365 solution*

The most obvious change in this environment is that the servers have been moved to a hosted environment. Instead of an on-site server running Exchange Server 2013, for example, you'll use Exchange Online 2013, which is hosted on a remote server farm. These online versions of the Office server products are implemented with the same code base as their on-site counterparts. When you set up an Outlook client, you must specify the location of the Exchange server. In an Office 365 environment, you provide the URL that was specified when your Office 365 account was created. The fact that the server is now hosted off-site is essentially transparent. You can send and receive e-mails, check the calendars of team members, and schedule meetings just like you would in a traditional on-site Exchange solution.

The file servers are removed from this diagram because the SharePoint server is used for this purpose. The document libraries in SharePoint are a great place to store most of your files for both on-premise and browser-based users.

■ **Note**   There are some limitations regarding the size of files you can store on Office 365. For more details, see the article at http://office.microsoft.com/en-us/sharepoint-online-enterprise-help/sharepoint-online-soft-ware-boundaries-and-limits-HA102694293.aspx.

There are a couple of really nice benefits that are inherent in a cloud-based solution: support for remote users and role-based access. Notice that there is no VPN support in Figure 1-2 because it is not needed. Clients access the Office 365 servers (Exchange Online 2013, SharePoint Online 2013, and Lync Online 2013) through an Internet connection. Office 365 doesn't care whether you are connecting from work, your home, the public library, or your favorite coffee shop.

■ **Note** You will need to be authenticated in order to access these servers, which is typically done through a login and password. If you are on an Active Directory domain, you can synchronize your AD users with Office 365, which will enable a single sign-on to your domain. Once authenticated in AD, you can access Office 365 without supplying your credentials.

Providing access to remote users in Office 365 is really easy. There's no need for VPN software or firewalls. Best of all, there's no threat of a remote user infecting your network with viruses or malware because they are not connected to your network.

The other inherent benefit is a little more subtle. In the network described in Figure 1-1, a public-facing web site was implemented using a dedicated web server that is separated from your internal network with a firewall. This is a standard practice that provides protection from someone hacking into the web server and accessing the internal network. In Office 365, the public-facing web site is implemented as a SharePoint site hosted on the same SharePoint Online server that is hosting your internal sites.

In a hosted environment, a SharePoint farm will contain potentially hundreds of sites. This is referred to as a multi-tenant environment. So how does someone@companyA.com have access to their site while someone@companyB.com does not? Providing separation of customer data is a core competency of hosting services. It is accomplished through advanced technology, including Active Directory, state-of-the-art anti-virus solutions, and continual monitoring and auditing.

As a result, you can create a public-facing SharePoint site that non-authenticated users can access while your internal sites are kept safely hidden. You can create multiple sites and configure each user's access using role-based security.

Office 365 Client Applications

In addition to hosting the server components you can also use the web-based Office applications. Your e-mails, for example, are stored in the Exchange Online server and you can access them either through the Outlook client application or the Outlook Web App that is available in the Office 365 environment. You can configure this differently for each user. You can also use both. A typical configuration would use the Outlook application from an on-site PC while using the web app from a remote laptop or mobile device, as demonstrated in Figure 1-3.

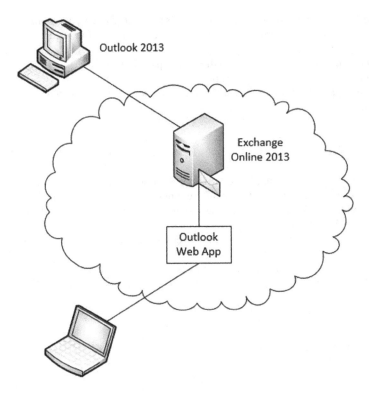

Figure 1-3. *Accessing Exchange Online*

The key point to remember here is that the data is stored in the cloud. Whichever application you use, it is accessing the same data.

■ **Tip**   In Chapter 6, we will show you how to build your own custom e-mail client. While the user experience will be different, the data resides on the server and can still be accessed through the other e-mail client applications.

Office 365 also provides a lightweight web-based version of Word, Excel, OneNote, and PowerPoint, called Office Web apps. These have a limited feature set compared to their client-based counterparts but read and write files in the same format. This allows you to create, view, and edit a file using the web app and then open it with the client application to perform advanced editing capabilities. Other users can then view the modified documents.

Storing Documents in SharePoint

Office 365 is designed to support browser-only clients. In this configuration there are no local applications; the client is simply a web browser. The benefit of this approach from an IT perspective is that there is no software to install or maintain and no data that needs to be backed up. From an application perspective, this means that all your documents must be stored in the cloud.

Office uses SharePoint Online as the document repository. When you create documents using the web apps, Office 365 automatically stores them in a document library on the SharePoint site. You can set up multiple document libraries configuring different levels of access to each. Libraries can also contain a hierarchy of subfolders so you can keep your documents organized. You can use this structure to control what documents are shared and with whom. Document libraries on SharePoint also provide advanced collaboration features such as checking out files and version tracking.

Storing documents on SharePoint is pretty much a necessity when using the web apps. It is also the recommended approach with full-featured client applications. These applications can be configured to access the document libraries directly, much like the web apps. This provides file sharing, data backup, and a consistent experience across both client and web applications.

Office 365 and Windows Azure

Both Office 365 and Azure are cloud-based offerings from Microsoft, and you might be wondering how they relate to each other. Can they be used together? Well, they were designed to solve two different needs. Azure is a platform that is primarily targeted towards mission-critical solutions. It provides an operating system, relational databases, and file storage. You must supply the application(s) that use these resources. In contrast, Office 365 provides a full-featured application suite that offers the features needed by most organizations. You can implement your own customizations, as we will demonstrate throughout this book.

Happily, the two platforms can be used together with each one serving the needs it was designed to address. A fully cloud-based infrastructure might look like Figure 1-4.

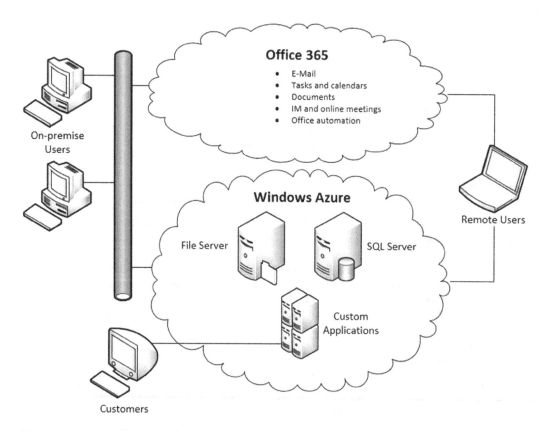

Figure 1-4. Using Office 365 and Azure

The Office 365 platform provides the office automation and team collaboration tools that you'll use to manage your business. Your mission-critical applications, including custom solutions, can be deployed on the Windows Azure platform. Users can then connect to both to perform their daily tasks.

Office 365 Online Servers

The server products (Exchange Online 2013, Lync Online 2013, and SharePoint Online 2013) form the core of the Office 365 platform. As a developer, you will be using and extending the features provided by the servers to implement custom applications. These products are very similar to their on-premise counterparts. The differences stem primarily from the fact that they are running in a multi-tenant environment. It's a little bit like living in a large apartment building; having close neighbors places some restrictions on what you're allowed to do.

We will get into this in more detail in the rest of this book but I wanted to give you an overview of these products. This will help you see what you're up against as you begin developing on the Office 365 platform.

SharePoint Online 2013

SharePoint is the workhorse of an Office-based collaborative solution. It's a great place to store and share documents, but it's also an effective platform for gathering and analyzing data. And workflows in SharePoint can automate processes and keep data flowing through your organization.

Using Custom Applications

In addition to the typical lists and document libraries that are synonymous with SharePoint, there are a large and growing set of custom applications that you can include in your SharePoint site. In SharePoint 2013 these are referred to as **Apps**. These apps can be added to a SharePoint site from the Site Contents page. You will be creating your own custom apps in subsequent chapters of this book. For now, to give a quick glimpse of how apps are used, you'll download, install, and configure one from the SharePoint store.

Go to the Team Site that was setup when you provisioned an Office 365 account. Click the Settings button in the ribbon and then select the Add an app link. You should see a page similar to Figure 1-5.

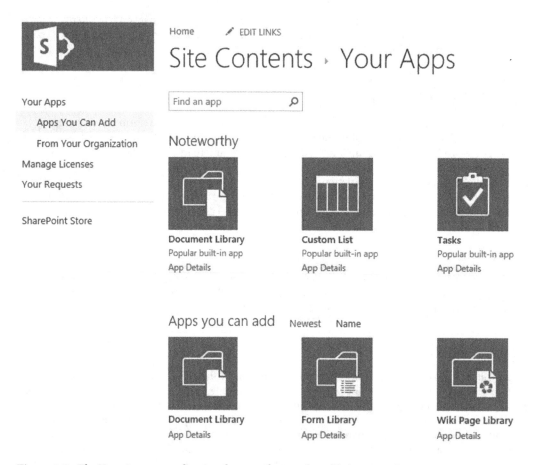

Figure 1-5. *The Your Apps page, showing the apps that can be added to your site*

■ **Note** In SharePoint there are often multiple ways to get to the same place and depending on how you navigate to a page, the contents may be filtered based on where you came from. Also, SharePoint Online 2013 is available in many different configurations with differing features sets and licensing options. Throughout this book, we will focus on development techniques that are applicable in most of these environments. Be aware however, that all of the options shown in the screenshots may not match what are available to you.

The "Noteworthy" section includes the most common apps which include the basic Document Library and Custom List that you are undoubtedly familiar with. The "Apps you can add" section contains more specialized lists and libraries such as a Picture Library, Calendar, Contacts, and Announcements.

You can also download additional apps from the SharePoint store. Click the SharePoint Store link on the left side of the page. You will see a collection of custom applications that are available for download. The "Featured Apps" are shown first as shown in Figure 1-6 but the page allows you to filter and search for an appropriate app.

Apress 365 Team Site ▸ Add Apps ▸

SharePoint Store

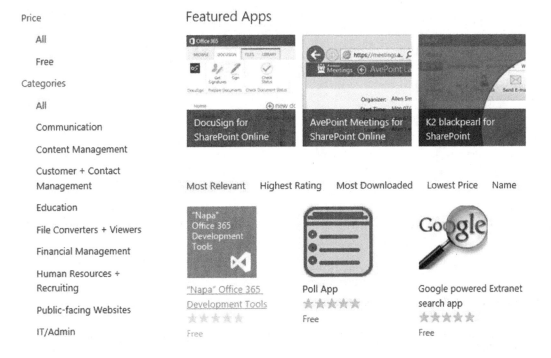

Figure 1-6. *The apps available in the SharePoint store*

If you find an app that looks useful just click on it and a page similar to the one shown in Figure 1-7 will be displayed with details about the app.

Poll App

from Shreyan Advisory Corporation

Find an app

Shreyan Poll App   · ☑

Select a Question to Activate or Deactivate

Select...   ▼

| Add a New Question | Set as Active Question |

Questions:

1 What is your mother toungh?   🖉 📊 ✖

2 Do you believe in politics?   🖉 📊 ✖

3 Which OS do you like the most?   🖉 📊 ✖

Free

ADD IT

By acquiring this app you agree to its permissions.

VERSION	1.0.0.0
RATING	★★★★★ (1)
RELEASE DATE	August, 2013
CATEGORY	Productivity,Content Management,Human Resources + Recruiting
SUPPORT	App Website

MORE ACTIONS ▾

Details   Reviews

DESCRIPTION
Shreyan Poll Web Part allows to quickly publish simple user polls/voting. The poll results

Figure 1-7. *Reviewing the details of the Poll App*

Select the Poll App and to install the app, click the ADD IT button. You will be presented with a confirmation page before the app is installed.

■ **Note** Depending on the SharePoint configuration that you are using and your access rights, some apps may not be allowed. In this case, you'll see a note explaining this and the ADD IT button will be disabled.

Installing the app makes it available to be included in your site. After it is installed you'll see a page like the one shown in Figure 1-8. To add this to your Team Site, make sure the check box is checked before clicking the Return to site button.

Apress 365 Team Site ▸ Add Apps ▸   **?**

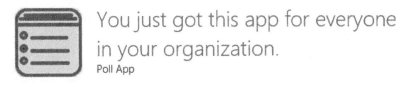

You just got this app for everyone
in your organization.
Poll App

☑ Add this app to Apress 365 Team Site

You can add this app later on any site you can manage, or return to the SharePoint Store to get
more apps.

[Return to site]

Figure 1-8. Confirming the installation

Go to the Team Site and select the Site Content link. You should see that this app has been added to your site.

Adding an App Part

There are three different types of SharePoint 2013 apps that are categorized by their **shape**. This is arguably a rather
poor name as the differences are not really related to shape but rather their footprint on the SharePoint UI. The
defined shapes are:

- Immersive (full-page): the app uses the entire area within the SharePoint page. The standard
  lists and document libraries are examples of full-page apps.

- App part: The app resides in an IFrame as part of a SharePoint page. From the users'
  perspective, app parts resemble the earlier web parts although they are functionally different.

- Extension app: These are not really applications, just custom actions that are provided as
  extensions to the ribbon or menu. These actions can call into your custom apps.

To use a full-page app, you can simply select it from the Site Content (or provide a link to it). However, the
Poll App that you just installed, uses the App part shape, so in order to use it, you need to include it on another page.
As we'll show you, this is a fairly simple task. You'll add it to the Home page of your Team Site.

1. Go to your Team Site and look just below the title bar. You should notice the Browse and
   Page links as shown in Figure 1-9.

Figure 1-9. *The Browse and Page links*

2. Click the Page link and you'll see a ribbon bar appear like the one shown in Figure 1-10. This contains an assortment of commands for modifying the page.

Figure 1-10. *The Page ribbon*

3. Click the Edit button in the ribbon and a couple more ribbon tabs will appear. Select the Insert tab and click the App Part button as shown in Figure 1-11.

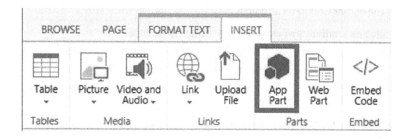

Figure 1-11. *Inserting an app part*

4. A list of available app parts will then appear. Select the Poll App from the list as shown in Figure 1-12 and then click the Add button.

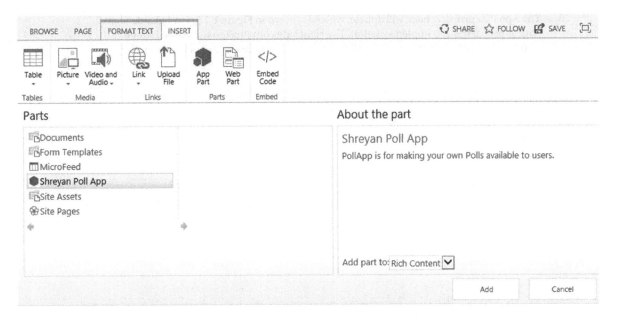

Figure 1-12. Selecting the App Poll app part

5. The app part is now included on the page and displays some instructions for configuring it. Like most app parts, there are some configuration options that allow you to define how it looks on the page and how it functions. In this case, you'll also need to enter the poll question and the allowed answers. There is a small triangle to the right of the app part. Click this to access a menu of options and then click the Edit Web Part link as shown in Figure 1-13.

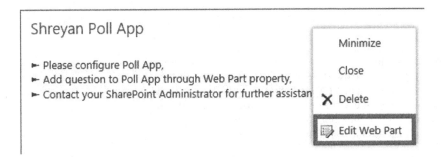

Figure 1-13. Using the app part context menu

■ **Tip** The terms **App Part** and **Web Part** seem to be used interchangeably. App Part is the new term that has been adopted but there are still vestiges of the old terminology. In Visual Studio 2013 they are still called Web Parts. Whichever term is used, just know that they are not the same thing as the old Web Parts from SharePoint 2010.

6. The App Part property page will appear, which is shown in Figure 1-14. The left side of this page is part of the app implementation. The right side contains the standard SharePoint App Part menu that allows you to configure some of the appearance and layout options.

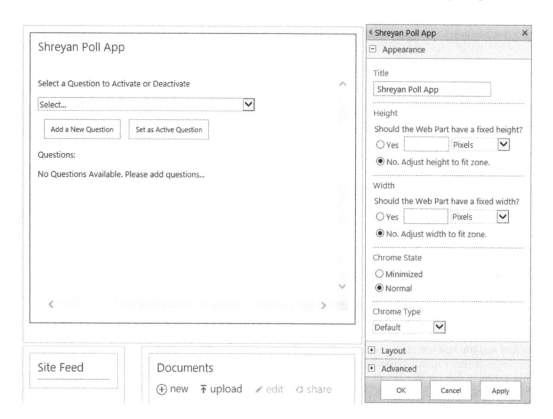

Figure 1-14. *Configuring the App Part*

7. Follow the instructions to add a question and define a set of responses. After setting up the questions, make sure you select the question in the drop down and click the Set as Active Question button. You don't need to change anything on the right-hand side but you might want to change title. We chose to call it **Apress 365 Daily Poll**. When you're done, click the Save button in the ribbon. You should now see the poll question displayed at the top of your page similar to Figure 1-15.

Apress 365 Team Site

Apress 365 Daily Poll

Question : What is your faviorite season of the year?

○ Winter

○ Spring

○ Summer

○ Fall

Vote

Figure 1-15. *The completed app part with the configured poll question*

8. Once a user has responded to the poll, the question is not presented to them again. You can configure the app so that the results are displayed once the question has been answered.

Developing Solutions in Visual Studio 2013

Visual Studio 2013 has made some significant improvements that will really help you create your own custom apps. To whet your appetite, we'll mention two of them now:

- One of the biggest changes is that you can build a SharePoint app and deploy to O365 without needing SharePoint installed on your development machine. This is a ***huge*** benefit (thank you Microsoft!). They've also improved the list designer in VS 2103 so creating a custom list in VS is now an attractive option that we will demonstrate in Chapter 3.

- There are also some major improvements in creating workflows in VS, which we'll explain in Chapter 4. Workflows are a powerful component of any office automation solution. However, in previous versions they were also very difficult to achieve, especially in SharePoint Online, due to the limitations of Sandboxed solutions.

When creating a SharePoint app in VS, you have essentially two available hosting options. They can either be hosted within SharePoint or somewhere else, such as Azure. SharePoint hosted apps are essentially client-side applications that can use familiar web development techniques such as MVC, HTML, JavaScript, and CSS. They have very little server-side code, except for declarative access to the SharePoint resources. However, this is ideal for many applications which do not need resources outside of the SharePoint environment.

Non-hosted applications run on a separate web server and can have full access to non-SharePoint resources such as databases and file systems. However, accessing SharePoint resources such as lists, will require authentication, which we'll cover in Chapter 9. Once you have setup a channel between your SharePoint site and your web application, your can read (and update) data in SharePoint.

Customization Scenarios

SharePoint Online provides a variety of ways to develop custom solutions. We will explain each of these in detail throughout this book with practical examples that you can follow. Some of the techniques we'll cover include:

- SharePoint Designer: This is a powerful tool for editing SharePoint sites. SharePoint Designer allows you to create and edit SharePoint objects such as lists, fields, and content types.

- Visual Studio: You can develop SharePoint solutions using Visual Studio 2013. This allows you to access the SharePoint object model using familiar C# syntax. Visual Studio 2013 provides project items for creating content types, lists, and Web Parts. These can be verified using standard F5 debugging and easily deployed to your O365 site.

- Workflows: You can use Visio and SharePoint Designer 2013 to build workflow solutions in O365.

- Access Web Databases: You can create a web database in Access 2013, including tables, forms, queries, and reports, and then export the database to SharePoint Online. This is a great way to quickly implement a sophisticated web application.

This is not an exhaustive list, but represents a broad coverage of the most common development scenarios.

Exchange Online 2013

Exchange Online 2013 exposes its features to client applications through a set of web services known as Exchange Web Services (EWS). You can use these web services by adding a service reference to the EWS. Visual Studio will then generate a set of proxy classes that you'll use to communicate with the web service. However, Exchange Online also provides a managed API that provides an easier and more intuitive way to use EWS. So your application can either call the web service directly or use the managed API, as shown in Figure 1-16.

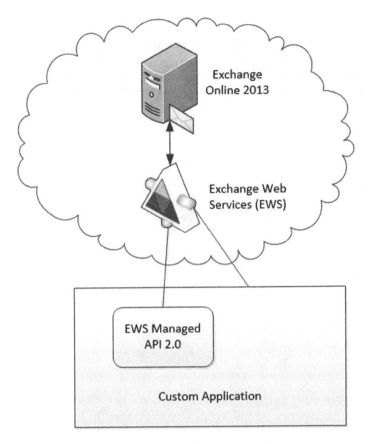

Figure 1-16. *Using the Exchange Web Services (EWS)*

Customization Scenarios

Exchange Online 2013 exposes many features through EWS to client applications such as Outlook and Outlook Web App. Your custom application can use these as well. Some of the more common ways you can integrate Exchange functionality in your application include:

- Accessing the mailbox items stored in Exchange. Think of Exchange as a specialized database containing objects such as e-mails, appointments, tasks, and contacts, which are organized in a hierarchy of folders. You can view, modify, and create these objects programmatically through EWS or the managed API.

- Availability is another Exchange feature that allows you to see when someone (or a group of people) will be available based on their calendars. You can also use this feature to suggest windows when the specified group of people and resources will be available.

- Exchange provides notifications when certain events occur, such as the arrival of a new message. Your custom application can receive these notifications and take appropriate actions.

Using Autodiscover

To optimize availability and capacity, especially in a cloud-based solution, the specific URL of the appropriate EWS can be dynamic. For this reason you should never hard-code this URL. Instead, when connecting to Exchange, you'll use a process called autodiscover. In this process, the managed API performs some handshaking with the Exchange Online servers to determine the optimum path to the appropriate server, as illustrated in Figure 1-17.

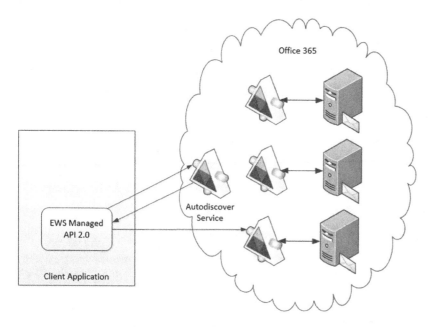

Figure 1-17. *The autodiscover process*

The managed API makes a request to the autodiscover service on Office 365. Through a series of callbacks, the URL to the appropriate web service is returned. The API then connects to the specified web server.

Lync Online 2013

Lync provides the ability for various types of conversations between two or more individuals. A conversation can include one or more of the following types (referred to as modality):

- Instant Message
- Audio
- Video
- Online meeting
- Desktop sharing
- File transfer

Lync Architecture

Lync Online 2013 provides the server component and is hosted by the Office 365 platform. The Lync 2013 Client must be installed on each device that will participate in a conversation. The overall architecture is shown in Figure 1-18.

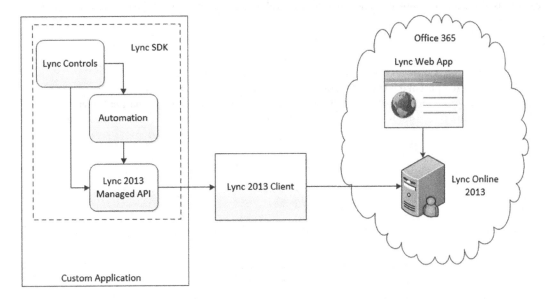

Figure 1-18. *Lync architecture*

The Lync 2013 client application controls the connection to the Lync Online 2013 server. It first provides the user's credentials to the server and establishes the connection. In many cases, it uses the current user's login credentials if this has been configured or cached credentials are enabled. In this case, this application performs its role in the background. If credentials are needed, it will display a window and prompt the user for a login and password.

Lync SDK

The Lync SDK provides some useful tools for developing custom applications that use Lync. The SDK consists of three components.

- Lync 2013 Managed API: A powerful yet easy-to-use API that allows your custom application to use the features provided by the Lync 2013 client application.

- Automation library: Provides the ability to launch and manage a conversation.

- Lync controls: A set of controls that can be dropped directly on your application, much like you would a TextBox or ComboBox control. The available controls include:

  - Presence indicator

  - Contact search results

  - Contact list

- Custom contact list

- Contact information

- Start IM or Audio Call controls

The Lync controls also support contextual conversations. This allows data from your applications to be passed into the conversation.

Automation

The Automation library, which is part of the Lync SDK, provides an easy way to embed Lync functionality in your custom application. You use the API to instruct the Lync 2013 client application to start a particular type of conversation. This will launch a new window that displays and manages that conversation. This is depicted in Figure 1-19.

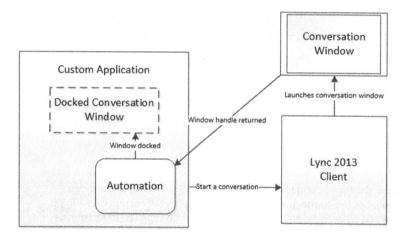

Figure 1-19. *Using Lync automation*

A handle to the new window is returned to your custom application so you can control the conversation in your code. You can also dock the new window inside your application's window so the UI will be completely contained by your application.

Contextual Conversations

Lync allows you to embed information into a conversation to help the participants better understand the context of your question. For example, if you wanted to ask a colleague about a particular product, the initial message can contain details of that product. There are two ways to do this.

- Launch Link allows you to include a link to launch an application from the conversation window. In this example, the link could load an inventory application and pre-load the specific product.

- Conversation Window Extension (CWE) allows you to host Silverlight application code inside the conversation window. In this case, this application could display details of the product in question.

You can use both of these techniques in the same conversation. You can include the details directly in the conversation window with a link to launch the application. The recipient can then view the details already provided but also have the option to use the application to browse for more information.

This requires that both the Silverlight application and the launched applications be configured with Lync using the Windows Registry. This is needed to prevent executing untrusted applications.

Unsupported Features

There are a couple of features in Lync Server 2013 that are not currently available in Lync Online 2013. These include:

- UCMA (Unified Communications Managed API)
- PSTN calls to an external number

These are server-side features that are locked down primarily due to the multi-tenancy of the Lync Online platform.

Summary

The Office 365 platform is a fully integrated Office solution that provides an enormous amount of functionality right out of the box. It provides the following cloud-based services:

- SharePoint Online
- Exchange Online
- Lync Online

Each of these services was designed to expose its features to custom applications. By utilizing this functionality, you can quickly implement some very useful custom applications. Throughout the remainder of this book I will be demonstrating ways to create custom Office 365 solutions.

CHAPTER 2

■ ■ ■

Creating Your Web Presence

In this chapter, we'll demonstrate an important feature of Office 365; it's a great platform to build an external public-facing web site. This is used as your online presence; the place where customers can find you, learn about your products and services, and ultimately contact you.

Designing a Web Site

Your public web site is primarily content based. The purpose of most of the other features you'll be working on in this book will be to create, modify, and use data. This one, however, is focused on displaying static content to a relatively broad audience. The pages are mostly read-only, and the majority of your work in building a content-based website is creating the content, which includes text, images, video, and other visual components.

With that in mind, you should start by deciding what the website needs to communicate. This includes the technical details such as contact information and a description of the products or services that you provide. This also includes more intangible aspects; what types of emotions should your site evoke? For example, the fictitious company for this project provides interior design services. So you'll want to include lots of pictures of pretty interiors. From the first look of the home page, you want your potential customers to say "Wow, I wish my home looked like that!"

Collecting the Content

The first step of the design process is to decide what information the web site needs to provide. Generally, this will include contact details like e-mail, phone number and physical address as appropriate. This will vary depending on the type of business and the way your organization operates. If you have one or more physical locations where you receive customers, including an interactive map will add a nice touch.

Another key content that you'll need to provide is a description of the products and/or services that you want to advertise. What do you have to offer and why should a potential customer consider doing business with you. If you have a lot of products, you should summarize the types of products that are available. You can highlight specific items that you want to promote or provide as examples. At this level, a lot of details will tend to send your audience elsewhere.

■ **Tip** If you have an e-commerce business where you sell products online, you will need a true shopping cart application. You won't be able to implement this on an Office 365 platform. The site I'm describing here will provide information about your company and then link to your shopping cart.

It's a good idea to provide some background information about your business. What is your vision, business culture, and mission? Perhaps a brief history of your organization would be helpful. Also, consider including corporate highlights and accomplishments. Mission statements, corporate strategies, and core beliefs can be used as content as long as they are written from the customer's perspective.

■ **Note**   I am using business terminology here but the same concepts also apply for non-profit organizations. What is the mission of your organization? What resources do you provide? What actions from potential constituents do you want to inspire? The content of your web site should answer these questions.

As you think through these topics, you should create a list of site pages. You don't have to finalize the content of each page but you should at least identify the pages that are needed. You can create pages from templates and fill in the details later.

If you have more than five or six pages you should also consider how these should be organized. The navigation controls provide several options for navigating to all of your site pages. Since we only have a few pages you'll use the default single-level control arranged vertically. However, if you have a lot of pages, you should think through how these can be grouped and then decide the best way to arrange the navigation controls.

In addition to the standard navigation controls, you should add custom links to key pages in your site. If your primary goal of your site is to drive potential customers to your shopping cart, then you should have easy to find buttons or links to take them there.

Uploading Images

As we said earlier, our site will have lots of pictures and the first step is to collect the images that we want to use and upload them to a document library. You don't have to do this; images can be used from your local computer. In this case, SharePoint maintains an asset library to store the images. Doing this yourself will allow you to better organize them and include additional metadata that will be helpful when maintaining your site.

Typically, when your Office 365 account is set up, two sites are created for you. The Team site is only available to authenticated users and is where you'll keep all your internal lists and libraries. The Public site can be made available to everyone and should contain the outward-facing content. Click the Sites link in the menu bar at the top of the Office 365 page and you'll see the available sites similar to Figure 2-1.

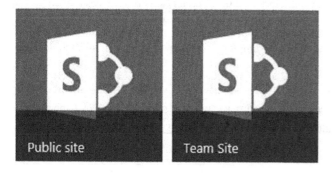

Figure 2-1. *Getting to the public website*

Click on the Public site button and your initial home page will be displayed.

■ **Tip** If you don't see the Office 365 menu bar at the top, click the Sign In link in the header.

The public site already has a picture library called Photos that you can use. To access that, click on the settings icon to the right of the menu bar (it looks like a gear). This will display a list of actions; click the Site contents link as shown in Figure 2-2.

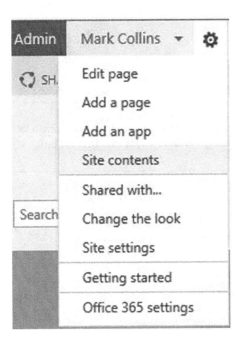

Figure 2-2. *Navigating to the site contents*

The Site Contents page shows all of the lists and libraries that have been created to store elements for your website. For example, the Pages library contain the pages used and the Posts library stores your blog posts. Click the Photos app to shows the contents of this library, which should be empty. Click the new link, which will display the Add a picture dialog box shown in Figure 2-3.

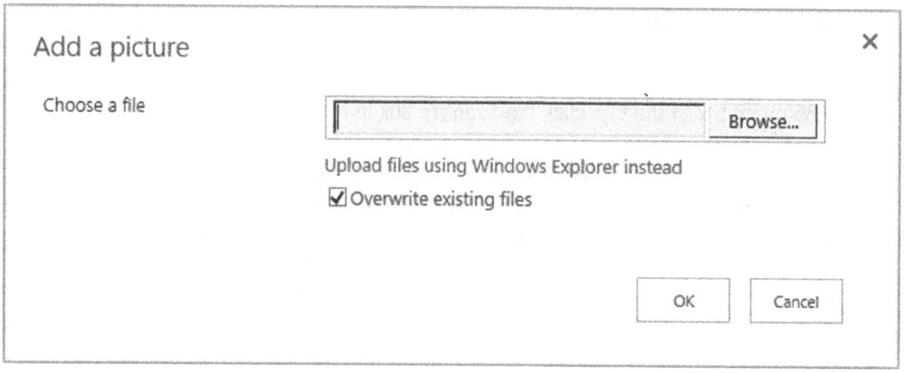

Add a picture   ×

Choose a file   [   ] Browse...

                                     Upload files using Windows Explorer instead
                                     ☑ Overwrite existing files

                                                        OK   Cancel

Figure 2-3. *The Add a picture dialog box*

Managing Images with Windows Explorer

You can click the browse button and then browse to a local folder and select an image to be uploaded. If you have a lot of files to upload, however, there's an easier way. Click the Upload files using Windows Explorer instead link.

■ **Note**   This feature is only available when using Internet Explorer.

You may see the warning shown in Figure 2-4. If so, just click the Allow button.

Figure 2-4. *Internet Explorer Security warning*

Also, this feature will only work if the Office 365 site has been configured as a trusted site. You will get an error similar to the one shown in Figure 2-5 if the trust has not been setup.

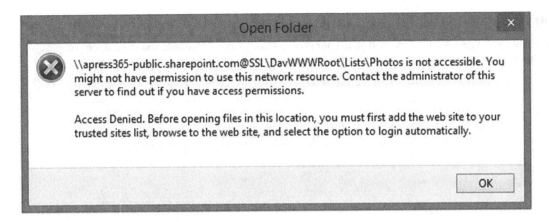

Figure 2-5. *Error displayed when the site is not trusted*

This is easy to fix. While on the Office 365 site in Internet Exporer, click the Tools menu and select the Internet Options link. Go to the Security tab and select Trusted sites. Click the Sites button and then click the Add button to include the current site in your list of trusted sites. Close these dialog boxes and then, from the Add a picture dialog box, click the Upload files using Windows Explorer instead link again. This will open Windows Explorer and it should look similar to Figure 2-6.

Figure 2-6. *Displaying your Photos library in Windows Explorer*

By going through these steps, you now have a path from Windows Explorer directly to this document library. Now you can view and edit its contents just like you would a local folder. Drag all of your images to this folder.

Managing Your Pictures

When you're done, close Windows Explorer and go to your Photos library from Office 365. You should see your images as shown in Figure 2-7.

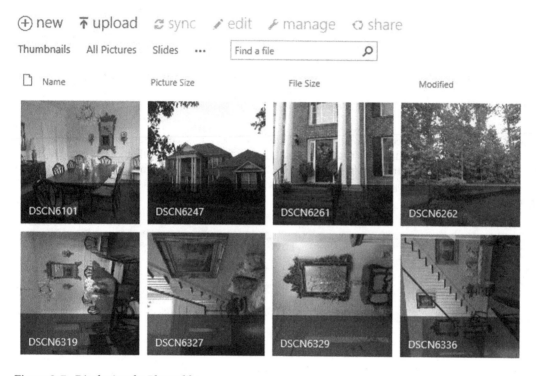

Figure 2-7. *Displaying the Photos library*

■ **Caution**   You may have noticed that some of the pictures are sideways. This is a bug in how Office 365 handles JPEG files that exists at the time of this writing, which may be fixed by the time you read this. Essentially, with newer JPEG files, when an image is rotated, instead of translating all of the pixels, an attribute is updated indicating the correct orientation. However, not all applications honor this attribute. For more information, there is a good article at http://office-watch.com/t/n.aspx?a=1766 that explains this. To resolve the issue, you'll need to convert your image to a different format such as PNG.

Once the files have been uploaded, you can append some metadata to help you organize them. If you hover over the thumbnail, you'll see an elipses that you can click to display a larger image. In this quick view pop-up dialog box there will be another elipses that you can click to bring up a context-sensitive menu. From this menu, select the Edit Properties link. Fill in the appropriate information as shown in Figure 2-8 and then click the Save button. You'll notice that the title you entered is now displayed instead of the file name.

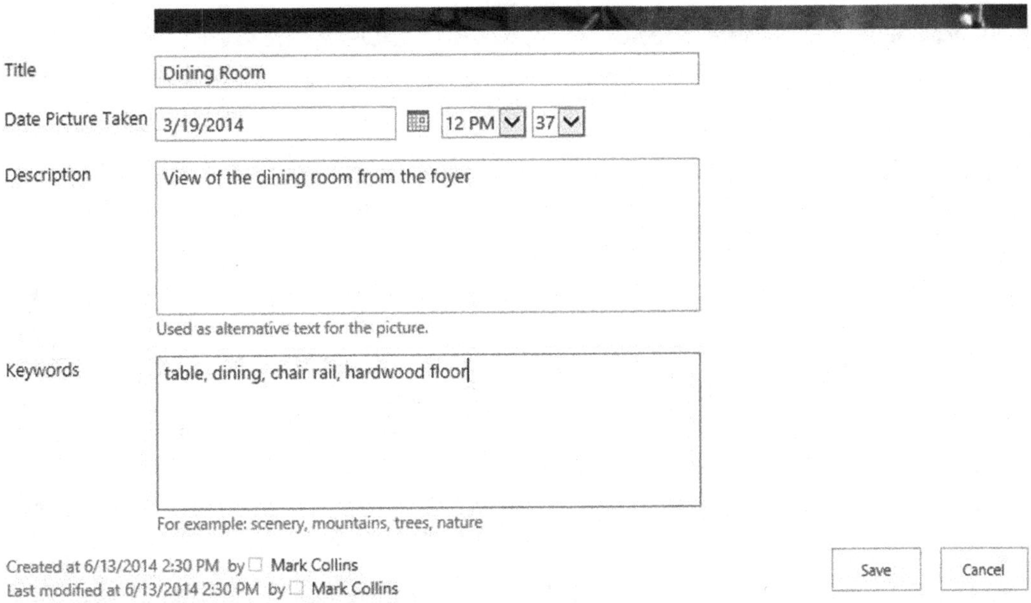

Title	Dining Room

Date Picture Taken | 3/19/2014 | 📅 | 12 PM ✕ | 37 ✕ |

Description

View of the dining room from the foyer

Used as alternative text for the picture.

Keywords

table, dining, chair rail, hardwood floor

For example: scenery, mountains, trees, nature

Created at 6/13/2014 2:30 PM by ☐ Mark Collins

Last modified at 6/13/2014 2:30 PM by ☐ Mark Collins

| Save | Cancel |

Figure 2-8. *Entering the image metadata*

Designing the Overall Site

SharePoint Online provides a design facility that allows you to easily modify the visual aspects of the web site. This tool only works with public-facing web sites. This is fairly intuitive to use so I will just walk through the steps we used to customize the site. Feel free to explore all of the capablities of the designer and try out several styles.

The initial home page will look similar to Figure 2-9.

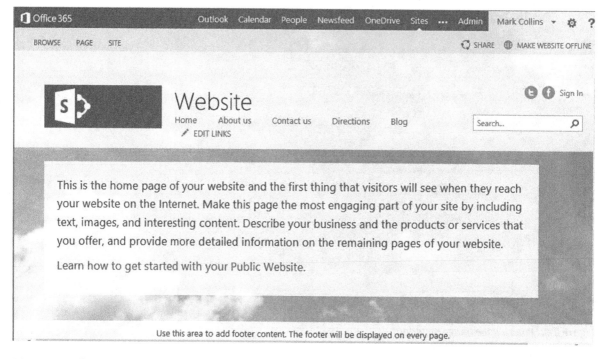

Figure 2-9. *The initial public website*

The light blue banner at the top is the page header, which is generally the same across all of your pages. The SharePoint icon on the left is the site logo. The header contains a title and a set of links which are used to navigate the site. There are also some social media links and a search field. We'll start by changing the logo and then reconfigure the site layout, color schemes, and fonts.

At the top of the page you'll find the BROWSE, PAGE, and SITE links. If you don't see these, click the Sign In link. These are only available to authenticated users. The SITE tab of ribbon is shown in Figure 2-10 and illustrates the things you can configure at the site level.

Figure 2-10. *The SITE tab of the ribbon*

Click the Edit Title button and enter a more suitable title for your site. In ours, we used **Apress Interiors**.

Changing the Logo

Click the Change Logo button, which will display the Change Logo dialog box shown in Figure 2-11.

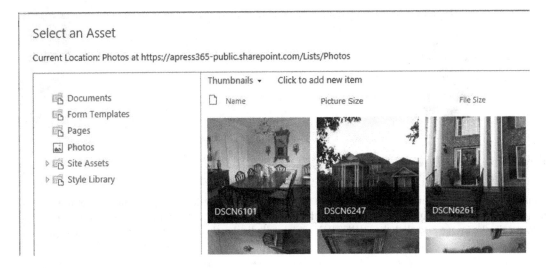

Figure 2-11. *Updating the logo image*

The dialog shows the image currently being used for the logo. Notice that there are two links for assigning an image: FROM COMPUTER and FROM SHAREPOINT. Since we have already uploaded all of our pictures, we'll use the later. This will display the Select an Asset dialog box. Select the Photos library and then click the image that you want to use as shown in Figure 2-12 and click the INSERT button.

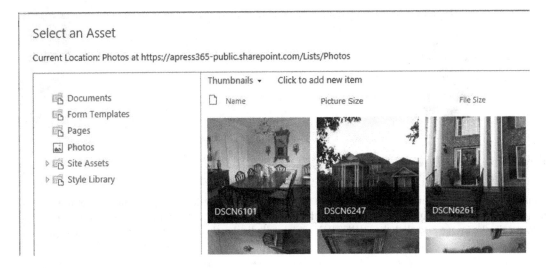

Figure 2-12. *Selecting an image from Photos library*

Changing the Look

From the SITE tab of the ribbon, click the Change the Look button. This will display a large collection of themes. You can thumb through over 50 pre-set themes and this may seem like a lot to choose from. However, each of these is simply a combination of four design elements:

- Background image
- Color scheme
- Layout (for example, where the links are located)
- Font set

We'll choose Estate since real estate is in a similar field, but we will later change all four of these elements individually. After this is selected, a sample page is displayed. On the left side you can set each of these elements individually. Select the Colors, Site Layout, and Fonts that are shown in Figure 2-13.

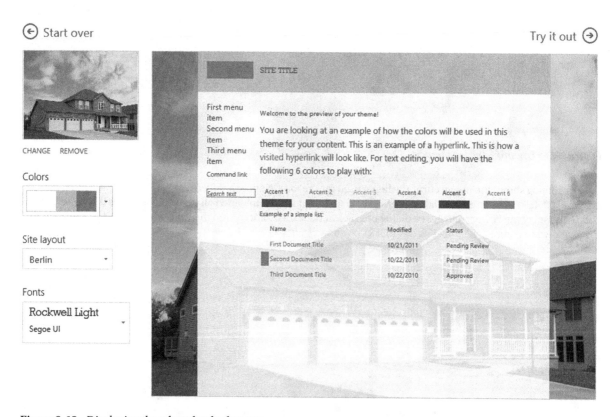

Figure 2-13. *Displaying the selected style elements*

Now you'll change the background image. If you don't want any image, just click the REMOVE link under the thumbnail image. To use a different image you can simply drag a file from Windows Explorer onto the thumbnail. Another way to specify the image is to click the CHANGE link, which will display the Add a document dialog box shown in Figure 2-14.

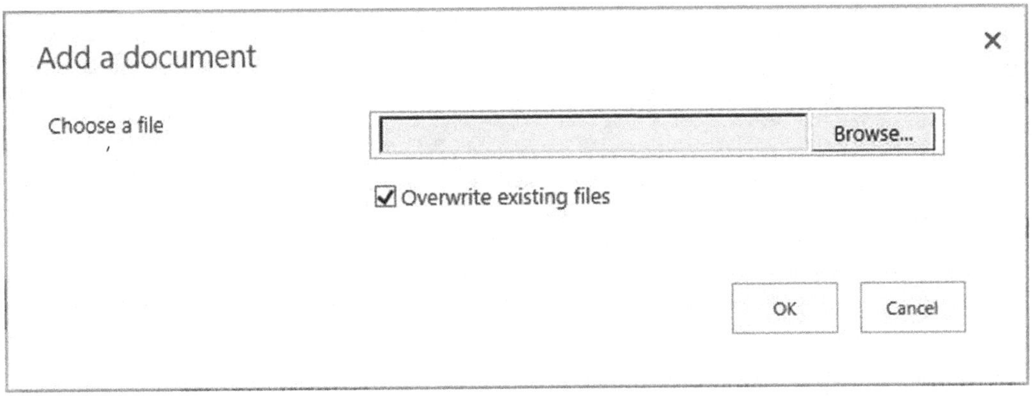

Add a document   ✕

Choose a file

[   ] [Browse...]

☑ Overwrite existing files

[OK]   [Cancel]

Figure 2-14. *Adding a background image*

■ **Note**   There is no option to select an image from SharePoint. This seems like an oversight and may be corrected in subsequent updates.

Click the Browse button and select an image from your local computer.

Adjusting the Menu

The layout we chose has the navigation links on the left site of the page. You can rearrange the order of the links, hide some of them, change the text that is displayed, and add new links. Notice the EDIT LINKS link below the menu; you'll use this to put the menu in edit mode where you can make adjustments. You can also click the Edit Menu button from the SITE tab of the ribbon; both actions do the same thing.

Click the EDIT LINKS link. Links that are hidden will have a dash icon to the right and those that are displayed will have an icon that looks like an eye as shown in Figure 2-15.

Figure 2-15. *Modifying the menu items*

You can click these icons to toggle whether a link is hidden or not. You can also click a link and drag it to a new location. We chose to hide the Directions link as this is not important to our site.

If you want to add a new link, click the link link. You'll see a dialog box where you enter the text to be displayed and the URL that the link should go to. You can create links that go to pages outside of your site if you want to.

When you have finished making changes, click the Save button.

Hiding the Search Box

For the next change, you'll remove the search field from the header. In our site, we decided not to enable this feature. From the SITE tab of the ribbon, click the Search Box button, which will display the Search Box dialog box shown in Figure 2-16.

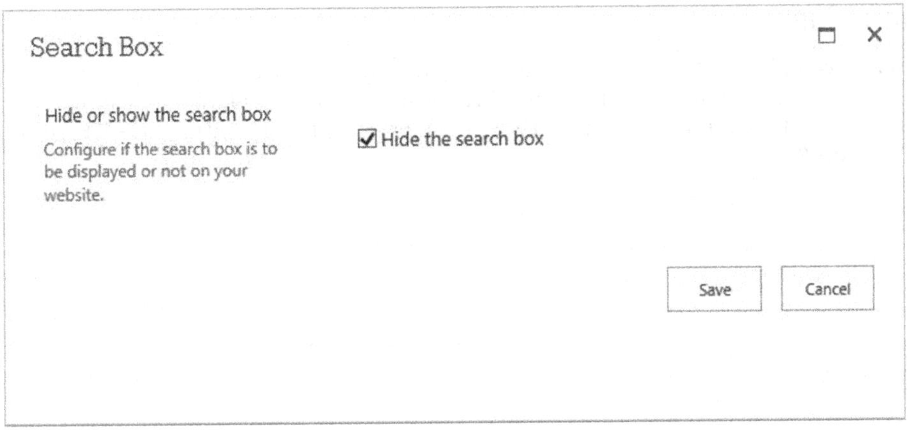

Figure 2-16. *Hiding the search box*

To remove the search box, just select the Hide the search box check box and click the Save button.

Modifying Site Elements

There are two site elements on the initial website, PageHeader and PageFooter. If you go to the Site Contents page, you'll find a Site Elements library with two items in it. Select this library and the edit the PageFooter elements. The dialog box will look similar to Figure 2-17.

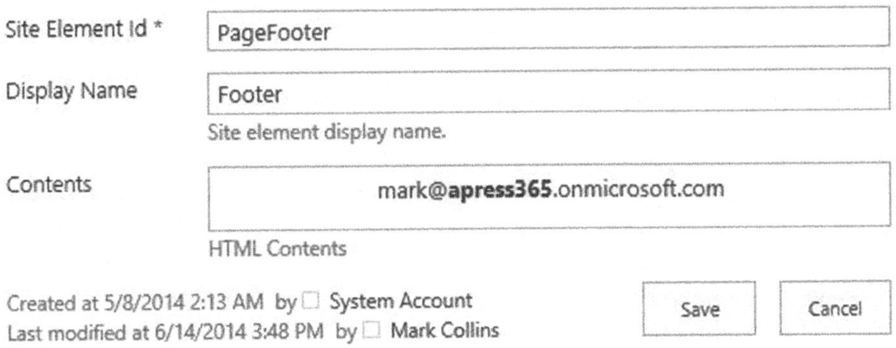

Figure 2-17. *Changing the footer text*

We modified the contents to include an e-mail address. We also used the format actions in the ribbon to make apress365 bolded. When you're done, click the site logo or the Home link to display the updated Home page.

You can also edit these site elements directly from any page. Go to the SITE tab of the ribbon and click the Edit Site Elements button. This will draw a border around both the PageHeader and PageFooter elements. You can edit the text, change fonts, and so on right from the page. The FORMAT tab of the riboon will also appear to give you various formatting options. Just click anywhere outside of these two elements to leave edit mode.

Modifying the Home Page

With the overall site configuration complete, you'll now modify the home page. Each page is stored in the Pages library, which you can see from the Site Contents page. From this library you can view and edit your existing pages as well as creating new ones. However, the easiest way to edit a page is to simply navigate to it, and use the PAGE tab of the ribbon, which is shown in Figure 2-18.

Figure 2-18. *The PAGE tab of the ribbon*

Go to the Home page, if not already there, and click the PAGE link to access the ribbon. The first thing you'll need to do is to put the page in edit mode by clicking the Edit button. The Home page will have a series of pictures on the right-hand side of the page. Then you'll add a large picture in the main part of the page along with some text.

Click the Page Layout button in the ribbon, which will show a list of available layouts as shown in Figure 2-19.

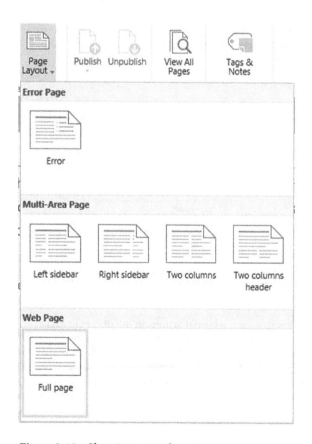

Figure 2-19. *Choosing a page layout*

Select Right sidebar. The page will be displayed with two areas labelled Page Content. Click inside the sidebar area and then select the INSERT tab of the ribbon. You'll notice that there are several types of elements that can be added, including pictures, videos, and app parts.

Click the Picture button and a dropdown will be displayed for you to specify where the picture will be loaded from as shown in Figure 2-20.

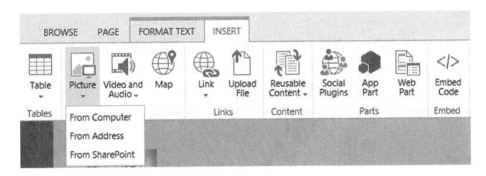

Figure 2-20. *Inserting a picture*

Click the From SharePoint link and then select one of the images in your Photos library. After the image is inserted, the IMAGE tab of the ribbon will appear. The images we're using are a bit large so we'll need to shrink them to a reasonable size. Select the Lock Aspect Ratio checkbox and then set the Horizonal Size to **200px** as shown in Figure 2-21.

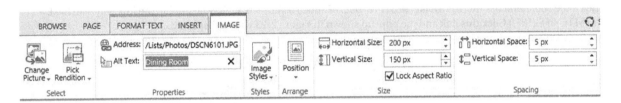

Figure 2-21. *Configuring the image properties*

When you tab off this field, the Vertical Size will be recalculated automatically. You can also adjust some of the spacing or alignment parameters, if necessary. Repeat this process to add several more images.

Then click inside the main content area and remove the existing text. Start typing some text in this area and the FORMAT TEXT tab of the ribbon will appear. Insert a picture in the main section and then add some more text. You can select the image and resize it to fit the width of the content area.

When you're done making changes, click the Save button in the ribbon. Several options will appear as shown in Figure 2-22.

Figure 2-22. *Saving the changes*

If you want to discard your changes, use the Stop Editing link. If you're done making changes use the Save link, which will return the page to a read-only state.

Making the Website Public

Initially, your website is not available to non-authenticated users. You'll now make it public so others can see it. In the Office 365 menu bar there is a MAKE WEBSITE ONLINE link. (If your site is already public, the link will read MAKE WEBSITE OFFLINE.) Click this link and the pop-up shown in Figure 2-23 will be displayed.

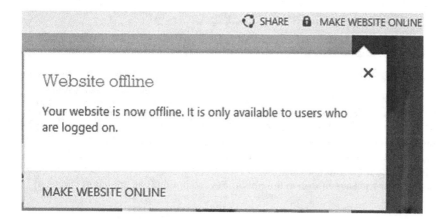

Figure 2-23. *Setting the website status*

Click the MAKE WEBSITE ONLINE link at the bottom of this window. The confirmation message shown in Figure 2-24 will appear. Click the Make online button to confirm.

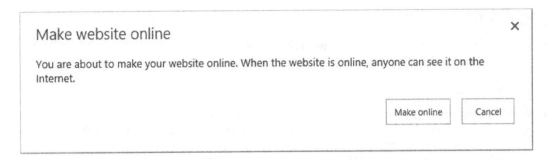

Figure 2-24. *Confirming public access*

The website is now public. Vistors can now see your site, which will look similar to Figure 2-25.

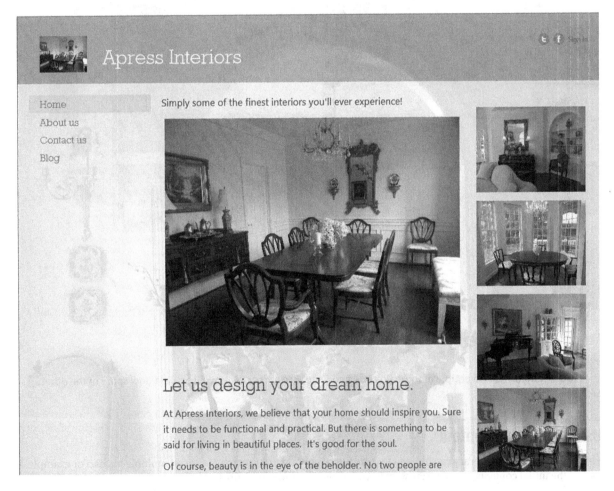

Figure 2-25. *The finished website*

Advanced Editing

With the basic website complete, we'll look at some advanced editing options.

SharePoint Content

All of the content for your public website is stored in a collection of lists and document libraries within SharePoint. You can view and edit all of this from the Site Contents page. You used this earlier to add images to the Photos library. Understanding these libraries will help you better utilize the features provided. Go to the Site Contents page (you can get there from the Settings icon). The default set of libraries will look similar to Figure 2-26.

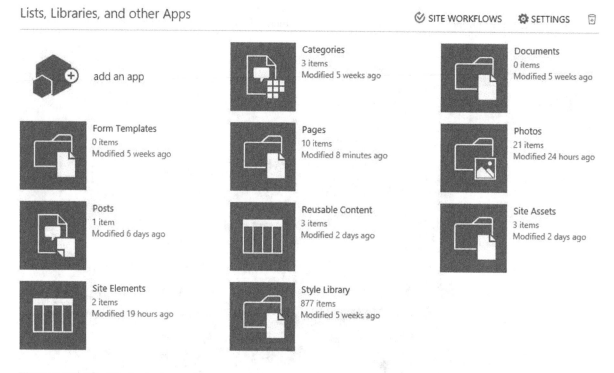

Figure 2-26. *The Site Contents page*

You've already used a couple of these (Photos and Site Elements). Now we'll explain how some of the others are used.

Using Reusable Content

The Reusable Content library can be used to store bits of content that you may reuse on multiple pages. For example, look at the initial contents that were created for you, which is shown in Figure 2-27.

Reusable Content ⓘ

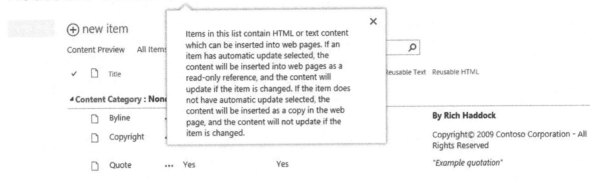

Figure 2-27. *The initial Resuable Content library*

The default library includes a Byline, Copyright, and Quote entries. If you want to include a byline on a page, for example, you can select it from the INSERT tab of the ribbon as shown in Figure 2-28.

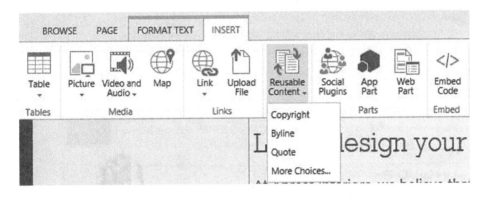

Figure 2-28. *Adding reusable content*

One nice benefit of using resuable content is that if you need to update it, just modify the text in the Reusable Content library and every page that uses it will be updated automatically. You can disable this feature, if you want to. If you edit one of the items in the Reusable Content library, the page will look like Figure 2-29.

Content Type   Reusable HTML ☑

Title *   Byline

Comments

A A̲ | B *I* U̲ | ▤ ▦ ▤ | ▤ ▤ ▸▤ ◂▤ | A̲ ◆ | ▸¶ ¶◂

Content Category   None ☑

Automatic Update   ☑

If this option is selected, the content of this list item will be inserted into web pages as a read-only reference. New versions of this item will automatically appear in the web pages. If the option is not selected, the content of this list item will be inserted into web pages as a copy that page authors can then modify. New versions of this item will not appear in the web pages. Any change to this setting will not affect existing web pages that are using this item.

Show in drop-down menu ☑

Select this option if you want this reusable content item to appear in a drop-down menu available during page editing. This will offer authors a quick way to add this item to a page.

Reusable HTML   by **Mark Collins**

Version: 2.0

Created at 5/8/2014 2:05 AM by ☐ System Account

Last modified at 6/15/2014 11:28 AM by ☐ Mark Collins

                                                [Save] [Cancel]

Figure 2-29. Modifying a resuable content item

You can also hide this item from the dropdown list in the INSERT tab of the ribbon. You will want to do this if an item is being discontinued. You can't delete it if it is already referenced, but you can prevent new pages from using it.

Notice that the Content Category dropdown only includes a None value. If you want to add more categories, you will need to modify the content type. To do this, while displaying the list of items, click the LIST tab of the ribbon and then click the List Settings button. In the Settings page, scroll down to the Columns section and find the Content Category column. Notice that the type is Choice, which means that this column has a fixed set of allowed values. Click the Content Category link, which will display the Edit Column page. In the Additional Column Settings section, add some other values to the existing None value and click the OK button at the bottom of the page. If you edit one of the existing Reusable Content items, you'll see that there are additional values in the category dropdown.

Adding Blog Categories

When you create a new blog post you can assign one or more categories to the post. The category is useful for searching or filtering posts in a blog. Initially, only Opinions, Events, and Ideas are supported. However, you can add more categories to the Categories list.

From the Site Contents page, select the Categories list, which will look similar to Figure 2-30.

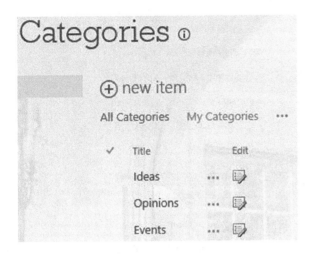

Figure 2-30. Showing the existing categories

Click the new item link to add other categories. These will then be available in the Category field when creating a new blog post.

Using the Pages Library

The actual content of each web page is stored in the Pages library. There are about ten pages created for you, which are listed in Figure 2-31.

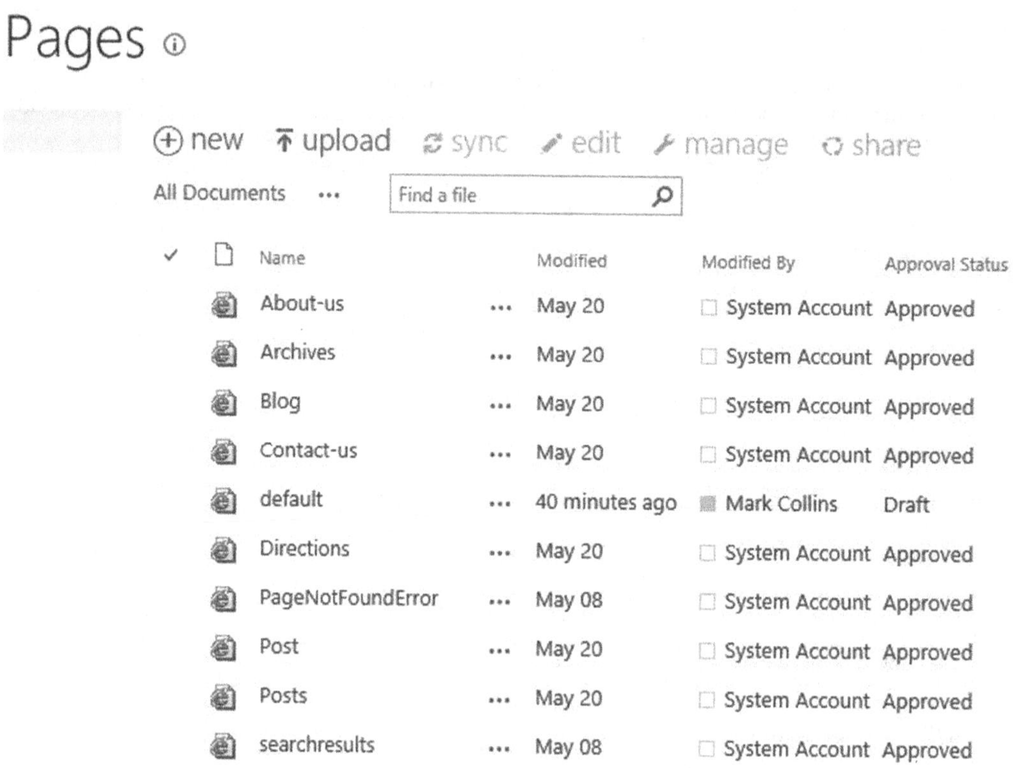

Pages ⓘ

⊕ new　↑ upload　⟳ sync　✏ edit　🔧 manage　↻ share

All Documents　⋯　| Find a file　🔍 |

✓	📄	Name		Modified	Modified By	Approval Status
		About-us	⋯	May 20	☐ System Account	Approved
		Archives	⋯	May 20	☐ System Account	Approved
		Blog	⋯	May 20	☐ System Account	Approved
		Contact-us	⋯	May 20	☐ System Account	Approved
		default	⋯	40 minutes ago	▦ Mark Collins	Draft
		Directions	⋯	May 20	☐ System Account	Approved
		PageNotFoundError	⋯	May 08	☐ System Account	Approved
		Post	⋯	May 20	☐ System Account	Approved
		Posts	⋯	May 20	☐ System Account	Approved
		searchresults	⋯	May 08	☐ System Account	Approved

Figure 2-31. *Listing the contents of the Pages library*

If you have a lot of pages, you'll find this very useful because it gives you a quick summary of all the pages, including when it was last updated, by whom, and its current status.

■ **Note**　The Draft status means that the page has been modified but these changes are not yet published to the live site.

Click the elipses next to the Home page (default) and then click the elipses in the quick view dialog and select the Edit Properties link. This will display the page shown in Figure 2-32.

Content Type	Multi-Area Page ▾
	Content type for additional page content fields used in Internet Websites.
Name *	default .aspx
Title	Home
Comments	
Contact	System Account x
	Contact is a site column created by the Publishing feature. It is used on the Page Content Type as the person or group who is the contact person for the page.
Hide physical URLs from search	☑
	If checked, the physical URL of this page will not appear in search results. Friendly URLs assigned to this page will always appear.
Page Image	Click here to insert a picture from SharePoint.
	Page Image is a site column created by the Publishing feature. It is used on the Article Page Content Type as the primary image of the page.
Page Content	Simply some of the finest interiors you'll ever experience!

Figure 2-32. *Editing the Home page properties*

This page includes both metadata fields such as Comments and Contact as well as the actual content, which is defined in the Page Content fields. Since this is a multi-part page (in this case with main and sidebar sections), there are multiple Page Content fields.

You can edit the content from this page. If you click inside one of these fields, the ribbon will automatically expand to include the appropriate editing commands. For example, if you click on an image, the IMAGE tab will appear. If you prefer to edit from the actual web page, from the Pages library, click the elipses on the page you wish to edit. Then, from the quick view pop-up, click the Open link. Then, use the PAGE tab of the ribbon to begin editing the page.

Modifying the Style Sheet

If you are comfortable with editing Cascading Style Sheets (CSS) you can have even more control over the look of your website. Ultimately, your web pages, which include HTML content, JavaScript, and CSS, are sent to a browser to be rendered. While some of the HTML includes in-line styles, most of it applies classes to an element and relies on the style sheets to define the layout, color, and fonts. By modifying the styles you can affect the look of your site.

■ **Note**   If you're new to cascading style sheets the W3C School provides a great tool for learning and practicing. Go to this site, http://www.w3schools.com/css/DEFAULT.asp to start. You can edit CSS and see in real time how these styles affect the rendering.

Go to the SITE tab of the ribbon and click the Edit Style Sheet button. A style sheet similar to the one shown in Figure 2-33 will be displayed.

Figure 2-33. *Editing the style sheet*

This is the actual style sheet that is included with your web pages. You can display a page, view the source, and verify this file is included. You'll find a link tag similar to this, and if you click on the href, the contents will be displayed.

```
<link rel="stylesheet"
      type="text/css"
      href="/_catalogs/masterpage/en-US/berlin-alternate.css?ver=29d6a5e7-b9f3-4817-a98a-0ea147d38fab"/>
```

However, notice that all of the styles have been commented out. The actual default styles are defined in other CSS files. The file displayed in Figure 2-33 is just a sample of the common elements that you might want to change. You can remove the comments, modify the styles, and click the Save button.

For our site, we want to make the logo a little bit bigger and change the background color of the side bar. Edit the style sheet and replace the SITE LOGO section with the following:

```
/* SITE LOGO */
.ms-siteicon-img{
height:60px;
}
```

Then replace the RIGHT SIDEBAR LAYOUT section with this:

```
/* RIGHT SIDEBAR LAYOUT */
.twoColumnRightLayout-right{
background-color:rgba(90,80,100,1.0);
}
```

Notice that as you type, the style changes are displayed immediately. If you're happy with the result, click the Save and Publish button to make these changes to the live site.

■ **Tip**   You are not limited to changing the styles in the sample file; you can modify the styles for any class. To find the appropriate class name, use an inspector in your browser tools or view the source.

Employing Search Engine Optimization

Search Engine Optimization (SEO) is a very broad and important topic. One popular SEO technique is to include metadata in your site pages that provide information to the search engine to help find relevant content and to influence what is displayed in the search results. We are not going to explain SEO in this book but we do want to show you how you can adjust the metadata to accomplish your SEO strategies.

Adding Meta Tags

Metadata is included in your pages using meta tags, which are look like this:

```
<meta name="" content="" />
```

■ **Tip**   This page provides a good overview of the meta tags that the Google search engine recognizes:
https://support.google.com/webmasters/answer/79812?hl=en

To add meta tags to your pages, you'll need to go to the Site Settings page You can get there by clicking the Settings icon in the menu bar and then selecting the Site settings link as shown in Figure 2-34.

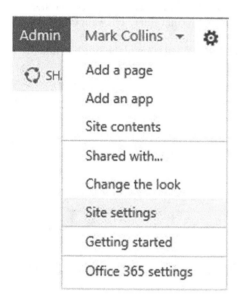

Figure 2-34. *Navigating to the Site Settings page*

The Site Settings page contains a number of links that navigate to pages that are used to configure various settings including user permissions and site collection administration. The two links related to SEO configuration are highlighted in Figure 2-35.

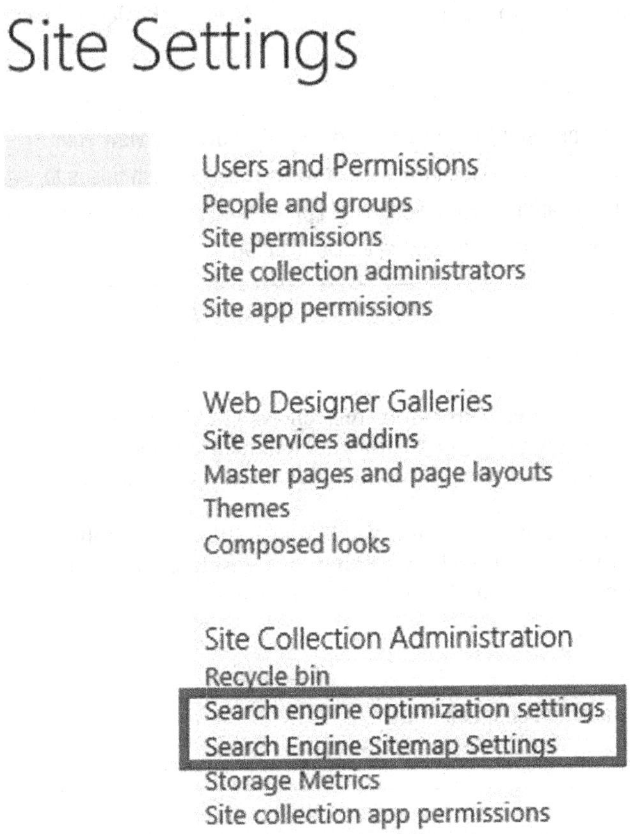

Site Settings

Users and Permissions
People and groups
Site permissions
Site collection administrators
Site app permissions

Web Designer Galleries
Site services addins
Master pages and page layouts
Themes
Composed looks

Site Collection Administration
Recycle bin
Search engine optimization settings
Search Engine Sitemap Settings
Storage Metrics
Site collection app permissions

Figure 2-35. *The Site Settings page*

Click the Search engine optimization settings link. The first part of this page is shown in Figure 2-36.

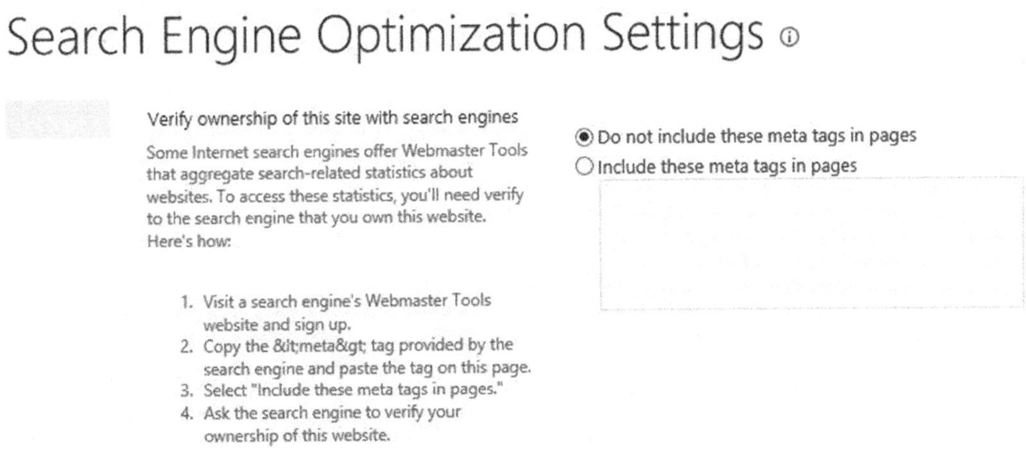

Search Engine Optimization Settings ⊙

Verify ownership of this site with search engines

Some Internet search engines offer Webmaster Tools that aggregate search-related statistics about websites. To access these statistics, you'll need verify to the search engine that you own this website. Here's how:

1. Visit a search engine's Webmaster Tools website and sign up.
2. Copy the <meta> tag provided by the search engine and paste the tag on this page.
3. Select "Include these meta tags in pages."
4. Ask the search engine to verify your ownership of this website.

◉ Do not include these meta tags in pages
◯ Include these meta tags in pages

Figure 2-36. *The Search Engine Optimization Settings page*

To embed meta tags, select the Include these meta tags in pages radio button and then enter the desired tags in the text box.

■ **Tip** You may want to use some of the search engine's webmaster tools to view and optimize how they view your site. In order to do this, you will need to prove that you "own" this site. One of the easiest ways to accomplish this is to generate a meta tag on their site and embed it into yours. The search engine's verification process will then look for the tag. The Search Engine Optimization Settings page is where you'll embed the verification tag.

Using Canonical URLs

Search engines will rate how popular a particular page is by how many times someone follows a link to the page. Sometimes a page may have different links to it. This is especially true when URL parameters are used. Some parameters are used to filter the content. In this case, diferent parameters will result in different content. For this reason, search engines generally treat these as different URLs.

However, some parameters may not have any affect on content. In this case, different URLs result in the same content but the URL's popularity rating will be artificially diluted because they are considered different pages. To improve the rating you'll want to combine these so the search engine treats this as a single, or canonical URL.

■ **Tip** This article explains the benefits and approach to using canonical URLs:

https://support.google.com/webmasters/answer/139066?hl=en&ref_topic=4617741.

The second half of the Search Engine Optimization Settings page allows you add parameter filters, which is shown in Figure 2-37.

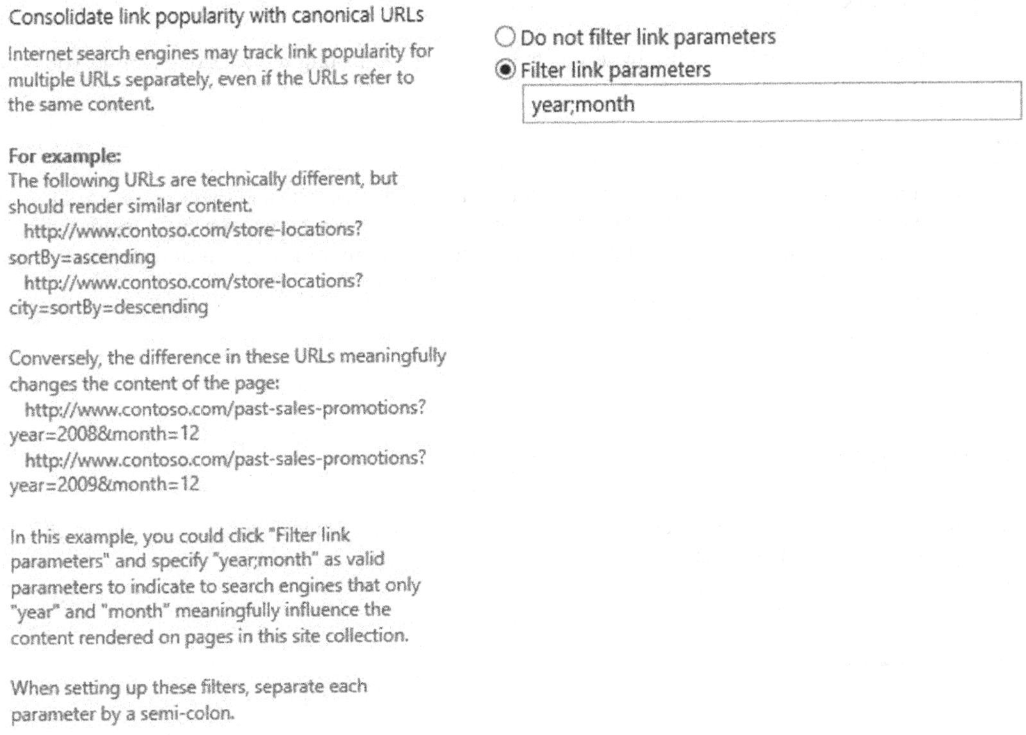

Consolidate link popularity with canonical URLs

Internet search engines may track link popularity for multiple URLs separately, even if the URLs refer to the same content.

For example:
The following URLs are technically different, but should render similar content.
 http://www.contoso.com/store-locations?sortBy=ascending
 http://www.contoso.com/store-locations?city=sortBy=descending

Conversely, the difference in these URLs meaningfully changes the content of the page:
 http://www.contoso.com/past-sales-promotions?year=2008&month=12
 http://www.contoso.com/past-sales-promotions?year=2009&month=12

In this example, you could click "Filter link parameters" and specify "year;month" as valid parameters to indicate to search engines that only "year" and "month" meaningfully influence the content rendered on pages in this site collection.

When setting up these filters, separate each parameter by a semi-colon.

○ Do not filter link parameters
◉ Filter link parameters
   year;month

Figure 2-37. *Entering filter parameters*

The page itself explains how to do this. Just select the Filter link parameters radio button and then enter the parameters that truly affect the content that is returned. These should be separated by a semicolon. In the example given, the filter should be **year;month**.

Adding Videos

As more people have access to broadband, video is becoming an increasingly important aspect of a web site. I'll show you two ways to add video to your site. A simple way to incorporate video is to take advantage of existing hosting services such as youtube.com. The video is uploaded to their site and streamed from there; you simply embed the video viewer in your web page. However, you can also host the video on your Office 365 site. I'll show you how to use both techniques.

Creating a Video Library

Before you start adding videos to your site, you'll create an asset library to store them. As you did with images, this will allow you to organize them and include metadata that will be helpful in maintaining your site.

Go to the Site Contents page and click the add an app link. In the section called Apps You Can Add, select the Asset Library app, and enter the name **Video** when prompted.

Linking to a Hosting Service

The easiest way to show a video is by simply adding a hyperlink to the URL of the hosting service. For example, you could add a hyperlink to this video:

```
https://www.youtube.com/watch?v=BQjBrt9LriY
```

However, you would have then navigated your potential customer away from your site and they would now be on the youtube site. There is a better way; instead of linking to the youtube site, you can embed the video inside your page using an iframe. When you view a video on one of these hosting sites, there are some controls underneath it similar to those shown in Figure 2-38.

👍 Like 👎   About   **Share**   Add to   🖨   ılıl   ⚑

Figure 2-38. *The video controls on youtube*

When you click the Share link, the window will open and show the URL for this video. If you click on the Embed link you'll see more options as shown in Figure 2-39.

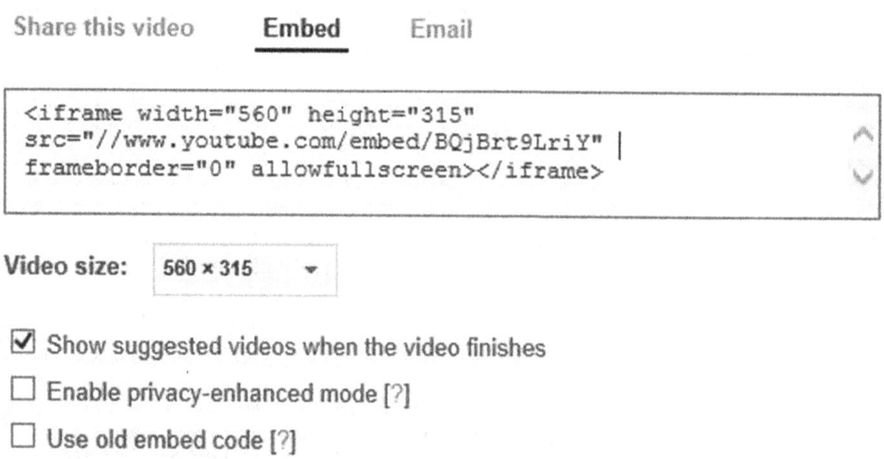

Share this video   **Embed**   Email

```
<iframe width="560" height="315"
src="//www.youtube.com/embed/BQjBrt9LriY" |
frameborder="0" allowfullscreen></iframe>
```

Video size: 560 × 315   ▼

☑ Show suggested videos when the video finishes

☐ Enable privacy-enhanced mode [?]

☐ Use old embed code [?]

Figure 2-39. *Generating the embed HTML*

You can select the options you want such as the window size and the embedded HTML will be generated for you. The generated HTML for embedding this video is:

```
<iframe width="560"
        height="315"
        src="//www.youtube.com/embed/BQjBrt9LriY"
        frameborder="0"
        allowfullscreen>
</iframe>
```

Go to the Videos library, which will be empty. Go to the FILES tab of the ribbon and click the New Document button. This will display the dropdown shown in Figure 2-40 where you can select the content type.

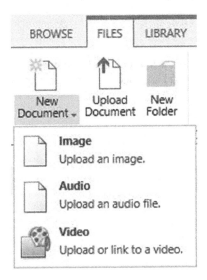

Figure 2-40. *Selecting the content type*

Select the Video link. In the edit page that is displayed, select the Provide code to embed a video from the web radio button. Enter a name for the video and paste in the embedded code as shown in Figure 2-41.

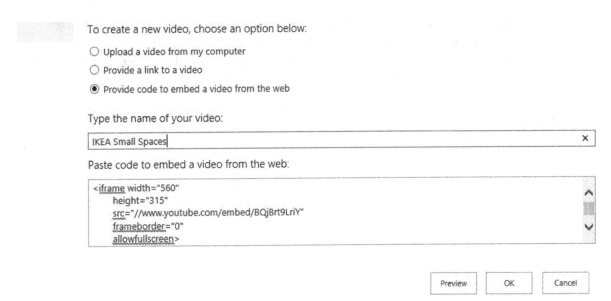

Figure 2-41. *Entering the video details*

You can click the Preview button to verify the embed code is correct. Click the OK button when you're done. The page will then display the intial video frame as well as all of the metadata fields that you can enter to organize your assets. You can also load a thumbnail image by clicking the Change thumbnail link.

Uploading Your Own Videos

Now you'll add a video that will be hosted within SharePoint. From the FILE tab, click the New Document button and then select the Video link just like before. In the page that is displayed, select the Upload a video from my computer radio button and browse to your video file as shown in Figure 2-42.

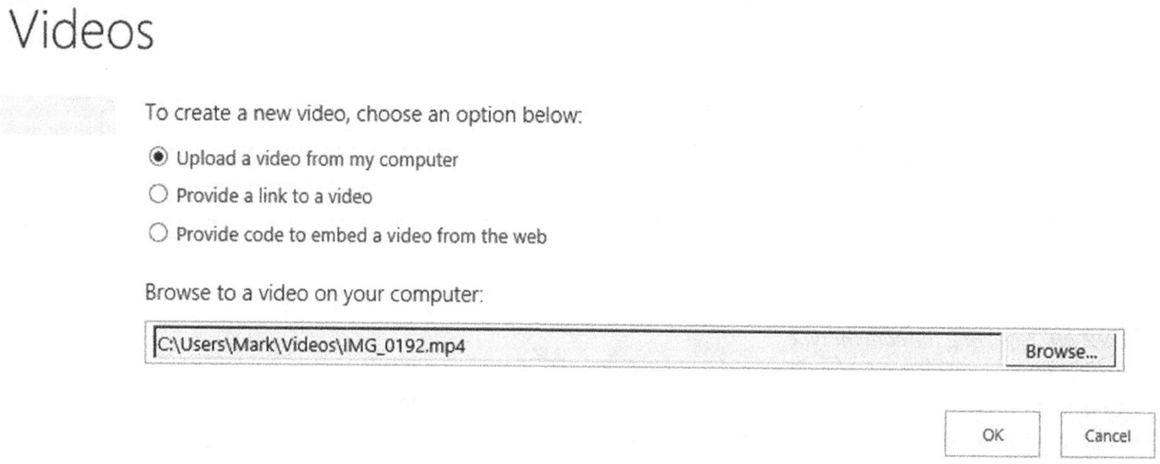

Videos

To create a new video, choose an option below:

● Upload a video from my computer

○ Provide a link to a video

○ Provide code to embed a video from the web

Browse to a video on your computer:

| C:\Users\Mark\Videos\IMG_0192.mp4 | Browse... |

| OK | Cancel |

Figure 2-42. *Uploading a video*

■ **Tip**   The only video format that is currently supported is MP4. This, of course, can change and more options may be available later. If you need to convert a video file to MP4, I found this free site to work very well: http://video.online-convert.com/convert-to-mp4. Convert your files to MP4 before trying to upload them to SharePoint.

With a SharePoint hosted video, you have the option of capturing a thumbnail from the video itself. Click the Change thumbnail link to see the available options, which are shown in Figure 2-43.

This video's thumbnail

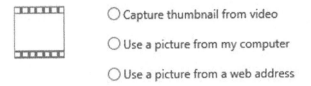

○ Capture thumbnail from video

○ Use a picture from my computer

○ Use a picture from a web address

Figure 2-43. *Thumbnail options*

Select the `Capture thumbnail from video` radio button and then click the play button on the video. When the video is displaying the desired frame, click the camera button at the top of the video as shown in Figure 2-44. You can also use the left and right arrows to step through the video.

This video's thumbnail

⦿ Capture thumbnail from video

　Use camera button above after starting video playback to capture thumbnail from video

○ Use a picture from my computer

○ Use a picture from a web address

Figure 2-44. *Capturing a thumbnail from the video*

As with images, you can enter metadata information for each video. The edit form is shown in Figure 2-45.

Video Properties

Content Type

Video ☑

Upload or link to a video.

Name *

Sunset

Description

A summary of the Video

Owner

☐ Mark Collins x

The owner of the Video

Show Download Link ☐

Specifies whether a button appears on the video player page that allows the user to download the video being played.

Show Embed Link ☐

Specifies whether a button appears on the video player that allows the user to get an embed code for the video being played.

People In Video

Enter names or email addresses...

The people appearing in the video.

Created at 6/15/2014 5:40 PM by ☐ Mark Collins
Last modified at 6/15/2014 5:43 PM by ☐ Mark Collins

Save   Cancel

Figure 2-45. *Editing the video properties*

Click the Save button when you have finished editing the properties. Go to the Videos library and you should have two videos as shown in Figure 2-46. One video uses an embedded link and the other is hosted on Sharepoint.

Videos

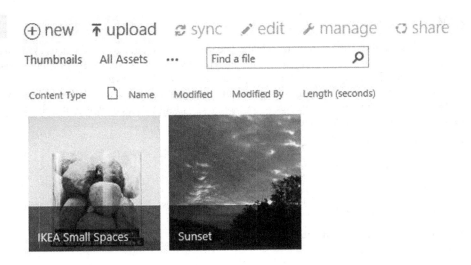

Figure 2-46. *The completed Videos library*

Adding Videos to Your Page

Regardless of where the image is hosted, once it is in your Videos library, the process for adding it to a page is the same. Go to one of your pages and click the Edit button from the PAGE tab of the ribbon. Then go to the INSERT tab and select the Video and Audio button. You'll see a dropdown with your options as shown in Figure 2-47.

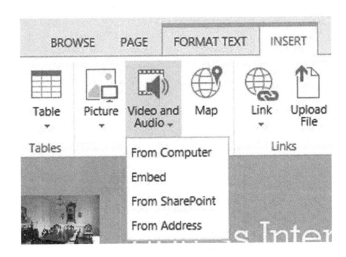

Figure 2-47. *Adding videos to your page*

Click the From SharePoint link and then select the Videos library. Select an image and the video will be added to the page.

Summary

In this chapter you created a professional looking website. The site uses color, images, and videos to make a great impression. A public-facing website is very different from the typical SharePoint site. It is more content based and less functional than most internal sites. The design facility provides some great features for designing public web sites. And with the ability to include custom images and videos you can implement a full-featured web site on your Office 365 platform. Also, the SharePoint libraries provide an exellent facility for managing all of your web content.

The techniques used in this chapter include:

- Customizing the look of the website
- Uploading and using custom images
- Using the SharePoint libraries to manage content
- Embedding video from other hosting services
- Planning and organizing content for a public-facing website

CHAPTER 3

■ ■ ■

Developing SharePoint Apps in Visual Studio

In this chapter we'll show you how to create SharePoint apps using Visual Studio 2013. An integrated SharePoint development environment was introduced with Visual Studio 2010 but, to be honest, it just wasn't that great. With the improvements in 2012 and 2013, Microsoft really raised the bar!

For starters, Visual Studio can now work directly with a cloud-hosted SharePoint server such as Office 365. Previously, you had to install the SharePoint products on your development machine in order to develop and test. Now, you can point Visual Studio to your Office 365 site and you're ready to go. They also made some really nice improvements to the tools for designing lists and content types. No more manually editing XML files and guids.

In this chapter, you'll first create a list using the list designer and deploy it to Office 365. This will leverage all of the standard SharePoint forms for viewing and editing your list using what is sometimes referred to as the "SharePoint way". This is simple, easy, and provides a consistent UI that your users are likely very familiar with.

However, you may want to provide a custom UI using the standard web development technologies like HTML, CSS, and JavaScript. With the JavaScript Client Object Model your UI can access and manipulate server components such as lists and list items. We'll show you how to leverage this to create a list with a custom UI. You'll also create a custom tab on the SharePoint ribbon. To round out the chapter, you'll create an App Part that provides a view into your list, which you can drop onto any SharePoint page.

Enabling the Developer Feature

The development experience is really sweet; you code the app, hit F5, and the app is automatically deployed and launched, allowing you to set breakpoints and step though your JavaScript code. Previously this was only available with a local installation of SharePoint. Now you can do this with a remote on-premise server or cloud-hosted server. This, however, may cause some legitimate concerns from your system administrators. Think about it: developers pushing out applications to a live production site without any sort of control process.

To address these concerns, this ability is turned off by default. You'll need to enable it before you can deploy your first app. This F5 deployment, also known as side loading, is only available on a SharePoint site that has the Developer feature activated. This is a hidden feature so you'll need to run a PowerShell script to enable it.

■ **Caution** The Development feature should only be enabled on sites that are used for development purposes. Enabling this on a production site can open up vulnerabilities. Also note that if your SharePoint site was provisioned as a test site using NAPA or other type of development platform, this feature may have already been enabled for you.

You will need to install the SharePoint Online Management Shell, which you can get from this site: http://www.microsoft.com/en-us/download/details.aspx?id=30359. The download page is shown in Figure 3-1. Click the Download button to start the installation.

 SharePoint Online Management Shell Preview

| Language: | **English** | | Download |

The SharePoint Online Management Shell is a tool that contains a Windows PowerShell Module to manage your SharePoint Online subscription in the Office 365 Preview.

⊕ Details

⊕ System Requirements

⊕ Install Instructions

Figure 3-1. *Downloading the SPO Management Shell*

Then select either the 32-bit or 64-bit version when prompted. You may have to enable pop-ups to start the download. Follow the instructions to complete the installation.

Now you're ready to create and execute the PowerShell script. Using a text editor, create a file with a .ps1 extension and enter the text shown in Listing 3-1. This file is also available in the download folder from the Apress site.

Listing 3-1. Power Shell script

```
$programFiles = [environment]::getfolderpath("programfiles")

add-type -Path $programFiles'\SharePoint Online Management Shell\Microsoft.Online.SharePoint.
PowerShell\Microsoft.SharePoint.Client.dll'
Write-Host 'To enable SharePoint app sideLoading, enter Site Url, username and password'

$siteurl = Read-Host 'Site Url'
$username = Read-Host "User Name"
$password = Read-Host -AsSecureString 'Password'

 if ($siteurl -eq '')
 {
    $siteurl = 'https://apress365.sharepoint.com'
    $username = 'mark@apress365.onmicrosoft.com'
    $password = ConvertTo-SecureString -String ********' -AsPlainText -Force
}
 $outfilepath = $siteurl -replace ':', '_' -replace '/', '_'
```

```
try
{
    [Microsoft.SharePoint.Client.ClientContext]$cc = New-Object Microsoft.SharePoint.Client.
    ClientContext($siteurl)
    [Microsoft.SharePoint.Client.SharePointOnlineCredentials]$spocreds = New-Object Microsoft.
    SharePoint.Client.SharePointOnlineCredentials($username, $password)

    $cc.Credentials = $spocreds

    #Write-Host -ForegroundColor Yellow 'SideLoading feature is not enabled on the site:' $siteurl

    $site = $cc.Site;

    # This guid identifies the Development Feature
    $developerFeature = new-object System.Guid "e374875e-06b6-11e0-b0fa-57f5dfd72085"
    $site.Features.Add($developerFeature, $true, [Microsoft.SharePoint.Client.
    FeatureDefinitionScope]::None);
    $cc.ExecuteQuery();

    Write-Host -ForegroundColor Green 'Developer feature enabled on site' $siteurl
    #Activated the Developer Site feature

    $test = Read-Host 'Enter to continue'

}

catch
{
    Write-Host -ForegroundColor Red 'Error encountered when trying to enable Developer feature'
    $siteurl, ':' $Error[0].ToString();
    $test = Read-Host 'Enter to continue'
}
```

The point of this script is that it enables the development feature, which is identified by a "magic" guid: e374875e-06b6-11e0-b0fa-57f5dfd72085. This script prompts for three pieces of information:

- Site Url: This is the root address of the Team Site

- User Name: The user name (email address) of a user with admin privileges on the SharePoint site

- Password:

The script was coded to provide default values so you don't have to enter them when the script runs. The listing includes the values we used (minus the password) as an example. Make sure to change these with appropriate values for your environment.

After creating the file, from Windows Explorer, right-click the file and select the Run with PowerShell link. If you have hard-coded the information in the script, just press Enter when prompted for the URL, name, and password. Otherwise, enter the valid values when prompted. The result should look like Figure 3-2.

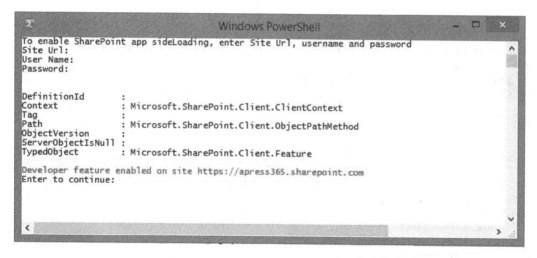

Figure 3-2. *Running the PowerShell Script*

Now go to your Team Site and you'll notice that a new Apps in Testing page, shown in Figure 3-3, has been created for you.

Apress 365 Team Site

Get started with Apps for Office and SharePoint REMOVE THIS

Apps in Testing

⊕ new app to deploy

✓   App Title   Version   Created   Modified

Figure 3-3. *The new Apps in Testing page*

This page has some links at the top that provide some developer resources. You can hide this by clicking the REMOVE THIS link. This page also lists all of the apps that have been deployed using the Sideloading (F5) feature. This list will be empty, for now.

Creating a SharePoint List

Now that your development environment is set up, let's build some SharePoint apps using Visual Studio 2013. The first one will be a list that includes the standard SharePoint UI. This is very simple process but will provide an opportunity to test the F5 deployment feature and also look at what is created for you, under the covers. Subsequent apps will demonstrate how you can develop your own UI using HTML, CSS, and JavaScript.

■ **Tip** In the new SharePoint 2013 model, everything is an "App". Even the basic Task List, Calendar, and Document Library that you are probably very familiar with are now called apps. Actually, they are both: there is underlying list with an app around it that provides the presentation layer. This is primarily a presentation shift in the SharePoint UI; underneath we still have the core list, library, and content type objects. Visual Studio, for the most part, still calls them lists.

Creating the Visual Studio Project

You'll now create a new project in Visual Studio, using the new project template to setup all of the SharePoint connections that are required.

1. Open Visual Studio 2013 and from the Start page, click the New Project link. In the Installed Template section you'll find the Office/SharePoint folder. Select the Apps sub-folder. We're using C# but if you want to use VB, you'll find a similar folder structure under the Visual Basic folder. Select the App for SharePoint template and enter **CustomTaskList** for the project name as shown in Figure 3-4.

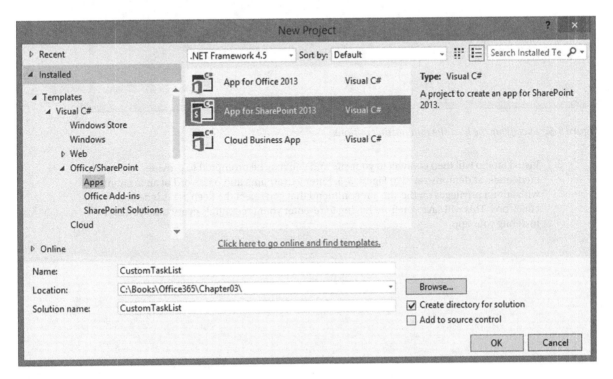

Figure 3-4. *Creating a SharePoint App project*

2. The project template needs a couple of pieces of information. First enter the URL of your SharePoint site. This is probably your domain name (without the `onmicrosoft.com`) with `sharepoint.com` appended to it. If you're not sure, just go to your team site and get its URL from the browser, ignoring anything after `.com`. Also, select the `SharePoint-hosted` option as shown in Figure 3-5.

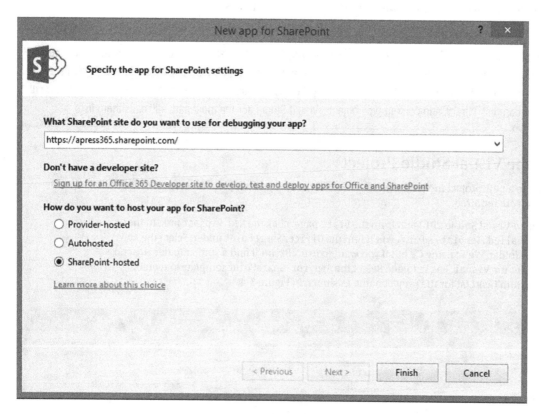

Figure 3-5. Specifying the host site and hosting options

3. Visual Studio will then connect to your site and you may be prompted to provide credentials as demonstrated in Figure 3-6. Enter a username and password of an account with admin privileges on the site. I recommend that you select the `Keep me signed in` check box. This will save you from having to re-enter your credentials every time you hit F5 to debug your app.

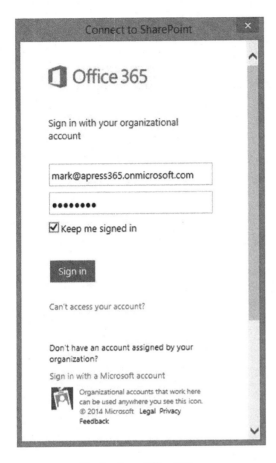

Figure 3-6. *Signing in to Office 365*

Now you have your Visual Studio project created and linked to your SharePoint site. Of course there's not much in it yet. We'll get to that shortly.

Exploring the Project Elements

Before we start designing the new list, let's briefly explore what was just created for you. Go to the Solution Explorer and expand the folders. You should see elements similar to Figure 3-7.

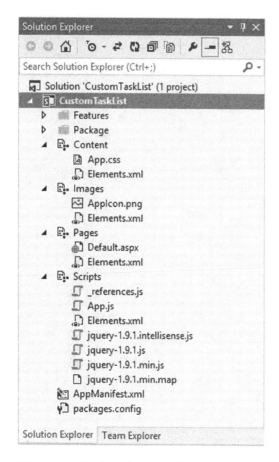

Figure 3-7. *The initial solution elements*

There are Features and Package folders that contain some SharePoint stuff. When your app is deployed to a SharePoint site, Visual Studio creates a deployment package and the contents of these folders are used to do that. If you have developed SharePoint apps before, this will be familiar to you. If not, the good news is that you rarely have to deal with these; Visual Studio takes care of most of this for you.

In the Content folder you'll find an App.css file and the Scripts folder contains some JavaScript files including jQuery. If you're a web developer that will be a hopeful sign.

Notice that in each folder there is an Elements.xml file. This is used to indicate the files that need to be deployed and where they need to go. Again, Visual Studio takes care of most of this for you. Here is a sample file:

```
<?xml version="1.0" encoding="utf-8"?>
<Elements xmlns="http://schemas.microsoft.com/sharepoint/">
  <Module Name="Images">
    <File Path="Images\AppIcon.png" Url="Images/AppIcon.png" ReplaceContent="TRUE" />
  </Module>
</Elements>
```

Now select the project and look at Properties window. This contains some of the information you entered when setting up the project such as the URL of the SharePoint site.

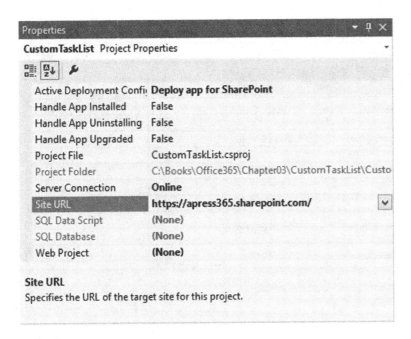

Figure 3-8. *The project properties*

■ **Caution** If you downloaded projects from the Apress site, you will need to change the Site URL properties. Just go to the Properties window and enter the correct URL here.

Adding a List

Let's add a list to your project. You can create a blank list without any columns and then add the needed columns. However, if your list is similar to an existing list, you can save some time by starting with this list and then make your modifications. In this project, we'll use the Tasks list as our starting point.

1. From the Solution Explorer, right-click the project and select the Add and then New Item links. In the Add New Item dialog box, the Office/SharePoint folder should already be selected. There are a number of different types of elements that can be added. For now, select the List item and enter **CustomTaskList** for its name, as shown in Figure 3-9.

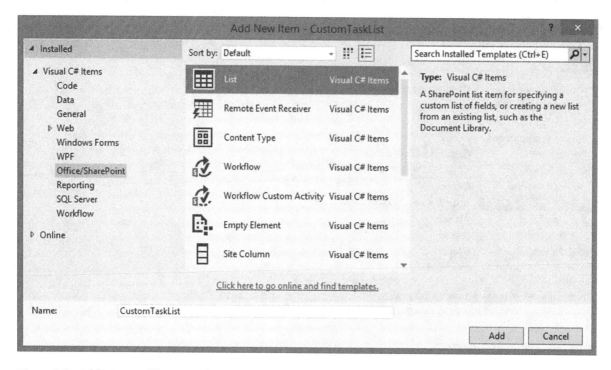

Figure 3-9. Adding a new List to a project

■ **Note** In this sample you'll create a list with a set of columns. However, in a properly architected SharePoint solution, you should create reusable columns (called Site Columns) and organize them into content types. A list can contain multiple content types and its set of columns will be a super-set of the columns in each of the content types. This is beyond the scope of this chapter, but will be covered, briefly, in Chapter 4. We have also provided a SharePoint Primer in Appendix A that explains site columns and content types. The tools in Visual Studio 2013 allow you to construct these elements.

---

2. The List template will then prompt you for some additional information. The name that is displayed will default to the name of the list. Enter **Custom Tasks** instead.

3. Then you have two options for creating a list. The first is to create a new list template and a new instance of it. This gives you the ability to customize the columns in your list. The second option is to create a new instance of an existing template. You can't modify the columns but simply create another copy of an existing list. For example, you'll use this option if you need a new task list for a different project but you don't need to change the columns. For this project, however, select the first option and select the Tasks list as shown in Figure 3-10 and click the Finish button.

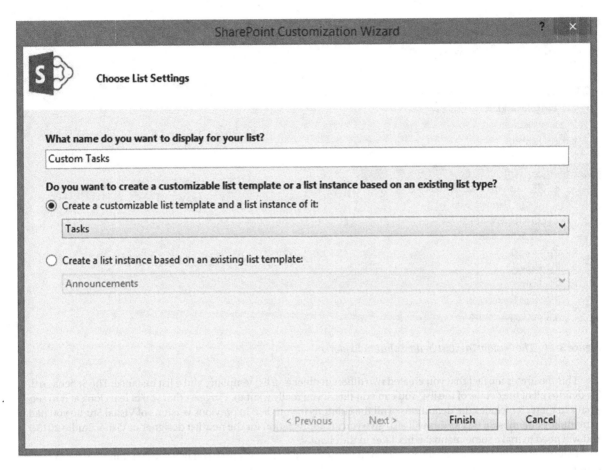

Figure 3-10. *Selecting the list to use as our starting point*

■ **Tip** Once you have created this list (and list template) you can create additional lists using the same template. For example, if you add another list to your project, and select the second option, you'll see the CustomTaskList in the dropdown list, which you can use to define the new list.

Modifying the List Definition

Now you're ready to define what your new list will contain. You'll also experience a nice improvement in Visual Studio 2013 in regards to SharePoint development.

If you look at the Solution Explorer you'll see a CustomTaskList has been added to your project. Within that you'll also find a CustomTaskListInstance as shown in Figure 3-11.

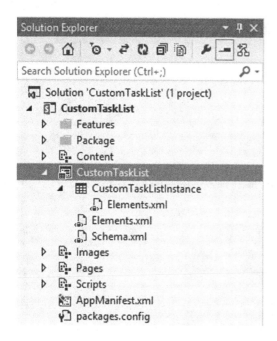

Figure 3-11. *The CustomTaskList in the Solution Explorer*

This illustrates the fact that you created two different objects: a list template, and a list instance. The Schema.xml file defines all of the details of the list. You can edit this, if you really want to. I suggest that you at least look at it to see what's in there. It includes the definitions of all the columns in your list. In previous versions of Visual Studio you had to manually edit most of this so this will also give you an appreciation for the new list designer in Visual Studio 2013. You will need to make some manual edits, later in the chapter.

Double-click the Schema.xml file to open it. If the designer is already open, you will get a warning similar to Figure 3-12.

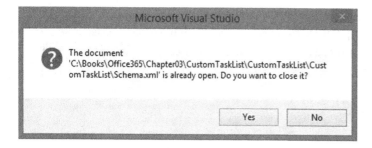

Figure 3-12. *Warning that the file is already open*

The designer is actually displaying and editing the Schema.xml file, with a much friendlier UI. Visual Studio will not let you open the file as both a text file and with the designer simultaneously, so you'll need to close the designer. If you choose No, the designer will stay open but the text-file version will not open.

Close the Schema.xml file an open the designer by double-clicking either the CustomTaskList or CustomTaskListInstance elements in the Solution Explorer. While these are two different objects (one a list template, the other an instance of that template), there is one definition (Schema.xml) for both. So opening either, will open the list designer. The list designer has three tabs: Columns, Views, and List. Let's go through each of these and customize your list.

Adjusting the List Columns

Select the Column tab and you'll see all of the columns that are on the existing Tasks list.

1. Scroll to the bottom of the column list. Select the Related Items column by clicking the empty grid column to the left of it. A green arrow will then appear in this column and the row will be highlighted. Right-click this row and click the Delete link to remove this column.

2. Using this procedure, remove the Previously Assigned To, Predecessor, and Parent ID columns.

3. The Task Name column is listed several times because there are multiple versions of it. Notice that one of these is defined with a Single Line of Text type but the others are Computed. The computed versions display the same information in a different format, such as with a hyperlink. On the row marked Single Line of Text, select the Required checkbox. This will make this column required.

4. Now you'll add an existing site column. Click the Type a new or existing column name link on the last row of the grid. All of the existing site columns will appear in a dropdown list. Select the Actual Work column. The Type attribute is automatically set to Numeric because this is an existing site column that was previously defined.

5. Click the Type a new or existing column name link again and enter **External Reference** for the name. Notice that as you type, the dropdown list is filtered with site columns that match. After entering the name press the Tab key. The Type will default to Single Line of Text, which will be fine for this project. If you needed a different type, you can select one from the dropdown list.

6. Click the Save button in the ribbon to save these changes. The Columns tab should look like Figure 3-13.

Columns	Views	List

Use the grid to configure columns for the list. Learn more about creating lists

◢ Column Display Name	Type	Required
Task Name	Computed	☐
Task Name	Computed	☐
Task Name	Single Line of Text	☑
Priority	Choice	☐
Task Status	Choice	☐
% Complete	Number	☐
Assigned To	Multiple Persons or Groups	☐
Description	Multiple Lines of Text	☐
Start Date	Date and Time	☐
Due Date	Date and Time	☐
Completed	Calculated	☐
Actual Work	Number	☐
External Reference	Single Line of Text	☐

Click Content Types to add columns from an existing content type to your list, or to change the default content type.

[Content Types]

Figure 3-13. The modified list columns

Adding a New View

The Task list that we started with has a lot of views defined. If you go to the Views tab you'll see them listed there. The All Tasks view is set as the default view and is shown in bold text to identify it as the default. This is the view that will be used when you first go to the list.

As you did with the column list, you can right-click a view and use the Delete link to remove it. You can also adjust the Row Limit value, which indicates how many items will be displayed on a page. You can also select the Read Only check box to prevent items from being modified from that view.

For this project you will create a new view. This view will display tasks that are not yet assigned to anyone.

1. Scroll to the bottom of the view list and click the Click here to add a view link. Enter the name **Unassigned Tasks**. Press the Tab key and enter **20** for the Row Limit.

2. Notice that there are no selected columns. You'll add them now. Select the following columns from the Available columns list and click the right-arrow button to move them to the Selected columns list. You can either move them one at a time or hold down the Ctrl key and select multiple columns and move them all at once.

   - Assign To
   - Priority
   - ID
   - Task Name (Link Title)

- Due Date
- Description
- Created By
- Created

3. Using the up and down arrows to the right of the Selected columns list, reorder the columns so that the ID, Priority, Task Name, Due Date, Assigned To, and Description columns are shown first, in that order.

4. Save the changes and the view definition should look like Figure 3-14.

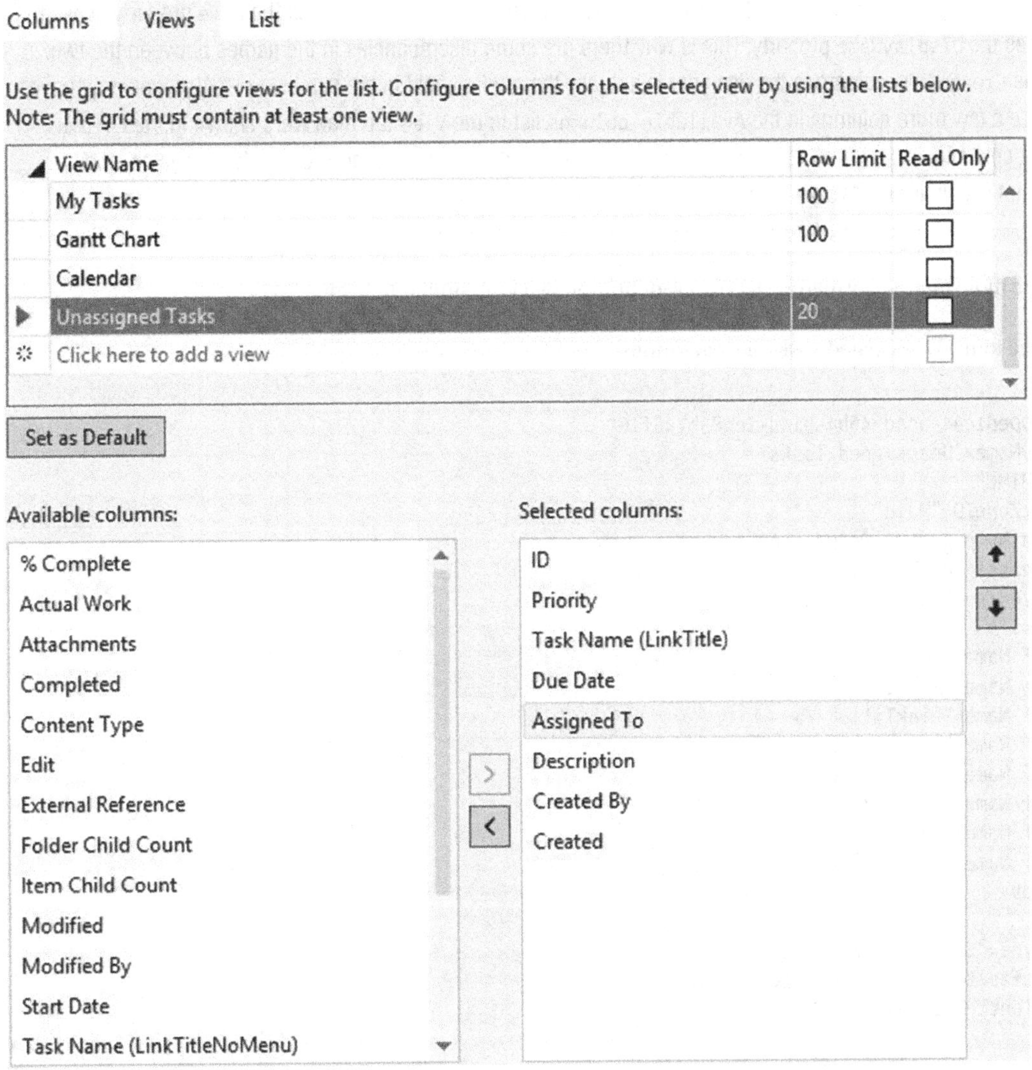

Columns	Views	List

Use the grid to configure views for the list. Configure columns for the selected view by using the lists below. Note: The grid must contain at least one view.

▲ View Name	Row Limit	Read Only
My Tasks	100	☐
Gantt Chart	100	☐
Calendar		☐
▶ Unassigned Tasks	20	☐
✲ Click here to add a view		☐

Set as Default

Available columns:

| % Complete |
| Actual Work |
| Attachments |
| Completed |
| Content Type |
| Edit |
| External Reference |
| Folder Child Count |
| Item Child Count |
| Modified |
| Modified By |
| Start Date |
| Task Name (LinkTitleNoMenu) |

Selected columns:

| ID |
| Priority |
| Task Name (LinkTitle) |
| Due Date |
| Assigned To |
| Description |
| Created By |
| Created |

Figure 3-14. *The new view definition*

So now you've defined a new view in terms of its contents, what columns are displayed, and in what order. But the point here is that this view should only show unassigned tasks. You will need to define a filter to make this happen. Unfortunately, the list designer does not provide this feature; you will need to modify the Schema.xml file manually to do this.

Open the Schema.xml file (closing the designer if prompted). You'll probably notice that the file has a lot of blank lines. Also, while some of the elements are properly indented, many are not. If you look for your new view, it will be near the bottom of the file and all on one line, which makes it hard to read. So the list designer edits this file but, while functional, is not formatted well. To resolve many of the formatting issues, from the Edit menu, select the Advanced link and then Format Document.

■ **Note** If you go to the Columns tab of the designer and select a column in the list, the Properties window displays all of its properties. There is both a Name and a DisplayName property. The Schema.xml file uses the Name property, while the list designer uses the DisplayName property. This is why there are some discrepancies in the names between the two. For example, the Created By column in the designer is actually the Author field in the Schema.xml. Also, you may have noticed there are a few more columns in the Available columns list in the View tab than were shown in the Columns tab. These extra columns are required columns such as Created and Created By. Since you can't remove or modify them, they are not shown in the Columns tab.

With a little more manual formatting your view definition will look similar to Listing 3-2.

Listing 3-2. The initial Unassigned Tasks view definition

```
<View BaseViewID="6"
      Name="00ed1e94-ac4d-46b4-914d-1eb83b736f16"
      DisplayName="Unassigned Tasks"
      Type="HTML"
      WebPartZoneID="Main"
      SetupPath="pages\viewpage.aspx"
      Url="Unassigned Tasks.aspx">
  <RowLimit>20</RowLimit>
  <ViewFields>
    <FieldRef Name="ID" />
    <FieldRef Name="Priority" />
    <FieldRef Name="LinkTitle" />
    <FieldRef Name="DueDate" />
    <FieldRef Name="AssignedTo" />
    <FieldRef Name="Body" />
    <FieldRef Name="Author" />
    <FieldRef Name="Created" />
  </ViewFields>
  <Query />
  <Toolbar Type="Standard" />
  <XslLink Default="TRUE">main.xsl</XslLink>
  <JSLink>clienttemplates.js</JSLink>
</View>
```

■ **Tip**   I wouldn't spend too much time cleaning up the format of this file. As soon as you make any changes with the designer, your formatting changes will be lost. The Format Document command will get your tags on separate lines and properly indented. That is generally sufficient.

Notice that there is an empty Query tag; this is where your custom filter will go. Replace the <Query />line with the following code:

```
<Query>
  <Where>
    <IsNull>
      <FieldRef Name="AssignedTo"></FieldRef>
    </IsNull>
  </Where>
  <OrderBy>
    <FieldRef Name="DueDate" Ascending="TRUE" />
  </OrderBy>
</Query>
```

The Query element includes a Where tag and an OrderBy tag. The Where tag uses the IsNull tag and inside that is the AssignedTo column. This query will only return rows where AssignedTo column is null. The OrderBy tag includes the DueDate column, setting the Ascending attribute to TRUE. This will order them with the tasks due soonest at the top. Save your changes to the Schema.xml file.

■ **Tip**   You may be wondering how do I know what query functions are available and what is the syntax for more complex queries. This is defined as part of the Collaborative Application Markup Language (CAML). For a reference of the Query portion of this, go to this article: http://msdn.microsoft.com/en-us/library/office/ms467521(v=office.15).aspx.

Modifying the List Properties

Now let's look at the List tab of the list designer. The first three fields Title, List URL, and Description are pretty self-explanatory. The default values of the first two are typically sufficient and are based on the details you entered when creating the list. The Description should be updated to something more appropriate. The two check boxes may need a little more explanation.

The Display list at Quick Launch adds a link to this list in the quick launch area so users can quickly navigate to this list. Using this link will display the default view, although the user can select a different view once the list is displayed. Users may prefer to add a link to a specific view such as My Tasks. Regardless, if this list is something that most users will need and you want them to find it easily, you should check this box.

If the Hide list from browser check box is selected, the list will not be included in the Site Content page. Assuming that you have also unchecked the Display list at Quick Launch check box, users will not be able to navigate to your list; it is essentially hidden from them. You may want to do this if you are providing some other way of accessing the data in this list, such as through an App Part, or from a custom page.

Leave the default values (Display list at Quick Launch checked and Hide list from browser unchecked) and save the change to the Description field. The List tab should look similar to Figure 3-15.

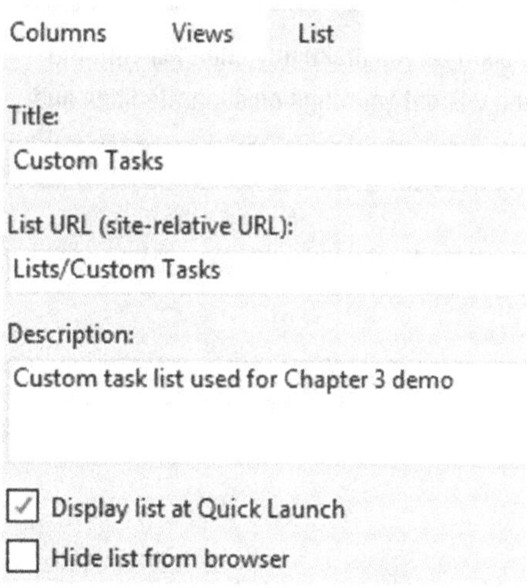

Columns   Views   List

Title:

Custom Tasks

List URL (site-relative URL):

Lists/Custom Tasks

Description:

Custom task list used for Chapter 3 demo

☑ Display list at Quick Launch

☐ Hide list from browser

Figure 3-15. *Modifying the List tab*

Modifying the Default Page

The project template created a Default.aspx page for you with some boilerplate content so that is can be displayed properly in the SharePoint site. It has no real content, however, which is what you'll need to add. But first we will briefly explain the initial page and how it works with the JavaScript that was created as well.

Exploring the Initial Page

Open the Default.aspx page from the Solution Explorer. At the top there are some Page and Register commands that enable it to work with SharePoint. You should generally leave these as is. The page then includes some standard JavaScript files. It first includes a jQuery library that is in your local Scripts folder. It then references two libraries (sp.runtime.js and sp.js). These are already installed on the SharePoint server and provide the JavaScript Client Object Model functions.

The page then includes the App.css file that is in your Content folder and the App.js file that is in your Scripts folder. You will be modifying these two files later in this chapter to implement a custom UI.

At the bottom of the page there is the following div with the initializing . . . text:

```
<div>
    <p id="message">
        <!-- The following content will be replaced with the user name
            when you run the app - see App.js -->
        initializing...
    </p>
</div>
```

It defines a paragraph tag with a "message" id. Now let's look at the App.js file to see what it is doing with this. The content of the initial App.js file is shown in Listing 3-3.

Listing 3-3. The initial implementation of App.js

```
'use strict';

var context = SP.ClientContext.get_current();
var user = context.get_web().get_currentUser();

// This code runs when the DOM is ready and creates a context object
// which is needed to use the SharePoint object model
$(document).ready(function () {
    getUserName();
});

// This function prepares, loads, and then executes a SharePoint query
//to get the current users information
function getUserName() {
    context.load(user);
    context.executeQueryAsync(onGetUserNameSuccess, onGetUserNameFail);
}

// This function is executed if the above call is successful
// It replaces the contents of the 'message' element with the user name
function onGetUserNameSuccess() {
    $('#message').text('Hello ' + user.get_title());
}

// This function is executed if the above call fails
function onGetUserNameFail(sender, args) {
    alert('Failed to get user name. Error:' + args.get_message());
}
```

The (document).ready() function specifies that the getUserName() function should be called when the page has been loaded. The getUserName() function executes a query to get the logged in user. Queries are executed asynchronously so when they are invoked, two callback methods are specified; one is called on success, the other on failure. The success function, onGetUserNameSuccess(), uses jQuery to replace the contents of the message tag with a welcome message that includes the user's name. You will use this querying technique more, later in this chapter.

Adding a List View Web Part

The content for this page will be very simple; you'll just add a web part onto the page that provides all of the standard SharePoint UI. Visual Studio provides a snippet to make this a snap.

In the Default.aspx page right-click just below the welcome div that we just discussed. In the menu that appears, click the Insert Snippet link, and then select SharePoint and then finally splistview. This will insert the following code to your page:

```
<WebPartPages:WebPartZone runat="server" FrameType="TitleBarOnly" ID="full"
    Title="loc:full">
    <WebPartPages:XsltListViewWebPart runat="server"
        ListUrl="Lists/List1"
        IsIncluded="True"
        JsLink="clientTemplate.js"
```

```
        NoDefaultStyle="TRUE"
        PageType="PAGE_NORMALVIEW"
        Default="False"
        ViewContentTypeId="0x">
    </WebPartPages:XsltListViewWebPart>
</WebPartPages:WebPartZone>
```

This code embeds a standard SharePoint web part on your page that displays a list as well as the normal view and edit forms. You'll need to change the `ListUrl` property to point to your list. To get the correct URL, just open the list designer and go to the `List` tab. For our project this is `Lists/Custom Tasks`.

There's one other minor change that you should make to this page. In the second `asp:Content` tag there is some default text, Page Title. Replace this with **Custom Task List**.

Testing the App

Your app is now ready to be deployed to your Office 365 site. Just press F5 to build and deploy it. After Visual Studio has built and deployed the app to SharePoint, the list will be displayed using the default view (`All Items`), which should look like Figure 3-16.

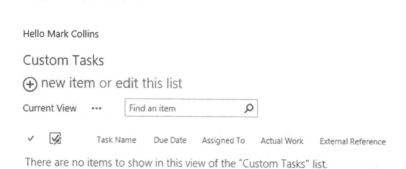

Figure 3-16. *The default view of the CustomTaskList*

Add a few items to the list but do not assign them yet. Notice that the forms for adding and viewing tasks look like the standard SharePoint forms. This all came for free, just by inserting the `splistview` snippet.

Now change the view to use the `Unassigned Tasks` view that you created. You should see the same items since nothing is assigned yet. However, the columns that are included will be different as demonstrated in Figure 3-17.

⊕ new item or edit this list

All Tasks	Calendar	Unassigned Tasks	•••	Find an item					

✓	ID	Priority	Task Name		Due Date	Assigned To	Description	Created By	Created
	1	(3) Low	Update the Bug List ✻	•••				▦ Mark Collins	About a minute ago
	2	(2) Normal	Perform code review ✻	•••				▦ Mark Collins	A few seconds ago
	3	(1) High	Check in the latest changes ✻	•••				▦ Mark Collins	A few seconds ago

Figure 3-17. *The Unassigned Tasks view*

Now edit one of these items and assign it to someone by entering a value in the Assigned To column. This task should then be removed from this view.

Creating a Custom UI

So you have created your first SharePoint app. You used the list designer to customize the list columns and defined a new view. You had to write a simple CAML query to implement a filter. Then you made a few minor changes to the web page and voila, hit F5 and you have an app.

This app is identical to a list that you could have created directly in the SharePoint site. But now you have another way of accomplishing the same thing. For the rest of this chapter we'll show you how you can create a SharePoint list and provide a custom UI using standard web development tools like HTML, CSS, and JavaScript.

Creating a Book List App

For this example, you will create a separate project in Visual Studio and create a simple list that you can use to store book titles. You'll use the list designer to define the columns and then create a custom page using CSS and JavaScript.

Defining the Book List

You'll start by defining a Books list that will store the book titles for your custom page. We'll go through these steps rather quickly as this will be similar to the first project.

1. Open Visual Studio 2013, and from the Start page, click the New Project link. Select the App for SharePoint template and enter **ReadingList** project name.

2. The template will prompt you for the site URL. Enter the address of your SharePoint site and select the SharePoint-hosted option, just like you did earlier in this chapter. You may be prompted for credentials to the site.

3. From the Solution Explorer, right-click the project and select the Add and then New Item links. In the Add New Item dialog box, the Office/SharePoint folder should already be selected. Select the List item and enter the name **Books**.

4. In the Choose List Settings dialog box, leave the display name as **Books**. Select the first option (Create a customizable list template and a list instance of it) just like you did before. This time, however, choose the Default (Custom List) option as shown in Figure 3-18. This will create a blank list that you will add columns to.

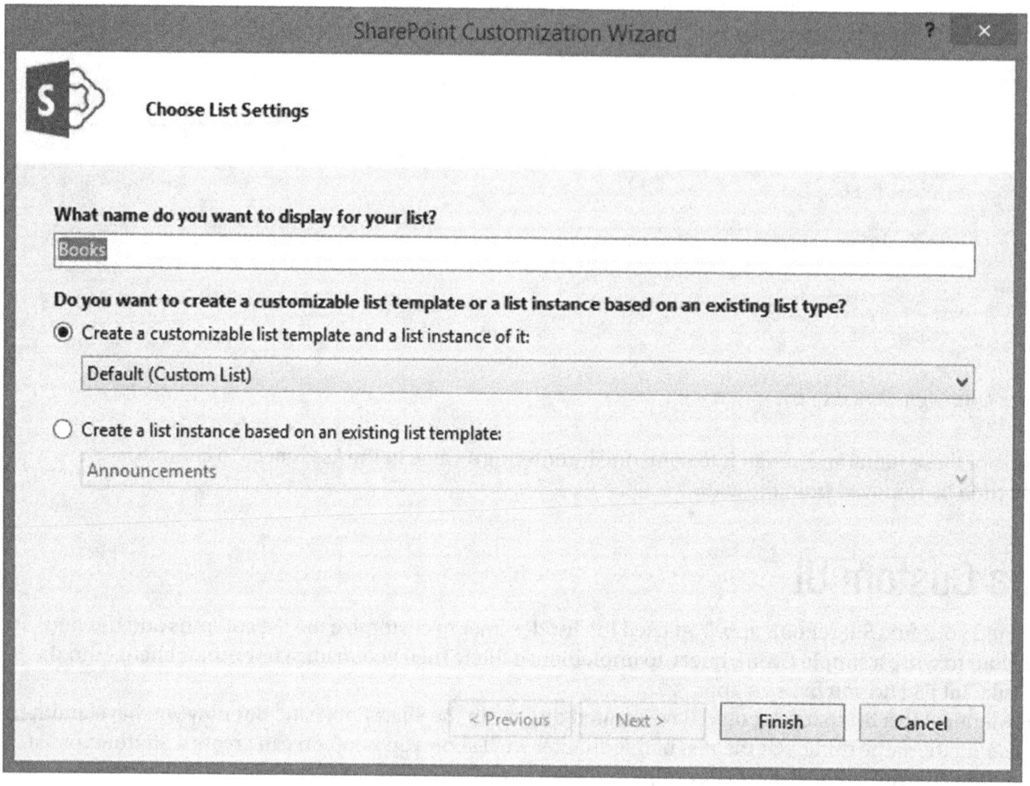

Figure 3-18. *Choosing a custom list*

5. The list designer should be displayed; if not, double-click the Books list in the Solution Explorer. The Title column is already added as all lists require a Title column. Add the following columns; the grid should look like Figure 3-19.

- URL - Hyperlink or Picture

- Background - Choice

- Order - Number

Columns   Views   List

Use the grid to configure columns for the list. Learn more about creating lists

Column Display Name	Type	Required
Title	Single Line of Text	☑
URL	Hyperlink or Picture	☑
Background	Choice	☐
Order	Number	☐
✿ Type a new or existing column name		☐

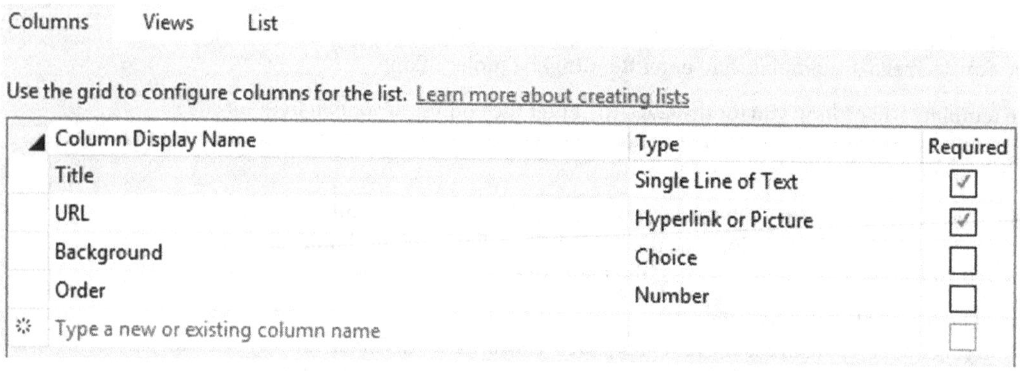

Figure 3-19. *Defining the list columns*

■ **Caution** There is an existing site column called URL. Make sure to select the one that is defined as a HyperLink or Picture. The other columns are Computed types. Background and Order do not already exist as site columns so you'll need to specify the type.

6. Go to the Views tab and add a new view called **Title List**. Select the Read Only check box and add the Order, Title (Link Title), and Created columns as shown in Figure 3-20.

Columns	Views	List

Use the grid to configure views for the list. Configure columns for the selected view by using the lists below.
Note: The grid must contain at least one view.

◢ View Name	Row Limit	Read Only
All Items	30	☐
Title List		☑
✷ Click here to add a view		☐

[Set as Default]

Available columns:

| Attachments |
| Background |
| Content Type |
| Created By |

Selected columns:

| Order |
| Title (LinkTitle) |
| Created |

Figure 3-20. Defining the Title List view

7. In the List tab, change the description to **My Reading List**. Click the Save button in the ribbon to save the list definition.

Defining Choice Values

In the previous project, you had to manually edit the Schema.xml file to enter the CAML query for the view filter. Now you'll need to edit this file to define the choice options.

You defined the Background column as a Choice type. This type of column is represented on the UI forms as a dropdown with a predefined set of values to choose from. The list designer does not give you the ability to define these values. We'll show you how to enter these manually.

Make sure you have saved your changes and then open the Schema.xml file, which will close the list designer. As you did before, format the XML first. From the Edit menu, select the Advanced link and then Format Document. This will make the file easier to read.

Search for the text **<Fields>** in the Schema.xml file. The Fields tag contains the definition of the columns (fields) used in your list. You should see four Field entries for the Title, URL, Background, and Order columns in your list. Within the Field tag for the Background column, add the following:

```
<CHOICES>
  <CHOICE>White</CHOICE>
  <CHOICE>Blue</CHOICE>
  <CHOICE>Red</CHOICE>
  <CHOICE>Green</CHOICE>
  <CHOICE>Orange</CHOICE>
  <CHOICE>Yellow</CHOICE>
  <CHOICE>Purple</CHOICE>
</CHOICES>
```

This defines the background colors that are available. Also, inside the Field tag, add the following attribute:

```
FillInChoice="FALSE"
```

This specifies that the user can only select from the existing list and not define any new values. The complete Fields tag is shown in Listing 3-4. The actual guid values may be different in your file. If so, use your values not the values in the code listing. The lines that you'll need to add or modify are shown bolded.

Listing 3-4. The final Fields tag

```
<Fields>
  <Field ID="{fa564e0f-0c70-4ab9-b863-0177e6ddd247}"
         Type="Text"
         Name="Title"
         DisplayName="$Resources:core,Title;"
         Required="TRUE"
         SourceID="http://schemas.microsoft.com/sharepoint/v3"
         StaticName="Title"
         MaxLength="255" />
  <Field ID="{c29e077d-f466-4d8e-8bbe-72b66c5f205c}"
         Name="URL"
         SourceID="http://schemas.microsoft.com/sharepoint/v3"
         StaticName="URL"
         Group="$Resources:core,Base_Columns;"
         Type="URL"
         DisplayName="$Resources:core,URL;"
         Required="TRUE" />
  <Field Name="Background"
         ID="{ec5bdad4-c9ef-45aa-8650-e6213fb1428d}"
         DisplayName="Background"
         Type="Choice"
         FillInChoice="FALSE">
    <CHOICES>
      <CHOICE>White</CHOICE>
      <CHOICE>Blue</CHOICE>
      <CHOICE>Red</CHOICE>
      <CHOICE>Green</CHOICE>
```

```
    <CHOICE>Orange</CHOICE>
    <CHOICE>Yellow</CHOICE>
    <CHOICE>Purple</CHOICE>
    </CHOICES>
  </Field>
  <Field Name="Order1"
         ID="{baf5e8e4-2c81-48b7-8185-f568c6a3d0d9}"
         DisplayName="Order"
         Type="Number" />
</Fields>
```

Save the changes to the `Schema.xml` file.

Populating the Books List

To test the custom page, you'll need some items in the Books list. You can add these manually after the app has been deployed to SharePoint. However, when deploying updates to the app you may find the list contents are removed and then you'll need to add them again. To make your life easier, we'll show you how to pre-populate the list every time the app is deployed.

■ **Note**   When you press F5 to deploy and debug, Visual Studio must first deploy the changes to the SharePoint site. If only client-side elements have been modified, such as CSS or JavaScript files, the deployment simply replaces the modified files. You'll notice that these types of deployments are much faster. However, if there are changes to the SharePoint elements, such as lists or views, the whole solution is retracted and then re-deployed. This will also cause you to lose whatever list contents were in the list.

As I mentioned earlier, when you create a list like this you are defining both a list template as well as an instance of that template. If you look in the Solution Explorer, the Books element is a list template, while the BooksInstance is the instance of this template. Both of these items have an `Elements.xml` file.

Open the `Elements.xml` file from the instance (`BooksInstance`). Inside this tag, enter the contents shown in Listing 3-5 to pre-populate the list instance with some test data.

Listing 3-5. Adding the Data element

```
<Data>
  <Rows>
    <Row>
      <Field Name="Title">Beginning WF</Field>
      <Field Name="URL">http://www.apress.com/9781430224853</Field>
      <Field Name="Background">Green</Field>
      <Field Name="Order1">1</Field>
    </Row>
    <Row>
      <Field Name="Title">Office 2010 Workflow</Field>
      <Field Name="URL">http://www.apress.com/9781430229049</Field>
      <Field Name="Background">Blue</Field>
      <Field Name="Order1">2</Field>
    </Row>
```

```
  <Row>
    <Field Name="Title">Pro Project Management with SharePoint 2010</Field>
    <Field Name="URL">http://www.apress.com/9781430228295</Field>
    <Field Name="Background">Orange</Field>
    <Field Name="Order1">3</Field>
  </Row>
  <Row>
    <Field Name="Title">Pro Access 2010 Development</Field>
    <Field Name="URL">http://www.apress.com/9781430235781</Field>
    <Field Name="Background">Yellow</Field>
    <Field Name="Order1">4</Field>
  </Row>
  <Row>
    <Field Name="Title">Pro Office 365 Development</Field>
    <Field Name="URL">http://www.apress.com/9781430240747</Field>
    <Field Name="Background">Red</Field>
    <Field Name="Order1">5</Field>
  </Row>
  <Row>
    <Field Name="Title">WinRT Revealed</Field>
    <Field Name="URL">http://www.apress.com/9781430245841</Field>
    <Field Name="Background">White</Field>
    <Field Name="Order1">6</Field>
  </Row>
  <Row>
    <Field Name="Title">HTML5 with Visual Studio 2012</Field>
    <Field Name="URL">http://www.apress.com/9781430246381</Field>
    <Field Name="Background">Purple</Field>
    <Field Name="Order1">7</Field>
  </Row>
  </Rows>
</Data>
```

This should be fairly self-explanatory. The Data tag defines data that should be uploaded to the SharePoint site during deployment. This contains a Rows tag, which has a collection of Row elements. Each Row element has a collection of Field tags to define the value of each column.

Deploying the Initial App

Let's deploy the App as it is currently so you can verify the list is working correctly. You'll add the custom UI later. Just Press F5 to build and deploy the Books list to your SharePoint site.

Since you've not modified the Default.aspx page, there won't be much content on this page. More specifically, it does not show the list of books or any way to navigate to such a list. The page will look like Figure 3-21.

ReadingList

Page Title

Hello Mark Collins

Figure 3-21. *The initial Default.aspx page*

However, there is a Books list in SharePoint and the standard UI for the defined views is available; you just need to find a way to get to it. If you look at your browser, there is a really long URL for the default page. You might want to paste it into notepad so you can view and edit it.

Start by removing all of the parameters starting with ?SPHostUrl=. With that gone the URL is easier to follow. It will end with something like /ReadingList/Pages/Default.aspx. Replace the Pages/Default.aspx with **Lists/Books/AllItems.aspx**. This will take you to the standard SharePoint page instead of your custom page. The final URL for our site is:

```
https://apress365-e2113008fe735a.sharepoint.com/ReadingList/Lists/Books/AllItems.aspx
```

Yours will be similar but with a different root address. Paste this into a browser to view the contents of the Books list, which should look like Figure 3-22.

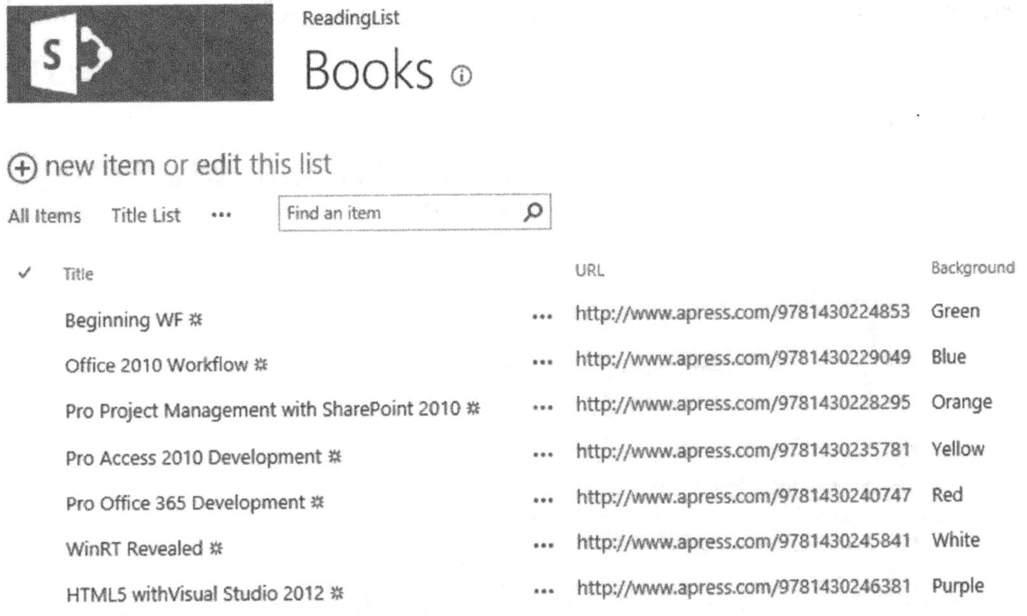

ReadingList

Books ⓘ

⊕ new item or edit this list

All Items   Title List   •••   [Find an item   🔎]

✓	Title		URL	Background
	Beginning WF ❄	•••	http://www.apress.com/9781430224853	Green
	Office 2010 Workflow ❄	•••	http://www.apress.com/9781430229049	Blue
	Pro Project Management with SharePoint 2010 ❄	•••	http://www.apress.com/9781430228295	Orange
	Pro Access 2010 Development ❄	•••	http://www.apress.com/9781430235781	Yellow
	Pro Office 365 Development ❄	•••	http://www.apress.com/9781430240747	Red
	WinRT Revealed ❄	•••	http://www.apress.com/9781430245841	White
	HTML5 withVisual Studio 2012 ❄	•••	http://www.apress.com/9781430246381	Purple

Figure 3-22. *The standard SharePoint AllItems page*

Notice the Title List view that you defined is also available.

Implementing a Custom Page

With the Books list defined, you're ready to build the custom UI. You'll start with the Default.aspx page. You'll just add a div here and then later use JavaScript to insert contents into it. The other change you will make here is to provide a way to navigate to the standard SharePoint UI. So you'll create a custom page but also provide a way to use the other views as well.

You'll then write some JavaScript code that uses both the SharePoint libraries as well as jQuery to create the dynamic content. This code will query data from the Books list and use this to format HTML content. Finally, you'll modify the App.css file to provide the necessary styling.

Modifying the Default Page

The Default.aspx page should look just like the one you worked with earlier in this chapter. Find the second asp:Content tag and replace the default Page Title text with **Reading List**.

Then, in the third asp:Content tag, where the message div is, remove this div and replace it with the following:

```
<a
    href="../Lists/Books/AllItems.aspx">Manage Books<img src="../Images/GearIcon.png" />
</a>
<div id="results"></div>
```

The anchor tag provides a link to the standard views. This will save your users the hassle you just went through to get to these pages. The results div is empty but you'll fill in content later.

You'll need a few images that the code will be referencing. We have included them in the download folder for Chapter 3, in the Images subfolder. The files are EditIcon.png, GearIcon.png, and ViewIcon.png. You can use your own images if you prefer. Drag these files into the Images folder in the Solution Explorer. Notice that the Elements.xml file in this folder is automatically updated to include these files.

Writing the JavaScript

Open the App.js file in the Scripts folder. This will be identical to the one you used earlier in this chapter. Replace the entire contents of this file with the code shown in Listing 3-6. We will then walk through this code function by function.

Listing 3-6. The App.js implementation

```javascript
$(document).ready(function () {
    SP.SOD.executeFunc('sp.js', 'SP.ClientContext', retrieveBooks);
});

function retrieveBooks() {
    var context = new SP.ClientContext.get_current();
    var oList = context.get_web().get_lists().getByTitle('Books');

    var camlQuery = new SP.CamlQuery();
    camlQuery.set_viewXml('<View><Query><OrderBy><FieldRef Name=\'Order1\' ' +
        'Ascending=\'TRUE\' /></OrderBy></Query><ViewFields><FieldRef Name=\'Id\' ' +
        '/><FieldRef Name=\'Title\' /><FieldRef Name=\'URL\' '+
        '/><FieldRef Name=\'Background\' /><FieldRef Name=\'Order1\' ' +
        '/></ViewFields></View>');
    this.collListItem = oList.getItems(camlQuery);
```

```
        context.load(collListItem, 'Include(Id, Title, URL, Background, Order1)');

        context.executeQueryAsync(Function.createDelegate(this, this.onQuerySucceeded),
                                  Function.createDelegate(this, this.onQueryFailed));
}

function onQueryFailed(sender, args) {
    SP.UI.Notify.addNotification('Request failed. ' + args.get_message() + '\n' +
                                                    args.get_stackTrace(), true);
}

function onQuerySucceeded(sender, args) {

    var listEnumerator = collListItem.getEnumerator();
    var listInfo = "";

    while (listEnumerator.moveNext()) {
        var oListItem = listEnumerator.get_current();
        listInfo +=
            "<div id='" + oListItem.get_id() + "' class='Book " +
                        oListItem.get_item('Background') + "'>" +
                "<a href='" + oListItem.get_item('URL').get_url() +
                    "' target='_blank'>" +
                    "<div class='BookDescription'>" + oListItem.get_item('Title') +
                    "</div>" +
                "</a>" +
                "<div class='EditIcon'>" +
                    "<a href='#' onclick='ShowDialog(" + oListItem.get_id() +
                        ")'><img src='../Images/EditIcon.png' /></a>" +
                "</div>" +
            "</div>";
    }

    $("#results").html(listInfo);
}

function ShowDialog(ID) {

    var options = {
        url: "../Lists/Books/EditForm.aspx?ID=" + ID,
        allowMaximize: true,
        title: "Edit Book",
        dialogReturnValueCallback: scallback
    };
    SP.SOD.execute('sp.ui.dialog.js', 'SP.UI.ModalDialog.showModalDialog', options);
    return false;
}
```

```
function scallback(dialogResult, returnValue) {
    if (dialogResult == SP.UI.DialogResult.OK) {
        SP.UI.ModalDialog.RefreshPage(SP.UI.DialogResult.OK);
    }
}
```

This may seem like a lot of code but if you break it down, it's fairly straightforward. As we described earlier, the $(document).ready() command specifies the function to be executed after the page is loaded, in this case it is the retrieveBooks() function.

The retrieveBooks() function gets the current SharePoint context and then uses that to get the Books list. It then executes a CAML query to access the data needed from the list. When formatted as a JavaScript string this may be a little hard to read, especially with the line wraps. Here is the actual query in XML format:

```
<View>
  <Query>
    <OrderBy>
      <FieldRef Name="Order1" Ascending="TRUE" />
    </OrderBy>
  </Query>
  <ViewFields>
    <FieldRef Name="Id" />
    <FieldRef Name="Title" />
    <FieldRef Name="URL" />
    <FieldRef Name="Background" />
    <FieldRef Name="Order1" />
  </ViewFields>
</View>
```

This is a pretty simple query that returns all rows sorted by the Order column. The ViewFields tag specifies the columns that should be returned by the query. This query is executed using the executeQueryAsync() method that we showed earlier. This requires two function delegates; one for a successful operation and one for errors. The results of the query will be stored in the collListItem variable.

The onQuerySucceeded() function is called when successful and it does all the interesting work. It gets an enumerator for the results and then iterates through all the items returned. Each iteration through the while loop processes one item from the list. For each book, the code generates HTML content, plugging in data returned from the list. Here is an example of what the HTML looks like (the variable text is shown bolded):

```
<div id="1" class="Book Yellow">
  <a href="http://www.apress.com/9781430246381" target="_blank">
    <div class="BookDescription">HTML5 with Visual Studio 2012</div>
  </a>
  <div class="EditIcon">
    <a href="#" onclick="ShowDialog(1)"><img src="../Images/EditIcon.png" /></a>
  </div>
</div>
```

The main div contains an anchor tag that links to the page with information about the book and within that another div that contains the book's title. There is also another div that contains an icon with an onclick event that calls the ShowDialog() function.

The contents for each book are accumulated in the listInfo variable. When all the books have been processed, the contents of the results div is replaced using the combined generated HTML.

The ShowDialog() function invokes the standard SharePoint EditForm. This allows the user to modify the details of a book from the custom page. When the EditForm is closed, the scallback() function is called. This refreshes the current page to reflect the modified details.

Modifying the CSS

The last step in this process is to define the appropriate styles in the App.css file. Open the App.css file and add the style commands shown in Listing 3-7.

Listing 3-7. The App.css contents

```
body {
    min-width: 520px;
}

.column {
    width: 170px;
    float: left;
    padding-bottom: 100px;
}

.Book {
    width:250px;
    height:80px;
    margin-top:5px;
    margin-left:0;
    margin-right:10px;
    margin-bottom:10px;
    cursor:pointer;
    padding:5px;
    float:left;
    text-align:left;
    font-family:Segoe UI, sans-serif;
    font-size:14px;
    background-repeat: no-repeat;
    background-position:center;
    overflow:hidden;
    position:relative;
    clear: both;
    border-style: solid;
    border-width: 2px;
    border-color: black;
    border-top-left-radius:10px;
    border-top-left-radius:10px;
    border-top-right-radius:10px;
    border-bottom-left-radius:10px;
    border-bottom-right-radius:10px;
}
```

```css
.BookDescription {
    color: #000;
    font-size: 12pt;
}

.EditIcon {
    float:right;
    text-align:right;
    background-color:black;
}

.Purple {
    background-color:#A200FF;
}
.Yellow {
    background-color:#efef42;
}
.Orange {
    background-color:#F09609;
}
.Blue {
    background-color:#1BA1E2;
}
.Red {
    background-color:#E51400;
}
.Green {
    background-color:#339933;
}
.White{
    background-color:#FFFFFF;
}
```

This is pretty much just basic styling. However, notice the color selectors at the end. The Background column contains a color name such as Purple or Yellow. This is included in the HTML as a class attribute for the main div. The CSS action sets the appropriate background-color property.

Also, the EditIcon selector aligns the icon to the right of the div with a black background (so it will show up well regardless of the main color).

Testing the App

With all the implementation complete, you're ready to test the app. Press F5 to build and deploy the app. The custom page should look like Figure 3-23.

ReadingList
Reading List

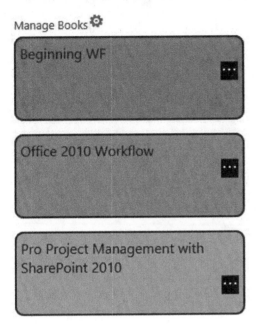

Figure 3-23. The custom Reading List page

If you click on the edit icon, the standard edit form will appear as shown in Figure 3-24.

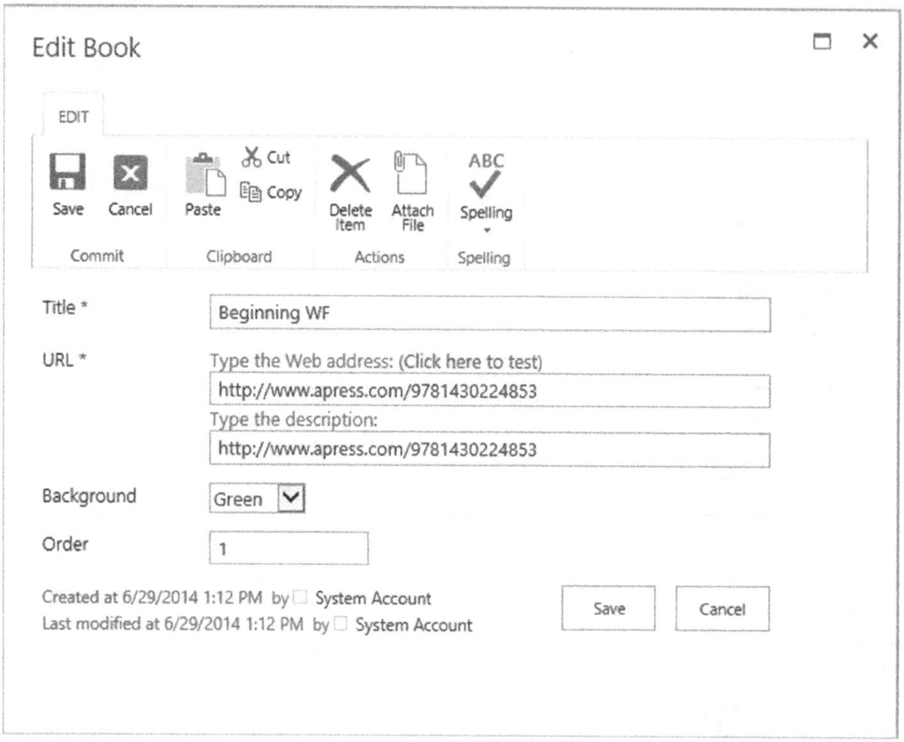

Figure 3-24. *The standard EditForm*

If you change the background color or the order, the page will be refreshed, reflecting the changes you have made. Also, notice the Manage Books link and icon at the top. If you click this, the All Items view that you looked at earlier will be displayed.

So you have a hybrid solution with a custom UI page combined with some of the standard SharePoint forms and pages. This allows you to create custom pages where needed and leverage the existing UI as well.

Adding a Custom Ribbon

You have the Manage Book link to navigate to the All Items view. Now you'll remove this and create a custom action in the ribbon instead. This is accomplished with some additional JavaScript code.

Open the App.js file and append the code shown in Listing 3-8.

Listing 3-8. Additional JavaScript code to add a custom ribbon

```
// Methods for the ribbon
function ModifyRibbon() {

    var pm = SP.Ribbon.PageManager.get_instance();

    pm.add_ribbonInited(function () {
        AddBookTab();
    });

    var ribbon = null;
    try {
        ribbon = pm.get_ribbon();
    }
    catch (e) { }

    if (!ribbon) {
        if (typeof (_ribbonStartInit) == "function")
            _ribbonStartInit(_ribbon.initialTabId, false, null);
    }
    else {
        AddBookTab();
    }
}

function AddBookTab() {
    var sTitleHtml = "";
    var sManageHtml = "";

    sTitleHtml += "<a href='../Lists/Books/Title%20List.aspx' >' ";
    sTitleHtml += "<img src='../images/ViewIcon.png' /></a><br/>Title List";
    sManageHtml += "<a href='../Lists/Books/AllItems.aspx' >";
    sManageHtml += "<img src='../images/ViewIcon.png' /></a><br/>Manage Books";

    var ribbon = SP.Ribbon.PageManager.get_instance().get_ribbon();
    if (ribbon !== null) {
        var tab = new CUI.Tab(ribbon, 'Books.Tab', 'Books',
            'Use this tab to view and modify the book list',
            'Books.Tab.Command', false, '', null);
        ribbon.addChildAtIndex(tab, 1);
        var group = new CUI.Group(ribbon, 'Books.Tab.Group', 'Views',
            'Use this group to view a list of titles',
            'Books.Group.Command', null);
        tab.addChild(group);
        var group = new CUI.Group(ribbon, 'Books.Tab.Group', 'Actions',
            'Use this group to add/update/delete books',
            'Books.Group.Command', null);
        tab.addChild(group);
    }
```

```
    SelectRibbonTab('Books.Tab', true);
    $("span:contains('Views')").prev("span").html(sTitleHtml);
    $("span:contains('Actions')").prev("span").html(sManageHtml);
    SelectRibbonTab('Ribbon.Read', true);
}
```

The ModifyRibbon() function initializes the ribbon, if it is not already initialized, and calls the AddBookTab() function. The AddBookTab() function is where the custom ribbon tab is generated. It will have two actions, one navigates to the All Items view and the other to the Title List view that you created. Each action is defined by an HTML block that includes an icon with a link to the appropriate view.

After generating the necessary HTML content, this method then uses the ribbon to create a new tab called Books that contains two groups called Views and Actions. Then the new tab is enabled. Finally, jQuery code is used to insert the generated HTML in the ribbon.

Now you'll need to modify the $(document).ready() command to also invoke the ModifyRibbon() function. Add the line shown bolded to your App.js file:

```
$(document).ready(function () {
    SP.SOD.executeFunc('sp.js', 'SP.ClientContext', retrieveBooks);
    SP.SOD.executeOrDelayUntilScriptLoaded(ModifyRibbon, 'sp.ribbon.js');
});
```

For the last step, you'll remove the existing Manage Books link. Open the Default.aspx page and remove the anchor tag from the third asp:Content tag. All that should remain is the empty result div.

With these changes done, you're ready to test the app. Press F5 to build and deploy the updated app to your SharePoint site. You should now see a Books tab as shown in Figure 3-25.

Figure 3-25. *The custom Books tab*

Click the Title List button, which will navigate to the custom Title List view shown in Figure 3-26.

ReadingList

Books ⓘ

⊕ new item or edit this list

All Items   Title List   •••   [Find an item   🔍]

✓	Order	Title		Created
	1	Beginning WF ❈	•••	27 minutes ago
	2	Office 2010 Workflow ❈	•••	27 minutes ago
	3	Pro Project Management with SharePoint 2010 ❈	•••	27 minutes ago
	4	Pro Access 2010 Development ❈	•••	27 minutes ago
	5	Pro Office 365 Development ❈	•••	27 minutes ago
	6	WinRT Revealed ❈	•••	27 minutes ago
	7	HTML5 withVisual Studio 2012 ❈	•••	27 minutes ago

Figure 3-26. *The Title List view*

To get back to the custom UI page, just click the ReadingList link at the top of the page.

Creating a Custom App Part

For the last feature in this chapter, you'll create an App Part. An App Part is like a regular web page but with a smaller footprint and can be placed onto an existing page. This allows the users to configure a page by including various App Parts. This works great for a home page or dashboard where you often want visibility into a number of things in one place.

Your reading list contains a collection of books in the order you intend to read them. Your App Part will simply display the one that's on the top of your list. You'll add an App Part to your Visual Studio solution using the Client Web Part template. This will create a web page in your Pages folder. You will then modify this file and include a JavaScript file to define your App Part.

■ **Note**   We explained in Chapter 1 about App Parts and Web Parts. The users will see them as App Parts. However as a developer you will refer to them as Web Parts because that is what Visual Studio calls them. We will call them either App Parts or Web Parts depending on the tools you're using.

Adding a Client Web Part

In Visual Studio, from the Solution Explorer, right-click the project and then select the Add and New Item links. In the Add New Item dialog box, select the Client Web Part template and enter the name **BookWebPart** as shown in Figure 3-27.

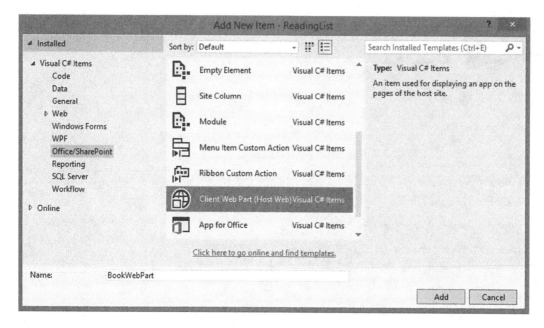

Figure 3-27. *Adding a client web part*

The template will prompt you for some additional details. Leave all the default values as shown in Figure 3-28.

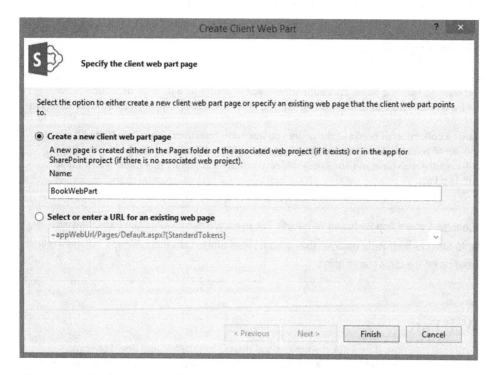

Figure 3-28. *Configuring the web part*

■ **Tip** When creating a new Web Part, the template gives you the option to base it on an existing page. If you have a page and you want the Web Part to look similar to that page, you can specify the page URL and it will use to define the web part.

Designing the Web Part

The template generated a BookWebPart.aspx file in your Pages folder. You'll need to include the existing App.css file as well as a new JavaScript file. As with the Default.aspx page, you'll add an empty div that you'll later fill in with JavaScript code. The html contents of this file are shown in Listing 3-9, with the additions shown bolded.

Listing 3-9. The BookWebPart.aspx implementation

```
<html>
<head>
    <title></title>

    <script type="text/javascript" src="../Scripts/jquery-1.9.1.min.js"></script>
    <script type="text/javascript" src="/_layouts/15/MicrosoftAjax.js"></script>
    <script type="text/javascript" src="/_layouts/15/sp.runtime.js"></script>
    <script type="text/javascript" src="/_layouts/15/sp.js"></script>

    <link rel="Stylesheet" type="text/css" href="../Content/App.css" />
    <script type="text/javascript" src="../Scripts/WebPart.js"></script>

    <script type="text/javascript">
        'use strict';

        // Set the style of the client web part to be consistent with the host web.
        (function () {
            var hostUrl = '';
            if (document.URL.indexOf('?') != -1) {
                var params = document.URL.split('?')[1].split('&');
                for (var i = 0; i < params.length; i++) {
                    var p = decodeURIComponent(params[i]);
                    if (/^SPHostUrl=/i.test(p)) {
                        hostUrl = p.split('=')[1];
                        document.write('<link rel="stylesheet" href="' +
                            hostUrl + '/_layouts/15/defaultcss.ashx" />');
                        break;
                    }
                }
            }
            if (hostUrl == '') {
                document.write('<link rel="stylesheet" ' +
                    'href="/_layouts/15/1033/styles/themable/corev15.css" />');
            }
        })();
    </script>
</head>
```

```
<body>
    <div id="bookList">Book List</div>
</body>
</html>
```

Now you'll need to add a JavaScript file that will contain the code needed to format the Web Part. In the Solution Explorer, right-click the Scripts folder and select the Add and New Item links. In the Add New Item dialog box, go to the Web folder and select the JavaScript File template. Enter **WebPart.js** for the file name and click the Add button.

Enter the code shown in Listing 3-10 into the WebPart.js file.

Listing 3-10. The WebPart.js implementation

```javascript
$(document).ready(function () {
    var spHostUrl = decodeURIComponent(getQueryStringParameter('SPHostUrl'));
    var layoutsRoot = spHostUrl + '/_layouts/15/';

    $.getScript(layoutsRoot + "SP.Runtime.js", function () {
        $.getScript(layoutsRoot + "SP.js", formatWebPart);
    }
    );
});

function formatWebPart() {
    context = new SP.ClientContext.get_current();
    web = context.get_web();

    retrieveBooks();
}

function retrieveBooks() {
    var context = new SP.ClientContext.get_current();
    var oList = context.get_web().get_lists().getByTitle('Books');

    var camlQuery = new SP.CamlQuery();

    camlQuery.set_viewXml('<View><Query><OrderBy><FieldRef Name=\'Order1\' ' +
    'Ascending=\'TRUE\' /></OrderBy></Query><ViewFields><FieldRef Name=\'Id\' ' +
    '/><FieldRef Name=\'Title\' /><FieldRef Name=\'URL\' ' +
    '/><FieldRef Name=\'Background\' /><FieldRef Name=\'Order1\' ' +
    '/></ViewFields></View>');
    this.collListItem = oList.getItems(camlQuery);

    context.load(this.collListItem, 'Include(Id, Title, URL, Background, Order1)');

    context.executeQueryAsync(Function.createDelegate(this, this.onQuerySucceeded),
                        Function.createDelegate(this, this.onQueryFailed));
}

function onQueryFailed(sender, args) {
    SP.UI.Notify.addNotification('Request failed. ' + args.get_message() + '\n' +
                                    args.get_stackTrace(), true);
}
```

```
function onQuerySucceeded(sender, args) {
    var listEnumerator = collListItem.getEnumerator();
    var listInfo = "";

    if (listEnumerator.moveNext()) {
        var oListItem = listEnumerator.get_current();
        listInfo +=
            "<div id='" + oListItem.get_id() + "' class='Book " +
                        oListItem.get_item('Background') + "'>" +
                "<a href='" + oListItem.get_item('URL').get_url() +
                  "' target='_blank'>" +
                  "<div class='BookDescription'>" + oListItem.get_item('Title') +
                  "</div>" +
                "</a>" +
            "</div>";
    }

    $("#bookList").html(listInfo);
}

function getQueryStringParameter(urlParameterKey) {
    var params = document.URL.split('?')[1].split('&');
    var strParams = '';
    for (var i = 0; i < params.length; i = i + 1) {
        var singleParam = params[i].split('=');
        if (singleParam[0] == urlParameterKey)
            return decodeURIComponent(singleParam[1]);
    }
}
```

This code is very similar to the App.js code that you implemented earlier. The code to query the Books list is identical and the code for generating the HTML is similar except it only processes the first item returned. Also, it does not include the EditIcon button so you can't edit the current book from this Web Part. There are also some minor differences in the way the context and list are obtained.

Deploying and Configuring the Web Part

Press F5 to build and deploy the app. In addition to the custom UI page, the Web Part will be installed. To access it, however, you'll need to add it to an existing page.

Go to the Home page of your Team Site. From the PAGE tab of the ribbon, click the Edit button to put the page in edit mode. Then put your cursor at the bottom of the page. Go to the INSERT tab of the ribbon and click the App Part button. You should see your new App Part as shown in Figure 3-29.

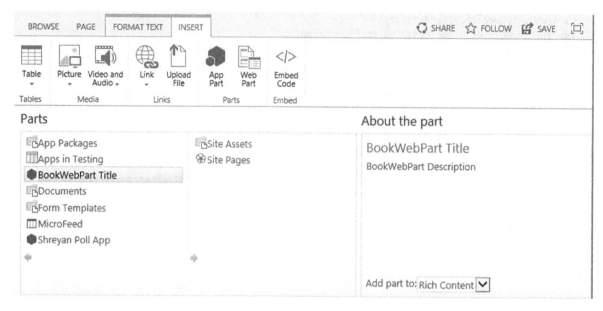

Figure 3-29. Adding the new App Part

Select BookWebPart and then click the Add button. In the App Part properties window, change the Title to **Current Book** and click the OK button. Click the Save button in the ribbon to save the changes. The modified home page should now look like Figure 3-30.

Figure 3-30. The updated Home page with new App Part

Summary

In this chapter you created two SharePoint apps. This first was a basic list using the standard SharePoint UI. You used the list designer to modify the list columns and to define a new view. You also wrote a CAML query to filter the list. With some fairly simple modifications you were able to quickly provision a functional list.

In the second app, you also created a custom list and modified the Elements.xml file to populate its initial contents. For this list you provided a custom page using JavaScript and CSS. While the implementation was somewhat trivial, you learned how to query data from a SharePoint list and render the contents with custom HTML.

You then implemented a custom ribbon using JavaScript. This is a really great way of providing custom navigation and user functions, within the standard SharePoint UI framework. Finally, you created a simple App Part that exposed some data from your custom list and included this in the Home page.

CHAPTER 4

Creating Declarative Workflows with Visio and SharePoint Designer

SharePoint is a versatile repository for all sorts of data including document libraries and various lists of data elements. Workflows are a great way to establish a process around that data. For example, when a new request is created, a workflow can be initiated to automate the processing of that request. SharePoint workflows are often referred to as human-centric workflows (or sometimes task-centric) because they are primarily concerned with the tasks that people will perform. When a request is received, for example, some of the typical tasks could be

- Review and approve the request.
- Assign and/or schedule the work.
- Fulfill the request.
- Verify (test) the end result.
- Provide feedback.

The workflow doesn't actually implement these tasks, people do. The workflow, however, enforces the business rules that determine what tasks are needed, what order they are performed in, under what conditions, and by whom.

The workflow infrastructure has been completely revamped in SharePoint 2013. From a developer's perspective, the most significant change is that only declarative workflows are supported in 2013. In SharePoint 2010, you could implement a workflow using .NET's Workflow Foundation, which was sometimes referred to as a "coded" solution since you wrote C# (or VB) code that was compiled into assemblies and executed within SharePoint. This was only supported in on-premise SharePoint servers, however, because of the access level required for them to run.

In SharePoint 2013 both the infrastructure and tools have been enhanced to make declarative workflow a much more viable solution and the coded solution is no longer supported. The good news, for Office 365 developers, is that workflows are fully functional in a cloud-based solution. For backward compatibility, SharePoint 2013 can still run the previous 2010-style workflows. In this chapter, we will be using only the 2013 platform.

Declarative workflows are designed by combining a fixed set of conditions and actions. Conditions allow you to take different actions based on data from various sources. For example, if a request is approved you may want to take different actions than if it was rejected. The available actions provide quite a bit of functionality including:

- Creating or updating a list item.
- Sending an e-mail.
- Checking in a document to a document library.
- Calling an external web service.

In this chapter you'll implement a workflow to automate the processing of requests using a custom Requests list that you'll create using SharePoint Designer 2013. You will then use a combination of Visio and SharePoint Designer to define the workflow process. In this chapter, we will show you how to

- Create a custom list using SharePoint Designer 2013.

- Design a workflow in Visio 2013.

- Implement a declarative workflow in SharePoint Designer 2013.

- Use content types and workflow variables to improve the user experience.

Creating the Requests List

Before getting started designing the workflow, you'll need to implement the Requests lists. You'll create the Requests list using SharePoint Designer 2013. SharePoint Designer is a desktop application that allows you to view and edit the objects in your SharePoint site such as lists, site columns, and content types. It is also used to define declarative workflows. With the 2013 release, it has been very nicely integrated with Visio 2013 as we will demonstrate later in this chapter.

Installing SharePoint Designer 2013

You can install SharePoint Designer on your client machine from the Office 365 site. Go to your Office 365 settings page. You can get there by clicking the settings icon (the gear-looking button) to the far-right of the menu bar. In the dropdown menu, select the Office 365 settings link. From the settings page select the Software link. From the Software page select the Tools & add-ins link. The page should look similar to Figure 4-1.

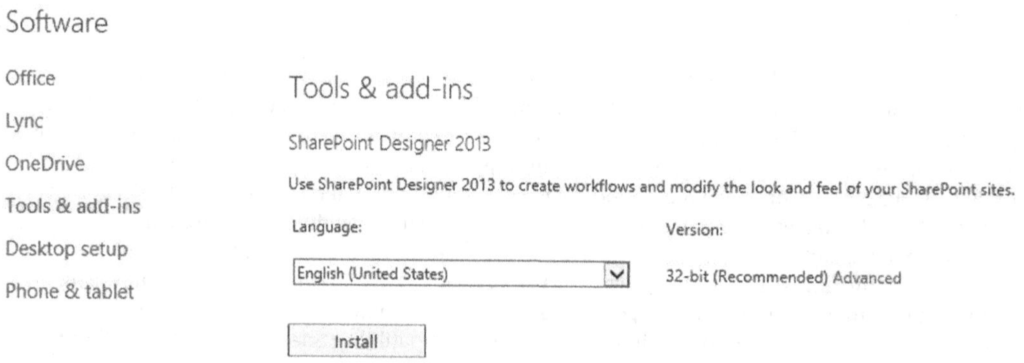

Figure 4-1. Finding the Install option

Click the Install button and follow the instructions to install SharePoint Designer.

■ **Caution**   You can also install SharePoint Designer 2013 directly from the Microsoft site (http://www.microsoft.com/en-us/download/details.aspx?id=35491). For some reason, however, this version doesn't seem to work with Office 365 on all machines. If you have any errors opening the SharePoint site, Microsoft recommends installing SharePoint designer using the Office 365 link.

You should also ensure that your site is configured to allow SharePoint Designer to access it. Go to your Team Site and click the settings icon and select the Site Settings link. In the Site Collection Administration section, you should find the SharePoint Designer Settings link near the end of the list. Click this to view the current settings. Make sure the Enable SharePoint Designer check box is selected as shown in Figure 4-2.

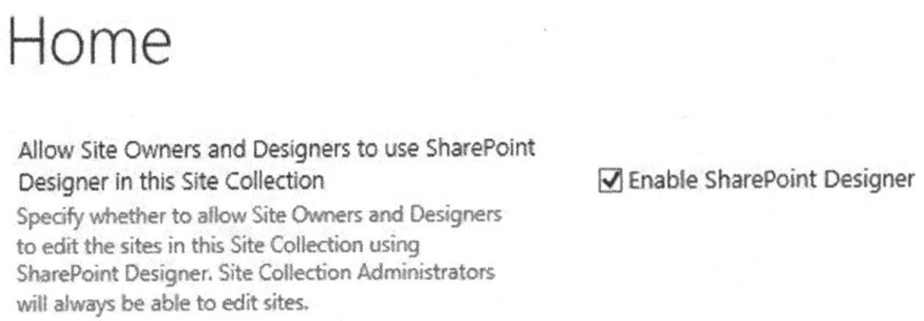

Home

Allow Site Owners and Designers to use SharePoint
Designer in this Site Collection
Specify whether to allow Site Owners and Designers
to edit the sites in this Site Collection using
SharePoint Designer. Site Collection Administrators
will always be able to edit sites.

☑ Enable SharePoint Designer

Figure 4-2. Enabling SharePoint Designer

Connecting to your Office 365 Site

Start SharePoint Designer 2013. The Sites tab should be selected. Click the Open Site button and, in the Open Site dialog box, enter the URL of your Team Site. In our case this is https://apress365.sharepoint.com. Click the Open button and, after downloading the information about your site, the contents will look similar to Figure 4-3.

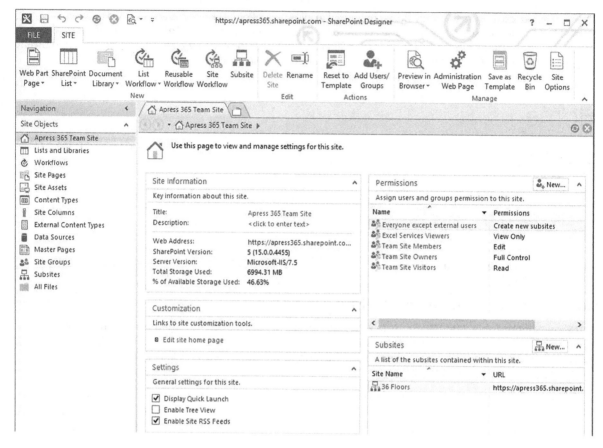

Figure 4-3. *The site information displayed in SharePoint Designer 2013*

Creating a Custom List

Now you'll create a new custom list by defining the columns that will be included. This is the same process that you followed using Visual Studio 2013 in the previous chapter, but you'll use a different tool to complete it.

1. Select Lists and Libraries from the Navigation bar and the details of your existing lists and libraries will be displayed similar to Figure 4-4.

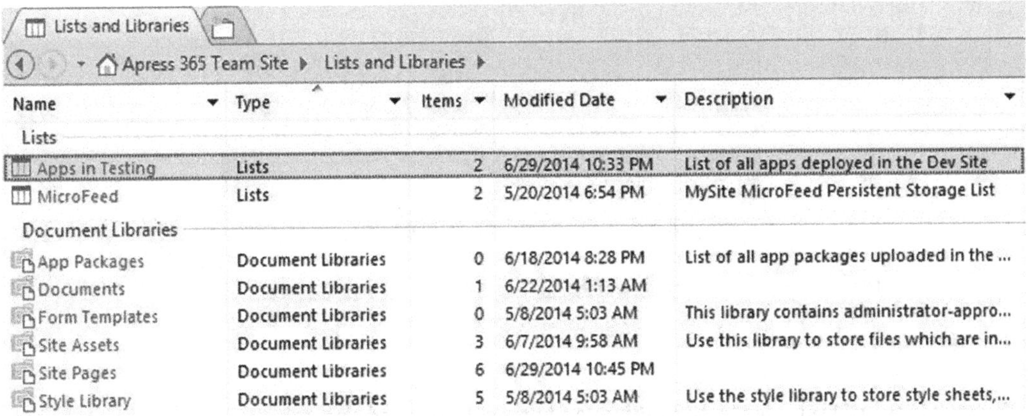

Figure 4-4. *Viewing the existing lists and libraries*

2. The ribbon contains several options for creating a new list or library. You can use the SharePoint List and Document Library buttons to create a new instance of one of the standard objects such as Tasks, Calendar, and Asset Library. For this project, click the Custom List button to define a list with a custom set of columns. Enter the Name and Description of this list as shown in Figure 4-5.

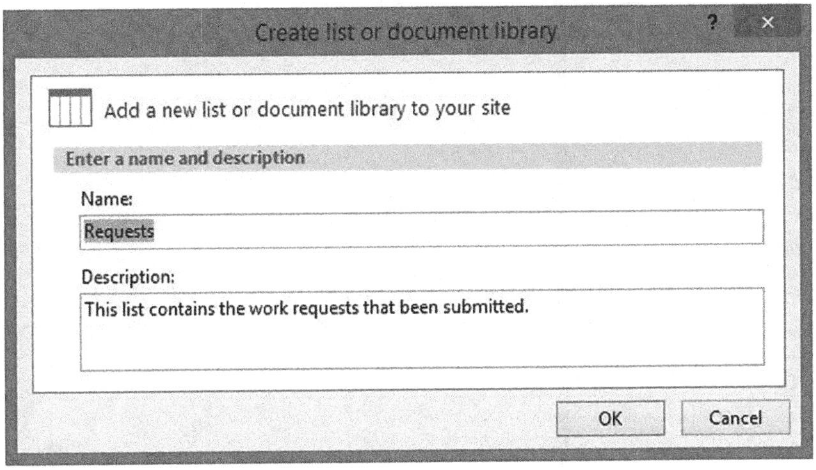

Figure 4-5. *Entering the list name and description*

3. The List and Libraries tab will now include the new Requests list. Select this list to view its details. In the Customization section, click the Edit list columns link. A Requests tab will be shown listing the existing columns, which, at this point, only contains the Title column as shown in Figure 4-6.

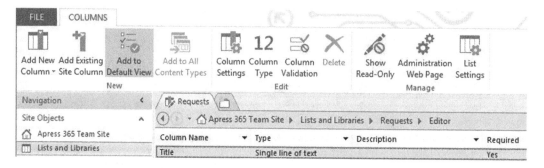

Figure 4-6. Viewing the initial list definition

4. The buttons in the ribbon provide the ability to add new columns and to configure them. The Add New Column button allows you to create a new column that is used only in this list. The Add Existing Site Column button is used to select one or more pre-defined site columns to your list. This is the same concept that we described in the previous chapter when defining columns in Visual Studio. Click the Add Existing Site Column button, which will display the Site Columns Picker dialog box shown in Figure 4-7.

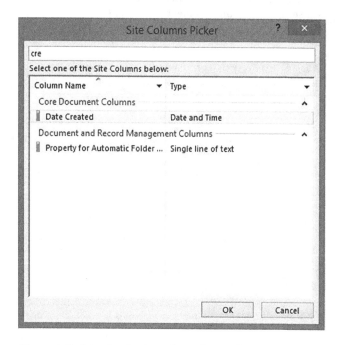

Figure 4-7. Selecting the Date Created site column

5. Notice that as you type in the search box, the list of columns are filtered to show the matching columns. Select the Date Created column and click the OK button.

6. Repeat this process to add the following site columns:

   - Due Date

   - Comments

   - Assigned To

   - % Complete

   - Date Completed

7. Click the Add New Column button to create a new column. You'll be prompted to select the type; select Choice. Enter the following values in the Choices list:

   - **Pending**

   - **Assigned**

   - **InProgress**

   - **Cancelled**

   - **Completed**

8. Unselect the Allow blank values? check box to make this a required column and set the default value as **Pending**, as shown in Figure 4-8. Click the OK button to add the column.

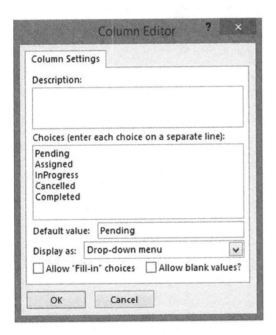

Figure 4-8. *Defining the Request Status column*

9. The column will be added as NewColumn1; you'll need to edit the name of this column. Highlight the Column Name cell in the Requests tab and enter **Request Status**. Click the Save icon in the title bar of the application window. The Requests list should look like Figure 4-9.

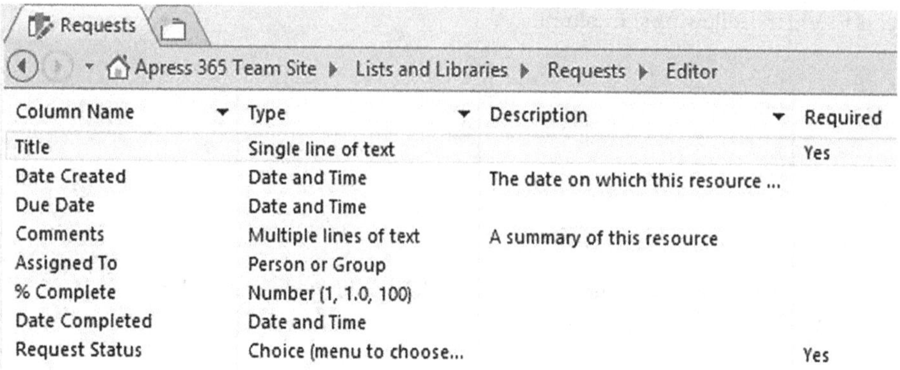

📝 Requests

◀ ▶ ▾ 🏠 Apress 365 Team Site ▸ Lists and Libraries ▸ Requests ▸ Editor

Column Name ▾	Type ▾	Description ▾	Required ▾
Title	Single line of text		Yes
Date Created	Date and Time	The date on which this resource ...	
Due Date	Date and Time		
Comments	Multiple lines of text	A summary of this resource	
Assigned To	Person or Group		
% Complete	Number (1, 1.0, 100)		
Date Completed	Date and Time		
Request Status	Choice (menu to choose...		Yes

Figure 4-9. *The completed list definition*

> 10. Now go to your Team Site and you should see the Requests list in your Recent folder. Select this list and click the new item link. The input form should look like Figure 4-10.

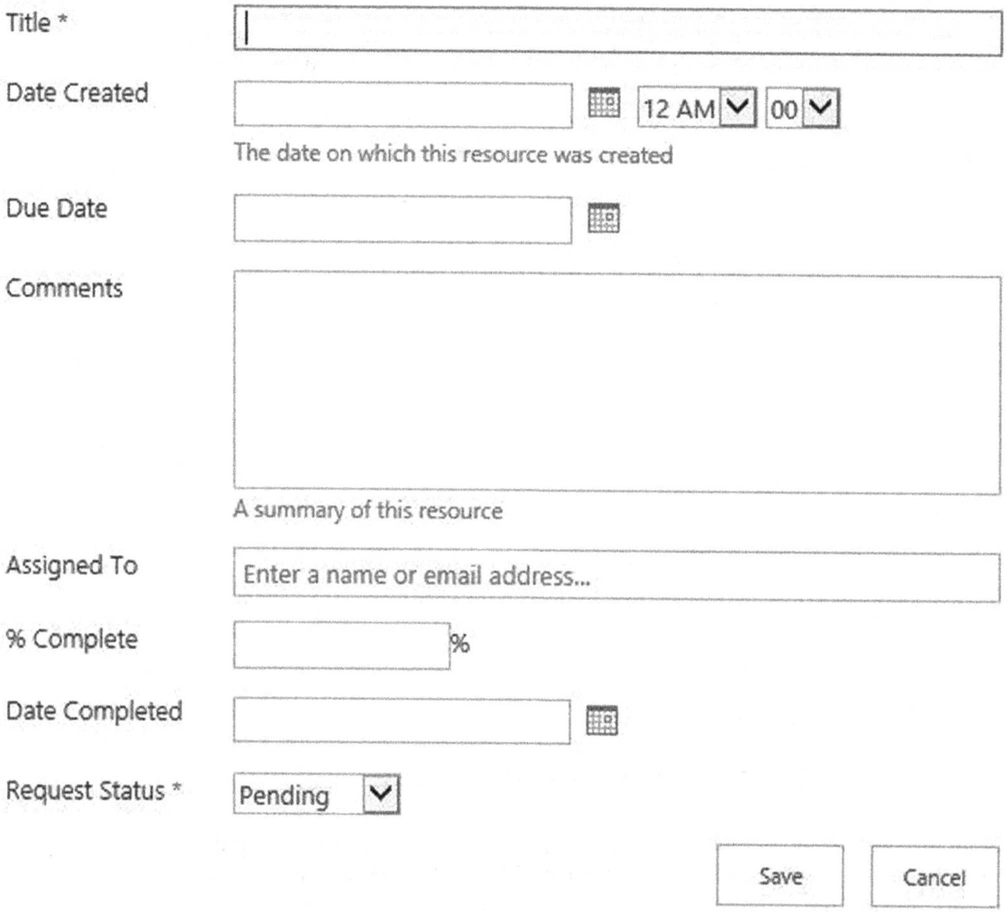

Title * [|]

Date Created [   ] 🗓 [12 AM ✔] [00 ✔]
The date on which this resource was created

Due Date [   ] 🗓

Comments [   ]
A summary of this resource

Assigned To [Enter a name or email address...   ]

% Complete [   ] %

Date Completed [   ] 🗓

Request Status * [Pending ✔]

[Save]   [Cancel]

Figure 4-10. *Displaying the new form for the Requests list*

Using Visio to Define a Workflow

You'll start the workflow design in Visio 2013. Visio is a great tool for creating diagrams and flowcharts, and with the 2013 release has been very well integrated with SharePoint 2013 workflows. It allows you to begin your workflow design at a high level, creating a flow diagram that describes the workflow process. It provides shapes that correspond with the actions and conditions available in SharePoint Designer. You will later use SharePoint Designer 2013 to add the specific SharePoint instructions onto these same shapes.

■ **Tip** You don't have to use Visio to create a declarative workflow. You can go directly to SharePoint Designer and add actions and conditions to implement the workflow logic using a text-based designer. We've included an overview of how to use the text-based workflows designer in Appendix B.

For more complicated workflows, there are several benefits to using Visio.

- Starting with the big picture is always a good idea.
- A Visio diagram will help you present the workflow design to end users or stakeholders.
- Configuring a workflow using the Visual Designer is more intuitive for end users.

■ **Note** You'll need Visio 2013 Professional to complete the next section of this exercise. You can download a trial version from Microsoft (http://office.microsoft.com/en-us/visio).

Designing a Workflow in Visio

Start Visio 2013. In the initial page you'll need to select a template for your drawing. Unless you have created workflow diagrams before, you probably don't have a SharePoint workflow option to select. Instead, type **SharePoint** in the search box and press the Enter key or click the search icon. You'll probably see an option for either SharePoint 2010 or SharePoint 2013; select the 2013 template. The template details will then be displayed as shown in Figure 4-11. Click the Create button to begin.

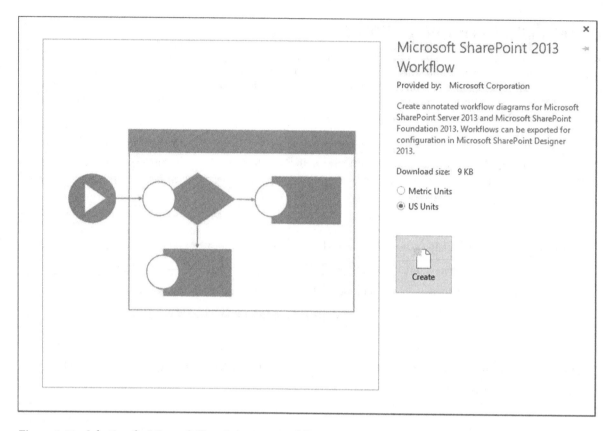

Figure 4-11. *Selecting the Microsoft SharePoint 2013 Workflow template*

The initial workflow will look like Figure 4-12.

Figure 4-12. *The initial workflow diagram with a single stage*

The PROCESS tab, shown in Figure 4-13, provides functions specifically for working with SharePoint workflows.

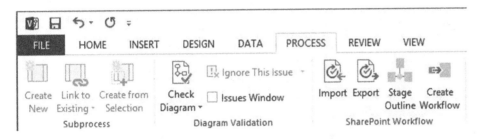

Figure 4-13. *The Process tab of the ribbon*

The Check Diagram button, for example, will verify your diagram is valid. Since this diagram will later serve as the actual workflow definition, it needs to be correct, logically.

Using Stages

To facilitate very large and complex workflows, Visio allows the process to be divided into stages. From a high level you can view the overall process as a series of stages. Consider a workflow that processes job applicants. You might organize into stages such as:

1. Intake

2. HR Prescreening

3. Position Match

4. Interviews

5. Employment Offer

6. Onboarding

This can be represented in Visio as shown in Figure 4-14. This is using the Stage Outline view, which you can select from the PROCESS tab.

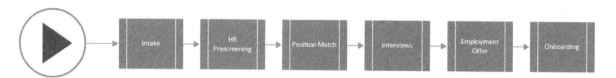

Figure 4-14. *Viewing the stage outline*

Using Steps

When designing the process for each stage, you can further break down the process into steps. Steps contain a set of actions that are related and are generally executed together. For example, the Intake stage can be comprised of two steps: 1) creating the candidate item in SharePoint and 2) sending an acknowledgement e-mail as illustrated in Figure 4-15.

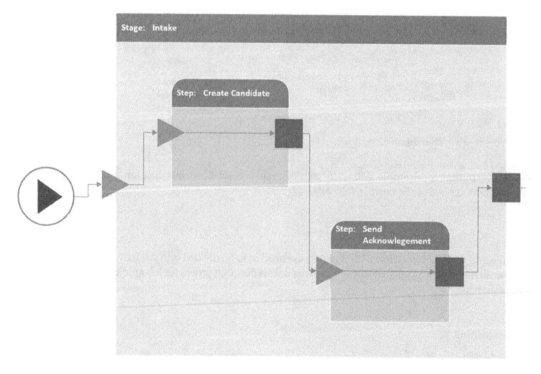

Figure 4-15. *The Intake stage with multiple steps*

You can also process steps in a loop repeating them as many times as needed. For example, the HR Prescreening stage, shown Figure 4-16, executes the Check qualification step for each guideline that needs to be checked.

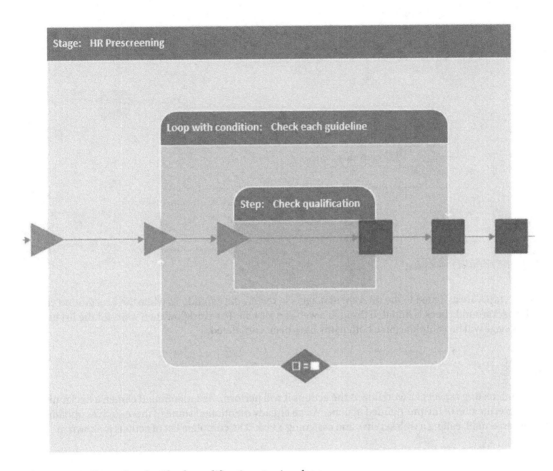

Figure 4-16. *Executing the Check qualification step in a loop*

Defining Parallel Processing

Some actions in a workflow need to be executed sequentially, that is, one at a time. But there are scenarios where multiple actions, especially long running actions, should be done in parallel. You can define the parallel processing in a workflow diagram using the Start parallel process and End parallel process components as shown in Figure 4-17.

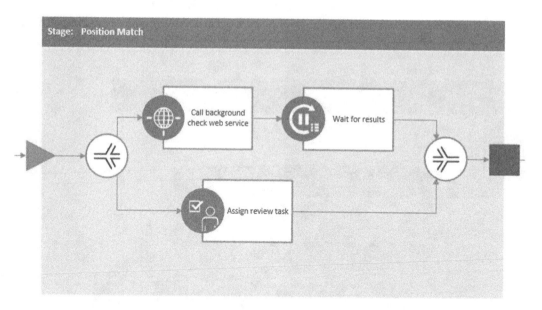

Figure 4-17. *Defining parallel processing*

In this example, tasks are assigned to the relevant managers to review the candidates while the background check is being done. The background check is initiated through a web service call. The workflow then waits for the list item to be updated. This stage will be complete once both paths have been completed.

Using Actions

Probably the most interesting aspect of a workflow is the actions it will perform. As I mentioned earlier, a declarative workflow can only execute one of the pre-defined actions. We've already mentioned some of these such as updating a list item, sending an e-mail, calling a web service, and assigning a task. The complete list of actions is shown in Figure 4-18.

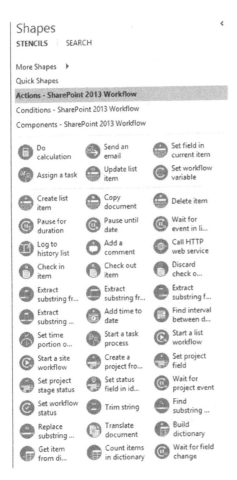

Figure 4-18. *The list of actions available in the stencil*

Designing the Request Process Workflow

For this project, you'll create a fairly simple workflow consisting of a single stage. To define the workflow, just drag the appropriate actions and conditions on to the initial stage, double-click each one to change its name, and then use a Connector to link them together. The completed diagram should look like Figure 4-19.

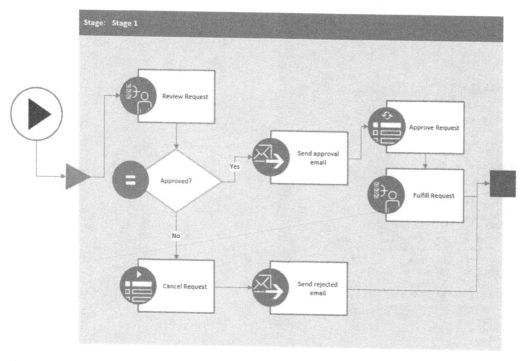

Figure 4-19. *The completed workflow diagram*

You can find the corresponding object in the stencil by matching up the icon. Some of the icons are very similar so, to avoid any confusion, these are the actions and conditions that you should use:

- **Review Request** – Start a Task Process

- **Approved?** – If any value equals value

- **Send approval email** – Send an e-mail

- **Approve Request** – Update list item

- **Fulfill Request** – Start a Task Process

- **Cancel Request** – Set field in current item

- **Send rejected email** – Send an e-mail

There are two branches coming from the Approved? condition; one for when the request is approved, the other for when it is not. To indicate, which is which, right-click the connector going to the Send approval email action and select the Yes link. Do the same for the other connector but select the No link. The Yes and No labels will then appear in the diagram.

■ **Tip** It is recommended that Yes branches go to the right and No branches go down as was done in this diagram. This allows the SharePoint visualization logic to better format the flow process.

When you have finished making the changes, go to the PROCESS tab and click the Check Diagram button. If there are any errors, they will be displayed in the Issues window. Fix any errors that may be reported and then save the diagram.

Configuring the Workflow

Now you'll go to SharePoint Designer and import this diagram and then configure it for your Requests list. If SharePoint Designer is not still open, start SharePoint Designer and open your Team Site as was described earlier. Select the Workflows item in the Navigator to show the current workflows. This list is probably empty.

In the WORKFLOWS tab of the ribbon, click the Import from Visio button and then select the Import Visio 2013 diagram link. In the file dialog box, select the Visio file that you just created. The Create Workflow dialog, shown in Figure 4-20, will appear. This is where you'll configure the workflow.

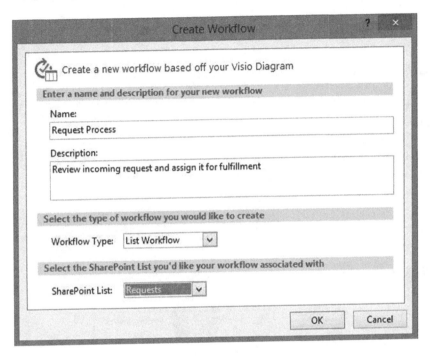

Figure 4-20. Configuring the workflow with the Requests list

Enter **Request Process** for the name and also add a description. For the Workflow Type, select List Workflow and then select your Requests list. This will configure this workflow to run specifically against the Requests list.

■ **Note** Generally a workflow is associated with a specific list or document library. When creating a workflow you can either associate it to a specific list or make it a reusable workflow. When creating a reusable workflow, you defer the list association until later. This workflow can then be reused and associated to multiple lists.

Implementing the Workflow

Now that you have created the workflow structure, you need to specify the details. Each of the shapes in the Visio diagram represents an action or condition and now you need to specify the specific parameters for each of them. We will take you through each of these and show you how to configure it.

The first thing you may have noticed is that it appears that you're now using Visio again. Actually, you are! This is a Visio control that is hosted inside of SharePoint Designer. The WORKFLOW tab of the ribbon, shown in Figure 4-21 is very specific to the functions of SharePoint Designer. But within the Visual Designer tab, this is actually running Visio.

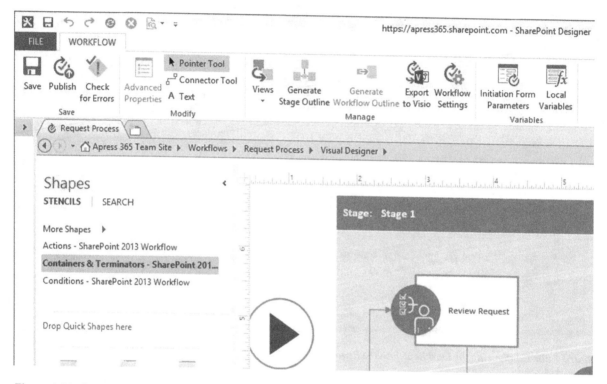

Figure 4-21. *Running Visio inside of SharePoint Designer*

If you hover over one of the shapes, a small gear-looking icon will appear on the lower-left corner. This is known as the SharePoint Designer Properties icon and it exposes the properties for this shape that you can configure. Click this icon to see a set of links that you can use to configure the shape as demonstrated in Figure 4-22.

Figure 4-22. Custom links for configuring the shape

■ **Note**   This icon and the links it exposes are also visible in the Visio application. However, the links are only enabled when running within SharePoint Designer.

The specific links will vary depending on the shape. Generally, the first link will display a dialog to configure all of the properties of the share. The last link, Properties, will display a list of all the properties and their values. Links in between will usually display the same dialog as the first link, or a subset of it.

Configuring the Approval Task

You'll start with the first action, Review Request, which will generate a task for someone to review and approve the associated request. Click the SharePoint Designer Properties icon and select the Process Settings link. This will display the Start a Task Process dialog box. This includes three collapsible sections: Task Options, Email Options, and Outcome Options. When fully expanded, the dialog box looks like Figure 4-23.

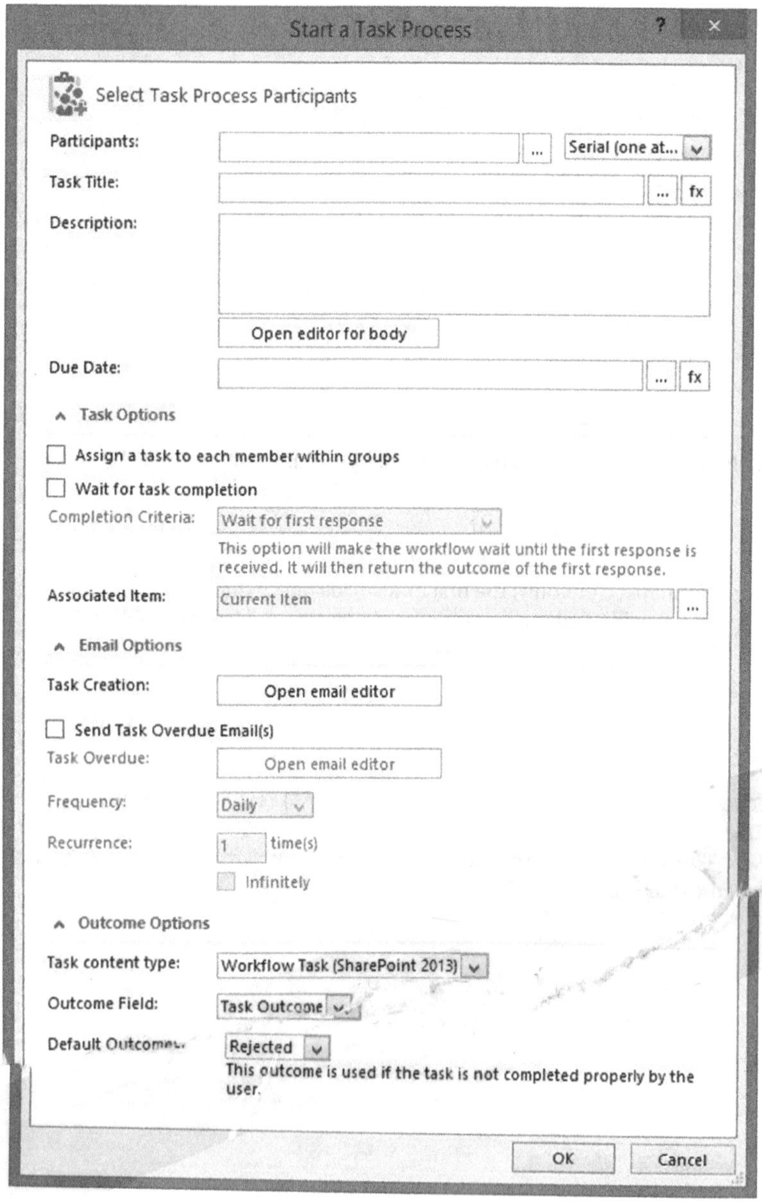

Figure 4-23. *The Start a Task Process dialog box*

This action starts a task process that we'll explain in more detail later in this chapter. But essentially, this creates a task that is assigned to one or more people. In this dialog box you'll configure the details of that task and how the workflow will process it.

1. Click the ellipses next to the Participants field to display the Select Users dialog box. This will list the users and groups that have been added to your Office 365 account. Just select your name from the list and click the Add button. Click the OK button to close the dialog box.

■ **Note**   For this example I just added myself as the approver. You could set up an Approvers group in SharePoint and then select that group. Anyone in that group would then be able to review the request. You can also assign multiple reviewers.

2.   The dropdown to the right allows you to select either serial or parallel approvals. If you are assigning the task to multiple people (or groups), you can either allow them to review the request simultaneously or one at a time. Since you're assigning a single person it doesn't matter which you select.

3.   For the Task Title, this should include some information about the request. The reviewer will likely receive tasks to review multiple request and the task title should indicate which request this task is for. Click the ellipses next to the Task Title field to display the String Builder dialog box. Enter **Request Approval –** and then click the Add or Change Lookup button.

■ **Tip**   You'll see the Add or Change Lookup button on a number of dialog boxes in SharePoint Designer. This is where you can retrieve data from a related list item or other data source. It will display the appropriate lookup dialog box, where you can enter the data source and specific field and format. The resulting expression is then embedded within your field value. The fx button, which you'll also see a lot, does the same thing, except the result replaces the entire field rather than just inserting the expression as part of a larger field definition.

4.   In the Lookup for String dialog box, select Current Item as the Data Source and then select the Title column as shown in Figure 4-24. In this context, the Current Item is the Requests item that is being reviewed. This will include its title in the task title. Click the OK button to close the dialog box.

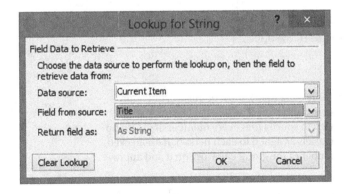

Figure 4-24. *Selecting the Title column*

■ **Tip** The dropdown contains all of the available lists including Calendar, Tasks, and Requests. It also includes a couple of generic references such as Current Item and Association: Task List. Since this workflow is associated with the Requests list, selecting Current Item is equivalent to selecting the Requests list. However, if you were implementing this as a reusable workflow you would need to use Current Item. Then the actual list that is referenced would be defined as whatever list the workflow is associated with.

5. The String Builder dialog box will now look like Figure 4-25. Click the OK button to close the dialog box.

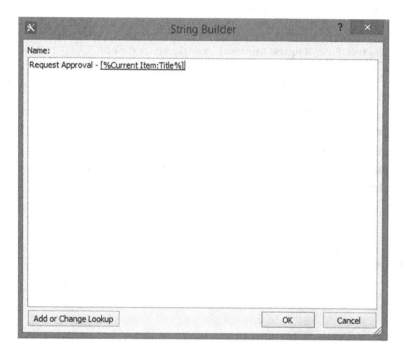

Figure 4-25. *The completed String Builder dialog box*

6. Expand the Task Options section (if not already expanded). Most of this will not apply since you're using a single person to perform the approval. The first check box, Assign a task to each member within groups, is used to specify that every member of the group needs to approve the request. In this case, a task is assigned to each person. If unchecked, the task is assigned to the group and any member of the group can work on it and approve the request.

7. The second check box, Wait for task completion, specifies that the workflow should pause until the task is completed, which is the typical scenario for an approval process. However, some tasks can run asynchronously while the workflow process continues. If the workflow must wait for the task, and there are multiple approvals, the Completion Criteria dropdown provides options such as waiting for all approvals, only the first one, or some percentage of approvals to complete.

8. Expand the Email Options section. An e-mail is sent to the user when a task is assigned to them. You can click the Open email editor button to configure the contents of that e-mail. You can also specify if a reminder e-mail should be sent when the task is overdue.

9. Expand the Outcome Options section. We'll explain task outcomes later in this chapter. Since you are using the standard approval task action, these options cannot be changed. You'll create a custom outcome later.

10. Click the OK button to close the Start a Task Process dialog box.

So now the workflow has started the approval process. As I said, this will create a task for someone (me) to review the request. In the meantime, the workflow will be idle waiting for the approval process to complete. The rest of the workflow will take the appropriate actions depending on whether the request was approved.

Designing a Condition

Hover over the Approved? shape and click the SharePoint Designer Properties icon. Then select the Value link to display the If any value equals value Properties dialog box. This has three fields to enter, two values and an operator. In this case, you'll want to see if the outcome from the previous task was approved.

1. Select the first Value field, and then click the lookup (fx) button. This will display the Define Workflow Lookup dialog box. The outcome from the approval task will be stored in a workflow variable. For the Data Source, select Workflow Variables and Parameters. For the Field from source dropdown, select Variable: Outcome as shown in Figure 4-26. Click the OK button to close the dialog box.

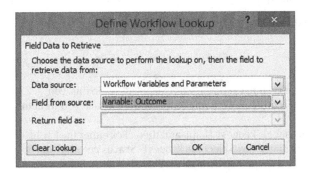

Figure 4-26. *Selecting the task outcome variable*

2. The Operator should default to equals, which is what you'll need for this condition.

3. In the second Value field, select Approved from the dropdown list. The completed condition criteria will look like Figure 4-27.

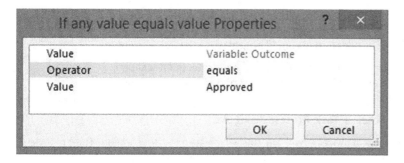

Figure 4-27. *The completed condition*

■ **Tip**   You can see from this dropdown list all of the available operations such as begins with, contains, and is empty. This dynamic list is based on the column type of the first value that was selected. If you had selected a numeric column you would see operations such as greater than and less than.

Handling the Rejected Request

If the request was rejected, there are two actions that will be performed by the Workflow:

- Update the Requests item to change its status to Cancelled
- Send an e-mail to the requestor informing them that the request was denied

Cancelling the Request

If the request was not approved you'll need to update the Requests item to show it was cancelled. To do this, you added a Set Field in Current Item shape in the workflow. To configure this, you simply select the field you want to update and then enter the new value.

Click the SharePoint Designer Properties icon on the Cancel Request shape and then click either the Field or Value link. In the Set Field in Current Item Properties dialog box, select the Request Status column. Since this was defined as a Choice column type, the Value field will be a dropdown listing the allowed options. Select Cancelled as shown in Figure 4-28. Click the OK button to close the dialog box.

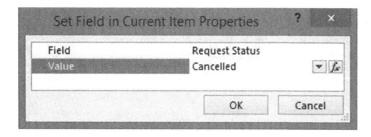

Figure 4-28. *Cancelling the request*

Sending an E-Mail

Now you'll need to inform the user that their request was cancelled by sending an e-mail.

1. Click the SharePoint Designer Properties icon on the Send rejected email shape and then click the Email link. This will display the Define E-mail Message dialog box.

2. The e-mail should go to the user who initiated the request. Click the lookup icon to the right of the To field to display the Select Users dialog box. You should find a User who created current item option. Select this and click the Add button as shown in Figure 4-29. Click the OK button to close the dialog box.

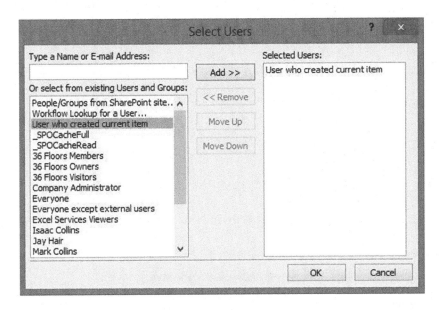

Figure 4-29. *Selecting the user who created the request*

3. For the Subject field, you'll want to include the title of the request just like you did with the task initiation e-mail. Click the fx button to display the String Builder dialog box. Enter **Request Denied -** and then click the Add or Change Lookup button to select the Title field from the Current Item source. When you're done, close the String Builder dialog box.

4. In the E-mail body add some static text like **Your request was denied**. The completed dialog box will look like Figure 4-30.

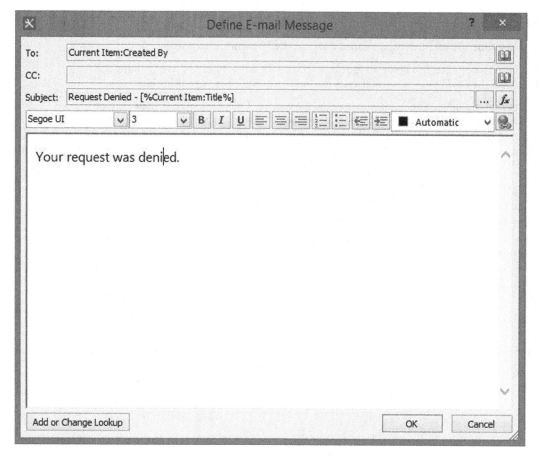

Figure 4-30. *The completed e-mail configuration*

Handling the Approved Request

If the request was approved, the workflow will need to perform similar actions, specifically it must send an e-mail and update the Requests list item. In addition, it will need to generate a new task to actually fulfill the request.

1. Configure the Send approval e-mail action just like you did for the rejected e-mail. The e-mail subject and body will have different text, obviously, but the process you'll use to configure it is the same.

2. To update the Requests list, you'll configure the Approve Request shape. This used a different action called, Update List Item. This action can be used to update other lists, not just the Current Item. It also allows you to update multiple fields in a single action.

3. Click the SharePoint Designer Properties icon on the Approve Request shape and then click the Item link. In the Update List Item Properties dialog box, select the Current Item column. This dialog box displays a grid of Field/Value pairs. Click the Add button and select the Request Status field and then select the Assigned value. Click the Add button again to add another field to be updated. This time, select the % Complete field and enter **.10** for the value. This will set the task to be 10% complete. The completed dialog box should look like Figure 4-31. Click the OK button to close the dialog box.

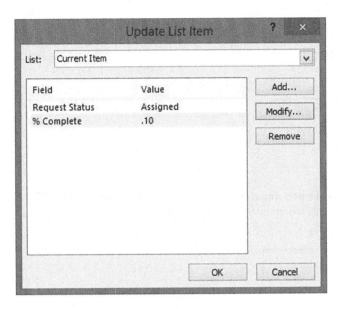

Figure 4-31. *Updating a List item*

4. The last action that needs to be configured is the actual fulfillment task. Click the SharePoint Designer Properties icon on the Fulfill Request shape and then select the Process Settings link. Configure this just like did for the approval task. Assign the task to yourself and configure the task title and e-mail subject to include the title of the request.

5. Click the Save icon in the Title bar to save all of your changes to the workflow.

Understanding a Task Process

As stated, workflows in SharePoint are normally human-centric. While the workflow performs some actions like sending an e-mail or updating a list item, the tasks that people do form the core of the workflow design. The other actions are used to keep everything organized and manageable. This workflow, for example, can be distilled down to the following:

- Review request.

- If approved, fulfill request.

You have implemented the first task, which is to review and approve (or deny) the request. You then implemented the second task that will fulfill the request.

SharePoint provides a generic task process that you can use for any human task. The approval action that you added to you workflow is called a task process and can contain multiple tasks. It is important to understand the distinction between these terms. A task process refers to an action in the workflow such as approve request. A task refers to a single person performing an action such as reviewing a request.

The distinction is more readily apparent when there is more than one approver. Suppose you require three people to review and approve a request. The task process refers to the entire approval process whereas a task refers to one person reviewing a request. This is illustrated in Figure 4-32.

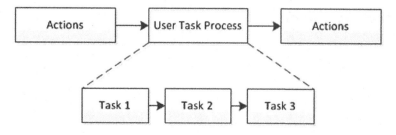

Figure 4-32. *User task process with serial execution*

SharePoint also allows tasks within a task process to be performed concurrently. With this approach, all three approvers are performing their review simultaneously. This is demonstrated in Figure 4-33.

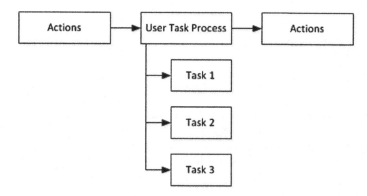

Figure 4-33. *User task process with parallel execution*

Using the Text-Based Designer

Using the Visual Designer, which is actually a Visio diagram, is convenient for configuring actions and conditions, especially for power users since they can manipulate the visual model of the workflow. However, there is also a Text-Based Designer that you might find useful as well. Prior to SharePoint 2013, this was how all declarative workflows were implemented. Appendix B provides an overview of how to use this designer.

You'll find a Views button in the WORKFLOW tab of the ribbon. Click the dropdown icon under this button and select the Text-Based Designer link as shown in Figure 4-34.

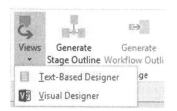

Figure 4-34. *Selecting the Text-Based Designer view*

The current workflow should now look like Figure 4-35.

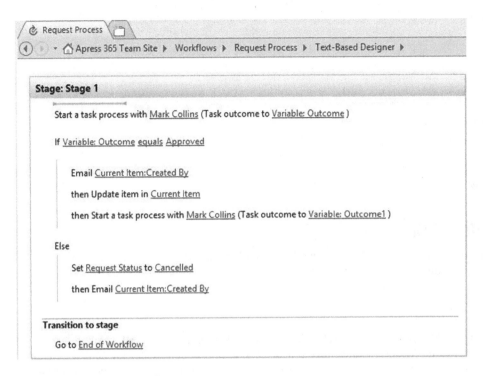

Figure 4-35. *The Text-Based Designer*

Configuring the Workflow Start Options

There is just one more step to complete before you're ready to test your workflow. You will configure the workflow to start automatically when a new item is added to the Requests list. As soon as someone submits a new request, a workflow will be started and the appropriate tasks added to the Workflow Tasks list. Go to the Workflow properties page for your workflow.

■ **Tip** You've probably noticed the breadcrumbs at the top of each SharePoint Designer page. This helps you keep track of where you are and how you navigated there. Your breadcrumbs probably look similar to Figure 4-36. Each of these items is also a link that will take you directly to that object. If you're currently displaying the Visual Designer page, you can click the Request Process link in the breadcrumbs to go to the Workflow property page.

Figure 4-36. *The SharePoint Designer breadcrumbs*

In the Start Options section, select the Start workflow automatically when an item is created check box, as shown in Figure 4-37.

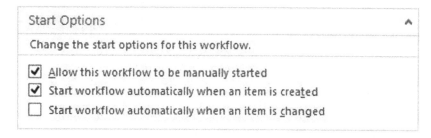

Figure 4-37. *The workflow start options*

Testing the Initial Workflow

Your workflow is done and ready to be published. Once is has been installed, you'll create a new request and watch the workflow generate tasks and update the Requests item.

Publishing the Workflow

Before publishing the workflow, it's a good idea to first check for errors. Click the Edit Workflow link in the Customization section to display the Visual Designer and the Check for Errors button should appear in the ribbon. Click this button and fix any errors that are reported. Once all errors are resolved, click the Publish button to install the workflow. This process can take a few seconds.

Now go to your Team Site and select the Requests list. Select the LIST tab of the ribbon and click the dropdown icon under the Workflow Settings button. Then select the Workflow Setting link as shown in Figure 4-38.

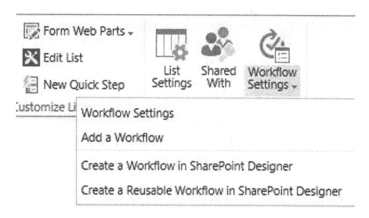

Figure 4-38. *Selecting the Workflow Settings link*

The Workflow Settings page is shown in Figure 4-39. You can use this page to see if there are any workflows currently in progress.

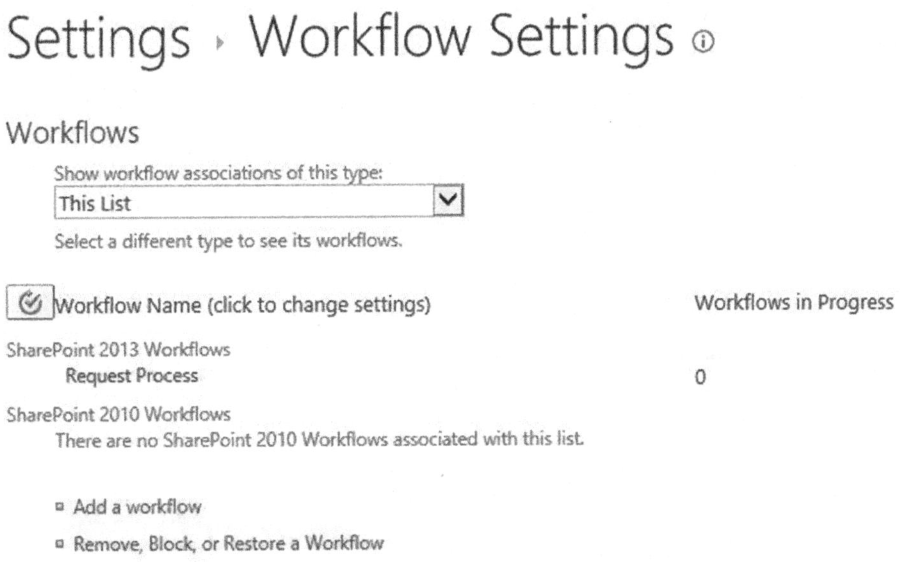

Settings ▸ Workflow Settings ⓘ

Workflows

Show workflow associations of this type:

This List ▼

Select a different type to see its workflows.

Ⓒ Workflow Name (click to change settings)   Workflows in Progress

SharePoint 2013 Workflows
    Request Process   0

SharePoint 2010 Workflows
    There are no SharePoint 2010 Workflows associated with this list.

   ▫ Add a workflow

   ▫ Remove, Block, or Restore a Workflow

Figure 4-39. *Viewing the associated workflows*

Processing a Request

Now you're ready to test the workflow. You'll add an item to the Requests list and then work the tasks that are generated by the workflow.

1. Go to the SharePoint site and select the Requests list. Click the new item link, which will display the New Item form. Enter a request. The only fields you need to enter are as follows (all the other fields should be left blank or have default values). The New Item form will look like Figure 4-40.

    - Title

    - Due Date

    - Comments

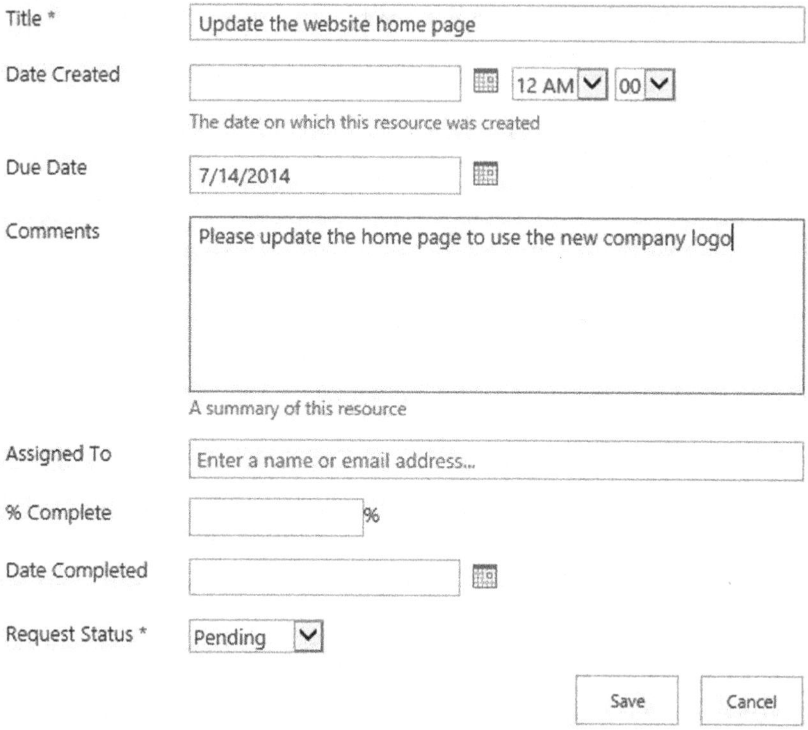

Title *	Update the website home page

Date Created

[ ] 12 AM ∨ 00 ∨

The date on which this resource was created

Due Date

7/14/2014

Comments

Please update the home page to use the new company logo

A summary of this resource

Assigned To

Enter a name or email address...

% Complete

[ ] %

Date Completed

[ ]

Request Status *

Pending ∨

Save   Cancel

Figure 4-40. *The initial New Item form*

2. The workflow will start as soon as the request is saved; however, it can take a few seconds before it has generated the first task. It is especially slow the first time it is run. Go to the Workflow Tasks list and you will eventually see a new task created.

3. Edit the new task; the task form should look like Figure 4-41. Click the Approve button to approve the request.

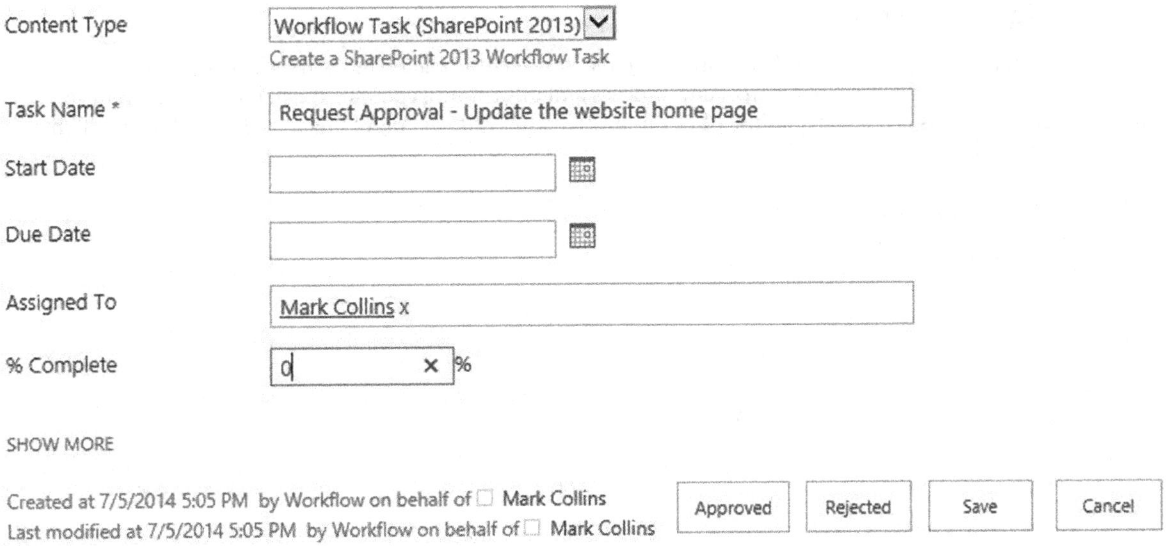

Content Type	Workflow Task (SharePoint 2013) ⌄
	Create a SharePoint 2013 Workflow Task
Task Name *	Request Approval - Update the website home page
Start Date	[ ] 🗓
Due Date	[ ] 🗓
Assigned To	Mark Collins x
% Complete	0 × %

SHOW MORE

Created at 7/5/2014 5:05 PM by Workflow on behalf of ☐ Mark Collins
Last modified at 7/5/2014 5:05 PM by Workflow on behalf of ☐ Mark Collins

Approved	Rejected	Save	Cancel

Figure 4-41. *The Approval task form*

4. Now go to the Requests list. After a few seconds or so, the Request Status will be updated
    to Assigned, and the % Complete will be set to 10% as demonstrated in Figure 4-42.

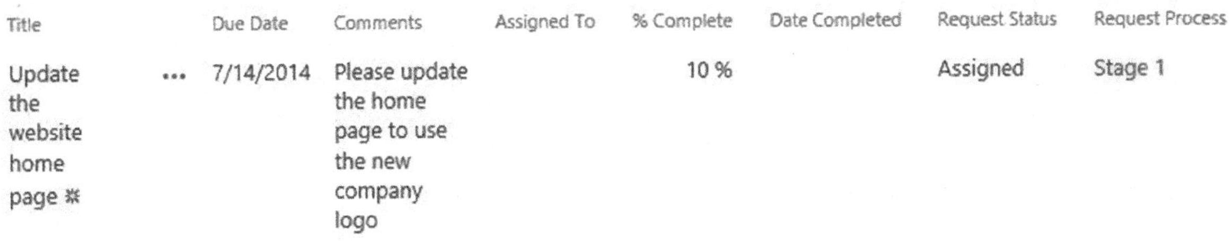

Title		Due Date	Comments	Assigned To	% Complete	Date Completed	Request Status	Request Process
Update the website home page ✳	...	7/14/2014	Please update the home page to use the new company logo		10 %		Assigned	Stage 1

Figure 4-42. *The updated Requests item*

Reviewing the Results

Now let's look at the artifacts of the workflow process. First, notice in the Requests list that there is a Request Process column. This is the name of the workflow process and this column contains the name of the current stage, Stage 1 in this case. This is also a hyperlink. Click this link to display the details of this workflow instance, which is shown in Figure 4-43.

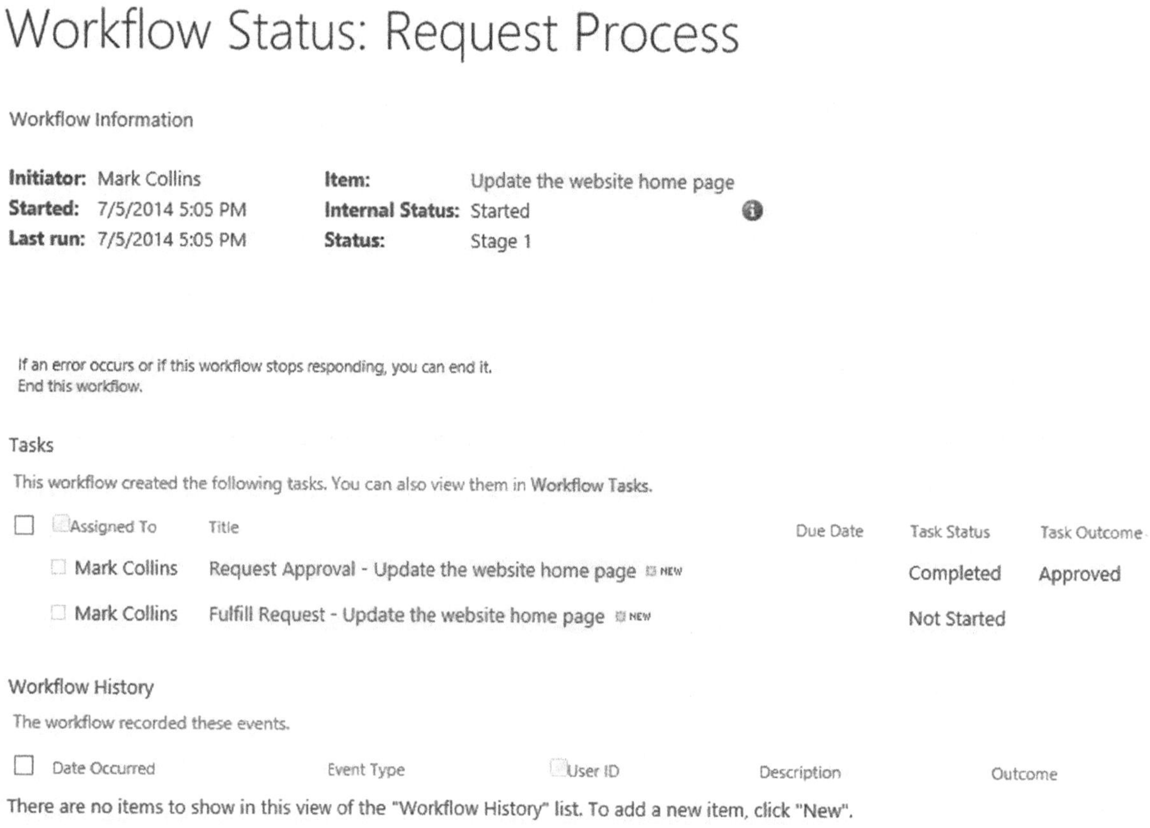

Workflow Status: Request Process

Workflow Information

Initiator: Mark Collins   **Item:**   Update the website home page

Started: 7/5/2014 5:05 PM   **Internal Status:** Started

Last run: 7/5/2014 5:05 PM   **Status:**   Stage 1

If an error occurs or if this workflow stops responding, you can end it.
End this workflow.

Tasks

This workflow created the following tasks. You can also view them in **Workflow Tasks**.

	Assigned To	Title	Due Date	Task Status	Task Outcome
	Mark Collins	Request Approval - Update the website home page ▣ NEW		Completed	Approved
	Mark Collins	Fulfill Request - Update the website home page ▣ NEW		Not Started	

Workflow History

The workflow recorded these events.

	Date Occurred	Event Type	User ID	Description	Outcome

There are no items to show in this view of the "Workflow History" list. To add a new item, click "New".

Figure 4-43. *The workflow instance details*

The Tasks section lists the tasks that have been generated. You can see the approval task was completed with an outcome of Approved. The fulfillment task has been created but not started yet. The Workflow History section shows the history log for this workflow. The workflow logic logs messages to this history log when certain events or errors occur. This log is a helpful feature for debugging workflows.

Check your inbox and you should see the e-mail letting you know that the request has been approved, similar to the one shown in Figure 4-44.

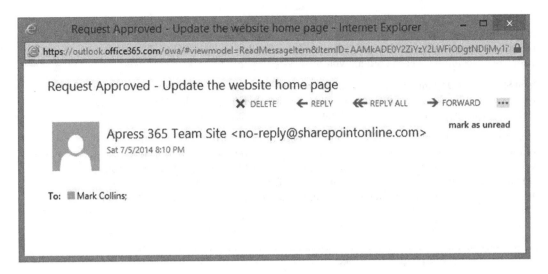

Figure 4-44. The approval e-mail

■ **Note**   There will be other e-mails in your inbox that the workflow generated. These e-mails are generated by the default implementation of the task and task process events.

Customizing the Workflow Tasks

You've created a simple workflow that creates and assigns tasks, sends e-mails, and moves list items through a defined process. However, there are a couple of enhancements that will make this a lot more useable. First, you may have noticed that there are two types of tasks, approval tasks and fulfillment tasks, in the same Workflow Tasks list. You would really like to perform different actions on these. For example, the Approved and Rejected buttons don't make a lot of sense on the fulfillment tasks.

The other feature that would be helpful is to use data entered from the approval task to influence the remaining process. For example, the person approving the request may want to decide who to assign the fulfillment request to. Or if the request was rejected, they should be able to enter some comments that are sent to the requestor as part of the rejection e-mail.

In the rest of this chapter, we'll demonstrate some techniques that you can use to improve the workflow process. First, you'll define two custom content types, which will enable you to have custom forms and actions for the different task types. Then you'll use workflow parameters to further enhance the process.

Creating New Content Types

Content types are an integral part of any SharePoint solution. They enable you to put disparate items in a single list and still handle each in a meaningful way. For example, you could have an asset library that contains text files, spreadsheets, pictures, and video clips. When an item is viewed or edited, the library will need to render each of these types differently. This is accomplished by assigning the appropriate content type to each and then configuring the appropriate action based on the content type.

Along the same lines, you'll define custom content types for the approval and fulfillment tasks. This will allow you to display different forms and support appropriate actions based on the task that is being worked on. You'll start by creating two new content types that are derived from the standard workflow task, Workflow Task (SharePoint 2013). Then you'll customize the columns of each content type.

1. Open SharePoint Designer 2013 (if not already opened) and connect to you Team Site. Select Content Types in the Navigator. You'll notice that there is a fairly long list of content types that have already been defined and they are organized into groups.

2. Click the Content Type button in the ribbon. Enter **Request Approval** in the name field. For the parent content type, first select the group that the parent is in, List Content Types, and then select the Workflow Task (SharePoint 2013) type. Select the New Group radio button and enter **Request** for the group name. This will create a new group and put the new content type in it. The dialog box should look like Figure 4-45. Click the OK button to create the new content type.

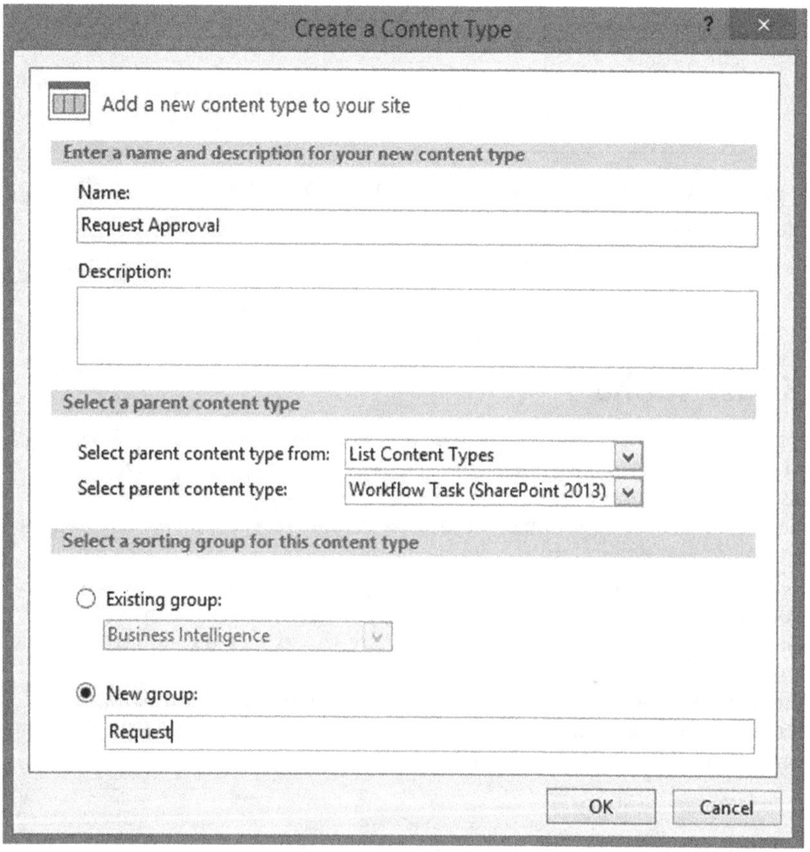

Figure 4-45. Defining the Request Approval content type

3. Click the Content Type button again to define another content type and enter
    Request Fulfillment for its name. Select the same parent content type, Workflow Task
    (SharePoint 2013) as the previous one. Then select the Existing Group radio button and
    select the Request group from the drop down. This group was created when you added the
    Request Approval content type. The dialog box should look like Figure 4-46. Click the
    OK button to create the new content type.

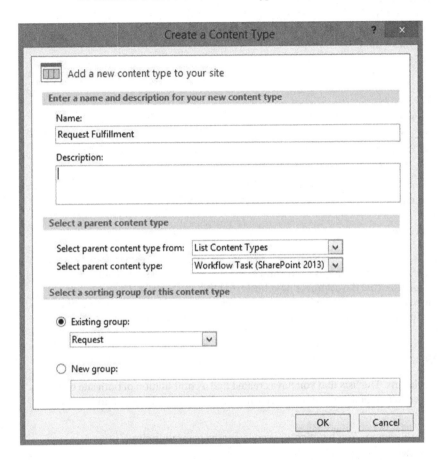

Figure 4-46. Defining the Request Fulfillment content type

4. You should now see the new content types listed in the Request group as shown in
    Figure 4-47.

List Content Types

Announcement	List Content Types	Item
Comment	List Content Types	Item
Contact	List Content Types	Item
East Asia Contact	List Content Types	Item
Event	List Content Types	Item
Issue	List Content Types	Item
Item	List Content Types	System
Link	List Content Types	Item
Message	List Content Types	Item
Post	List Content Types	Item
Reservations	List Content Types	Event
Schedule	List Content Types	Event
Schedule and Reservations	List Content Types	Event
Task	List Content Types	Item
Workflow Task (SharePoint 2013)	List Content Types	Task

Request

Request Approval	Request	Workflow Task (SharePoint 2013)
Request Fulfillment	Request	Workflow Task (SharePoint 2013)

Figure 4-47. *Showing the new content types*

Now you'll need to modify each of these content types to customize the columns of each. You'll add two columns to Request Approval. One will store the user that the approver has chosen to fulfill the request. The other is a comment that will be included in the rejection e-mail. The Request Fulfillment will be changed to use a different column to store the task outcome, which will have different options to replace the Approved and Rejected buttons.

Adding New Site Columns

Content types can only contain site columns. The lists that you have created had a combination of both site column and list-specific columns. So you'll need to first define the new site columns and then later add them to your new content types.

1. Select Site Columns in the Navigator. You'll notice an even larger list of existing site columns, which are also organized by groups.

■ **Note** These group names may be the same as the groups that you saw for the content type, but they are different groups. So, even though you created a Request group for content types, there is no Request group for site columns. You'll need to create a separate site column group.

---

2. Click the New Column button in the ribbon. You'll be prompted for the type before the dialog box appears. Select the Person or Group type.

3. In the Create a Site Column dialog box, enter the name **Assign To** and a description for this column. Select the New Group radio button and enter **Request** for the group name. The dialog box should look like Figure 4-48. Click the OK button to create the new site column.

Figure 4-48. *Creating the Assign To site column*

4. Click the Save icon in the title bar. Unlike content types, new site columns are not saved automatically.

5. Click the New Column button in the ribbon again. When prompted for the type, select Task Outcome.

6. In the Create a Site Column dialog box, enter **Request Completed** for the name and a description. Select the Existing group radio button and then select the Request group that you just created, as shown in Figure 4-49.

Figure 4-49. *Defining the Request Completed site column*

7. Because the Task Outcome type defines a set of choices, you'll be prompted with a Column Editor dialog box. Enter the following values as shown in Figure 4-50. Click the OK button to enter these changes.

- Completed

- On Hold

- Need Info

Figure 4-50. *The completed dialog box for the Request Completed site column*

8. Click the Save button to save all of the changes. You should see the new site columns as demonstrated in Figure 4-51.

Figure 4-51. *Listing the new site columns*

Customize the Content Types

Now you're ready to adjust the columns in your custom content types. You'll add the new columns to the appropriate content type and also remove one of the existing columns.

1. Select Content Types in the navigator and then select the Request Approval content type. Click the Name column to open the content type in its own tab.

2. In the Customization section, click the Edit content type columns link. This will show the existing columns defined for this content type. (You could also click the Edit Columns button in the ribbon).

3. Click the Add Existing Site Column button in the ribbon, which will display the Site Columns Picker dialog box, shown in Figure 4-52. Start typing the column name and the list is automatically filtered to only matching columns. Select the Assign To column and click the OK button.

Figure 4-52. *The Site Columns Picker dialog box*

4. Repeat this step to add the Comments column. The list of columns should look like Figure 4-53.

Request Approval

Apress 365 Team Site ▶ Content Types ▶ Request Approval ▶ Editor

Column Name ▼	Type ▼	Property
Task Name	Single line of text	Required
Start Date	Date and Time	Optional
Due Date	Date and Time	Optional
Assigned To	Person or Group	Optional
% Complete	Number (1, 1.0, 100)	Optional
Body	Multiple lines of text	Optional
Predecessors	Lookup (information already on ...	Optional
Priority	Choice (menu to choose from)	Optional
Task Status	Choice (menu to choose from)	Optional
Related Items	Related Items	Optional
Task Outcome	Task Outcome	Optional
Instance Id	Single line of text	Hidden
Assign To	Person or Group	Optional
Comments	Multiple lines of text	Optional

Figure 4-53. *The Request Approval columns*

5. Click the Save button in the title bar.

6. Open the Request Fulfillment content type and then click the Edit Columns button in the ribbon.

7. Select the Task Outcome column and then click the Delete button in the ribbon.

8. Click the Add Existing Site Column button in the ribbon and select the Request Completed site columns. The list of columns should look like Figure 4-54.

Request Fulfillment

Apress 365 Team Site ▶ Content Types ▶ Request Fulfillment ▶ Editor

Column Name ▼	Type ▼	Property
Task Name	Single line of text	Required
Start Date	Date and Time	Optional
Due Date	Date and Time	Optional
Assigned To	Person or Group	Optional
% Complete	Number (1, 1.0, 100)	Optional
Body	Multiple lines of text	Optional
Predecessors	Lookup (information already on ...	Optional
Priority	Choice (menu to choose from)	Optional
Task Status	Choice (menu to choose from)	Optional
Related Items	Related Items	Optional
Instance Id	Single line of text	Hidden
Request Completed	Task Outcome	Optional

Figure 4-54. *The Request Fulfillment columns*

9. Click the Save icon in the title bar.

Adding the Content Types to the Workflow Tasks List

Your custom content types are now created and customized with the appropriate set of columns. For a final step, you need to configure the Workflow Tasks list to allow these new content types.

1. Select Lists and Libraries in the navigator and then select the Workflow Tasks list (clicking the Name column to open this list in its own tab).

2. In the Content Types section you'll see the content types that are currently supported, which should be similar to Figure 4-55.

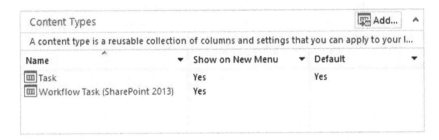

Figure 4-55. *The initial list of supported content types*

3. Click the Add button and then select the Request Approval content type in the Content Types Picker dialog box. Click the OK button to close the dialog box.

4. Repeat this step to add the Request Fulfillment content type.

5. The Content Types sections should now look like Figure 4-56.

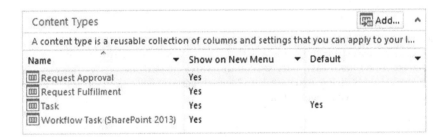

Figure 4-56. *The final set of supported content types*

Modify the Assign Task Actions

At this point you have new content types defined, but you'll need to modify the workflow to use the appropriate content type when creating a task. Go back to your Request Process workflow. If you don't still have this open, you can access it by selecting Workflows in the Navigator and then selecting the Request Process workflow, and finally, clicking the Edit workflow link in the Customization section. If the Text-Based Designer is displayed, you can change to the Visual Designer using the Views button in the ribbon.

1. Hover over the Review Request shape and click the SharePoint Designer Properties icon. Then select the Process Settings link. Expand the Outcome Details section. The standard Workflow Task (SharePoint 2013) content will be configured for this task. The new content types that you created should now be included in this dropdown list. Select the Request Approval content type. A warning will be displayed reminding you that the task list, Workflow Tasks in this case, needs to be configured to support this content type, as demonstrated in Figure 4-57. You took care of this earlier so you can ignore the warning. Click the OK button to close this dialog box.

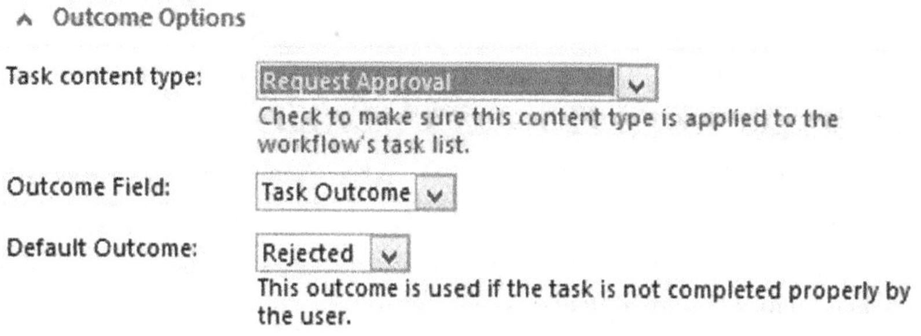

∧ Outcome Options

Task content type: Request Approval ⌄
                      Check to make sure this content type is applied to the
                      workflow's task list.

Outcome Field: Task Outcome ⌄

Default Outcome: Rejected ⌄
                      This outcome is used if the task is not completed properly by
                      the user.

Figure 4-57. *Using the new Request Approval content type*

2. Now you'll modify the other task process, Fulfill Request. Click the SharePoint Designer Properties icon and then select the Process Settings link and expand the Outcome Details section. For this task, select the Request Fulfillment content type. In this content type, you replaced the standard Task Outcome column with a custom one. After the content type is selected in this dialog, make sure the Request Completed column is selected as the Outcome Field as shown in Figure 4-58.

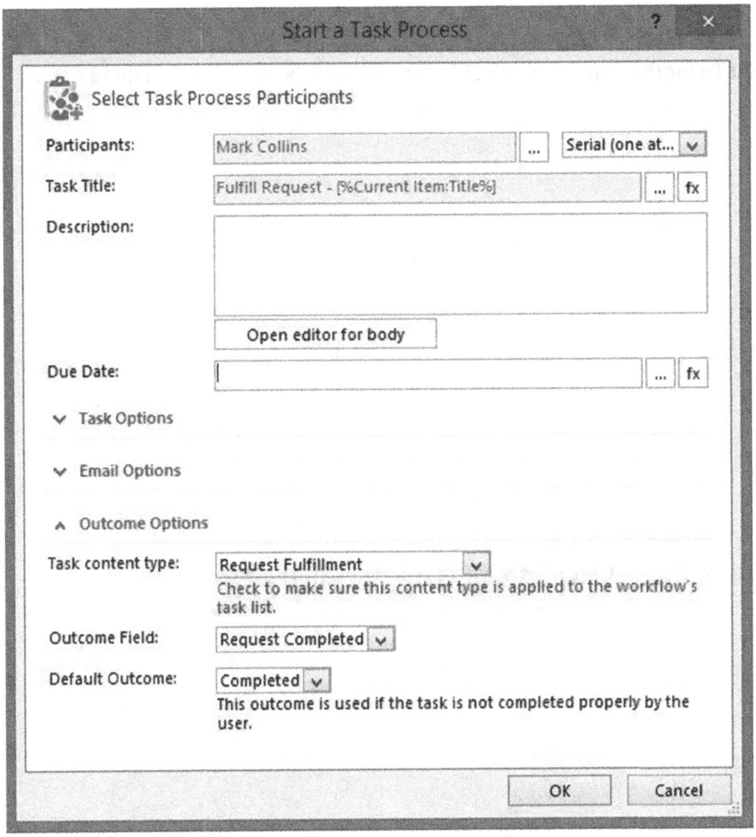

Figure 4-58. *Select the Request Fulfillment content type*

With these changes in place, you'll have a different form displayed when you edit a task. Most notably, the Approved and Rejected button will be replaced with more suitable options when working on a fulfillment task. But before we test this out, let's make a few more enhancements.

Defining Workflow Variables

The workflow process supports variables that persist across activities. This enables you to set a variable in one activity and then later use that in another action or condition. In fact, the Approved? condition used a workflow variable that was set by the preceding action. Now you'll define some custom variables that you can use to improve the request process.

You added two columns to the Request Approval content type, Assign To and Comments. The person working on the approval task can set these from the task form. These variables will be used later, when assigning the fulfillment task or sending the rejection e-mail.

Click the Local Variables button in the WORKFLOW tab of the ribbon. You'll see there are two variables, Outcome and Outcome1. These were set by the two Assign Task actions, Review Request, and Fulfill Request. Click the Add button to define a new variable. Enter **Assign To** for the name and select String as the type as shown in Figure 4-59. Click the OK button to save the variable.

Figure 4-59. *Adding the Assign To variable*

Repeat this process to add a second variable named **Comments** with a type String. The final variable list will look like Figure 4-60.

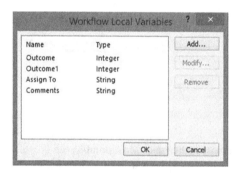

Figure 4-60. *The completed variable list*

Setting the Workflow Variables

To set these variables, you'll need to use the Set workflow variable action. You can edit the Visio diagram from within SharePoint Designer. You should have stencils already available to you that include the action and condition shapes. If not, click the SEARCH link in the Stencil window and enter **SharePoint**.

1. Drag two Set workflow variable shapes onto your diagram. One will be connected to the Yes branch and the other to the No branch. Rename the shape in the Yes branch to **Set Assign To variable** and the one in the No branch should be named **Set Comments variable**. You'll need to re-arrange the shapes a little and add some connectors. The diagram will look similar to Figure 4-61.

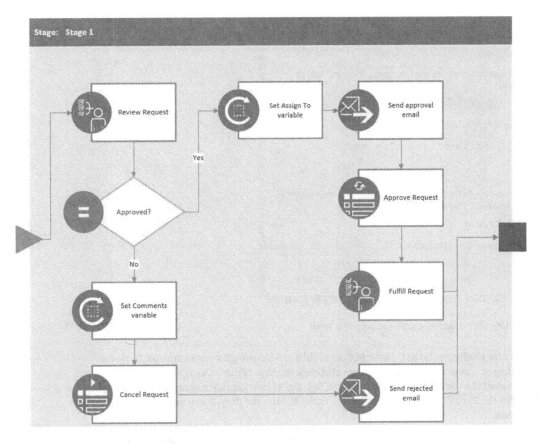

Figure 4-61. *Adding new shapes to the diagram*

2. Now you'll configure these actions to set the variables with the appropriate data. Hover over the Set Assign To variable shape and click the SharePoint Designer Properties icon. Select the Variable link to display the Set Workflow Variable Properties dialog box. This has two properties: 1) the variable to be updated and 2) the value to update it with. For the Variable, select the Assign To variable from the drop down. For the Value, click the fx button. This will display the Lookup for String dialog box.

3. In the top part of this dialog box you'll specify the source for the data and then the specific field within that source. For this variable, the data will come from the Assign To column of the Workflow Tasks list. In the Data source dropdown, select the Workflow Tasks list, then select the Assign To column. Since this column represents a Person or Group, there are multiple ways that this data can be formatted. Select Login Name.

4. Since the source is not from the current item you'll need to define how the specific item should be selected. This is done in the bottom part of the dialog box. You'll use the workflow's Instance Id, which is stored on each task. The Field dropdown lists the columns in the selected source, Workflow Tasks in this case. Select the Instance Id column. Then, in the Value field, click the fx button. Now you'll specify how the value is obtained. Select Workflow Context for the source and then select Instance ID. The completed dialog box should look like Figure 4-62.

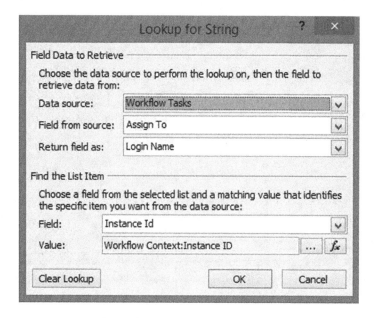

Figure 4-62. *Defining the value to update the variable with*

5. You'll now configure the Set Comments variable action using the same approach. Hover over the Set Comments variable shape and click the SharePoint Designer Properties icon. Select the Variable link to display the Set Workflow Variable Properties dialog box. For the Variable, select the Comments variable from the drop down and then click the fx button.

6. Configure the Lookup for String dialog box just like you did for the previous action, except select the Comments field. The completed dialog box should look like Figure 4-63.

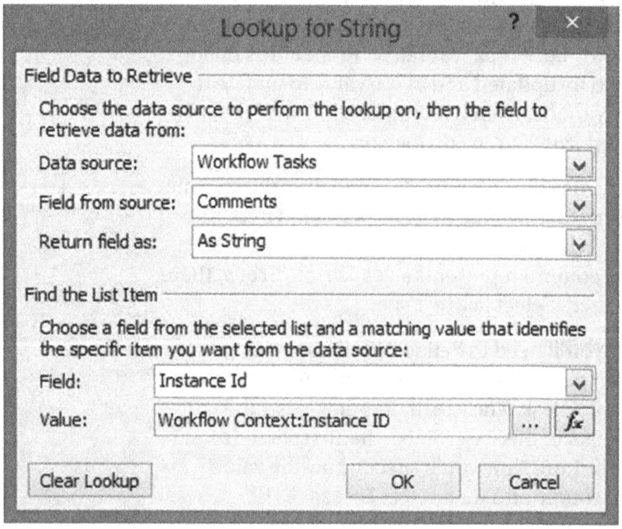

Figure 4-63. *Configuring the Set Comments variable action*

Enhancing the Workflow Logic

So now you have variables defined and their values have been set. The last step is to use these in your workflow. The Assign To variable will be used when creating the fulfillment task and the Comments variable will be used when sending the rejection e-mail. Let's start with the Assign To property. First, you'll modify the Requests item to store the user that will be assigned the fulfillment task.

1. Hover over the Approve Request shape and click the SharePoint Designer Properties icon and select the Items link. You are currently setting the Request Status and % Complete fields. Click the Add button, which will display the Value Assignment dialog box. Select the Assign To field and then, for the value, click the fx button. In the Define Workflow Lookup dialog box, select Workflow Variables and Parameters as the source and then the Assign To variable as the field. Click the OK button to close the Value Assignment dialog box. The completed dialog box will look like Figure 4-64. Click the OK button to save the changes to this action.

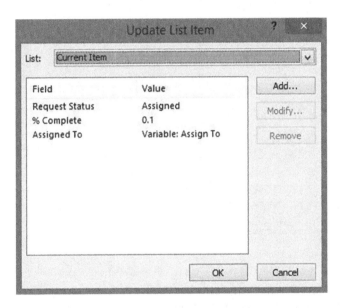

Figure 4-64. *The completed Update List Item dialog box*

2. Next, you'll adjust the actual task assignment. Hover over the Fulfill Request shape and click the SharePoint Designer Properties icon and select the Process Settings link. This will display the Start a Task Process dialog box. Click the ellipses next to the Participants field. In the Select Users dialog box, select the hard-coded user that is currently being used and click the Remove button. Then select Workflow Lookup for a User and click the Add button.

3. The Lookup for Person or Group dialog box will appear, select the Workflow Variables and Parameters for the source and then select the Assign To variables. Click the OK button to close the dialog box.

4. Then click the OK button again to close the Select Users dialog box. The Start a Task Process dialog box should look similar to Figure 4-65. Click the OK button to close this dialog box.

Figure 4-65. *The updated Start a Task Process dialog box*

5. Hover over the Send rejected email shape and click the SharePoint Designer Properties icon and select the Email link. In the body text enter the following:

   [%Variable: Comments%]

6. This will include the approver's comments in the body of the e-mail. The completed dialog box should look like Figure 4-66. Click the OK button to close the dialog box.

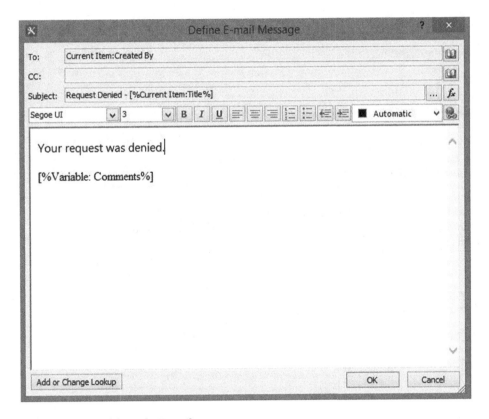

Figure 4-66. *Modifying the E-mail contents*

■ **Tip**   You could click the Add or Change Lookup button, which displays the Lookup for String dialog box if you're not sure of the exact syntax for this.

---

7. With these changes done, you're ready to test. Click the Save button in the ribbon and then click the Publish button to deploy these changes to your SharePoint site.

Testing the Revised Workflow

Now you're ready to test these changes.

1. Start by creating a new Requests item as you did earlier.

2. After the approval task is created, edit it and select a different user in the Assign To column and click the Approved button.

3. Go back to the Requests list. You should see the approval task completed and the fulfillment task assigned to the person you selected as demonstrated in Figure 4-67.

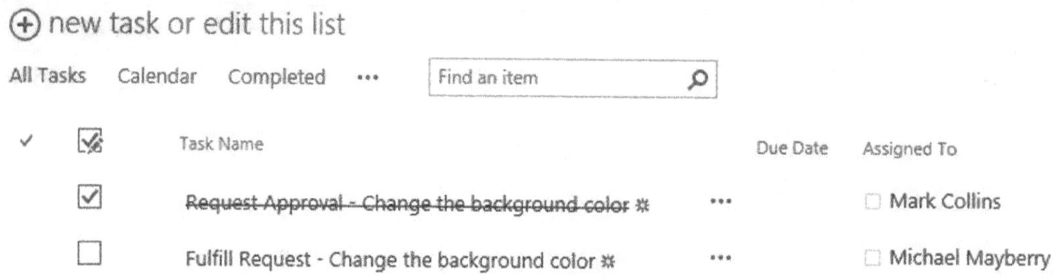

⊕ new task or edit this list

All Tasks   Calendar   Completed   ••• | Find an item   🔍 |

✓	☑	Task Name		Due Date	Assigned To
	☑	~~Request Approval - Change the background color~~ ✻	•••		☐ Mark Collins
	☐	Fulfill Request - Change the background color ✻	•••		☐ Michael Mayberry

Figure 4-67. *The fulfillment task assigned to the selected user*

4. Then, go to the Workflow Tasks list and edit the fulfillment task. Notice that the Approved and Rejected buttons have been replaced with Completed, On Hold, and Need Info buttons as shown in Figure 4-68.

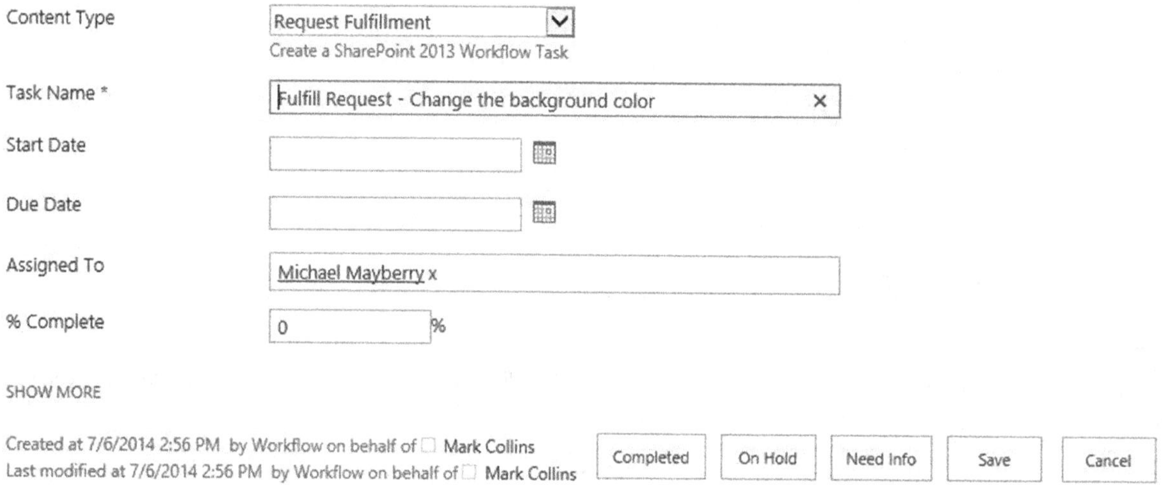

Content Type	Request Fulfillment ▾
	Create a SharePoint 2013 Workflow Task
Task Name *	Fulfill Request - Change the background color ✕
Start Date	[ ] 🗓
Due Date	[ ] 🗓
Assigned To	Michael Mayberry x
% Complete	0 %

SHOW MORE

Created at 7/6/2014 2:56 PM by Workflow on behalf of ☐ Mark Collins
Last modified at 7/6/2014 2:56 PM by Workflow on behalf of ☐ Mark Collins

| Completed | On Hold | Need Info | Save | Cancel |

Figure 4-68. *The fulfillment task with custom buttons*

5. Create another Requests item and edit the approval task when it has been created. This time, enter a comment and click the Rejected button. Then go to your e-mails and find the rejected e-mail, which should look similar to Figure 4-69.

Figure 4-69. *The rejection e-mail*

Updating the Visio Diagram

In this project you created an initial workflow diagram using Visio 2013. You then opened the same file with SharePoint Designer to implement the specific workflow logic. During the implementation you needed to add a couple of actions to the diagram. For convenience you did this in SharePoint Designer. This is a fairly typical scenario.

Now you want to share this diagram with the users. However, if you open the original diagram in Visio, it does not reflect the recent changes. SharePoint Designer actually imported the diagram into its own internal copy. To get an updated Visio diagram you just need to export it.

From the WORKFLOW tab of the SharePoint Designer ribbon, click the Export to Visio button. This will save the internal copy to a file that can be opened by Visio.

Summary

In this chapter I explained how to implement a declarative workflow to automate the processing of requests. Workflows can be used to automate common processes and make them more efficient and manageable. The workflow presented combines the capability of several tools including:

- SharePoint Designer 2013 to create a list as well as content types and site columns.
- Visio 2013 to provide a visual representation of the workflow.
- SharePoint Designer's workflow editor to implement the workflow logic.

Hopefully I have given you a sense of what you can do with declarative workflows and how to implement them. In the next chapter, I'll show you how to build a web database in SharePoint Online using Access 2013.

CHAPTER 5

■ ■ ■

Creating a Web Database with Access 2013

In this chapter you'll create a web database using Access 2013, which will be published to SharePoint Online in your Office 365 platform. This database implements a simple job tracking application that allows you to create, estimate, and track customer jobs. Publishing a special type of Access database, called a web database, is probably the easiest way to create a form-based SharePoint site. In this chapter you will create a fully working website with numerous tables and forms (views).

Out of necessity, I will cover this briefly without explaining every detail as much of it is fairly repetitive. You can also download the complete Access database from www.apress.com and then follow along as you read this chapter.

You will implement this application using the typical approach of designing the tables first. Then you'll add a few queries that will simplify some of the form development. You'll also create a fairly complex data macro that will compute the estimated job total by adding up the products and services included. You will then customize the forms for each of these tables. Finally, you'll implement a custom form for displaying a summary of all of the jobs.

Designing the Tables

Start Access 2013 and create a new database using the Custom web app template. When using this template, Access will create new objects such as tables and forms that are compatible with SharePoint. You'll be prompted to enter a name for your app as well as the web location where this will be deployed. Enter **JobTracking** and the address to your Team Site as shown in Figure 5-1.

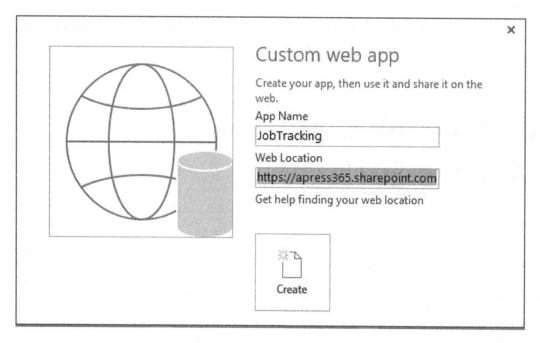

Figure 5-1. *Setting up the Access app*

Access will then connect to your SharePoint site and setup your new app. This includes provisioning a SQL Server database on Azure and may take several seconds to complete. The initial, empty, database will look like Figure 5-2.

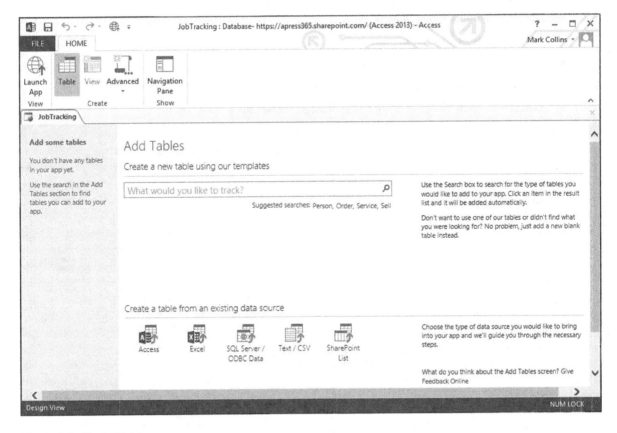

Figure 5-2. *The initial Access app*

Access 2013 provides several ways to get started building your database. You can search through the available table templates or you can import a data structure from an existing source such as previous versions of Access, a SQL Server database, or a SharePoint list. For this exercise, you will create your own custom tables.

■ **Note** You can import the table definition from Access 2010 into Access 2013, but the forms cannot be imported; you will need to recreate them in Access 2013.

Data Model Overview

The logical starting place for creating a web database is to design the tables. You will need the following tables to support the job tracking application. Figure 5-3 shows how these tables are related.

- Customer – contains current or potential customers
- Phone – stores customer phone numbers
- Address – stores customer and job addresses
- Product – defines products that may be included in a job

- Service - defines services offered

- Job – contains job or proposal summaries

- JobProduct - specifies products included in a job

- JobService - specifies services included in a job

- Contact - records incoming or outgoing contacts (phone calls, e-mails, etc.)

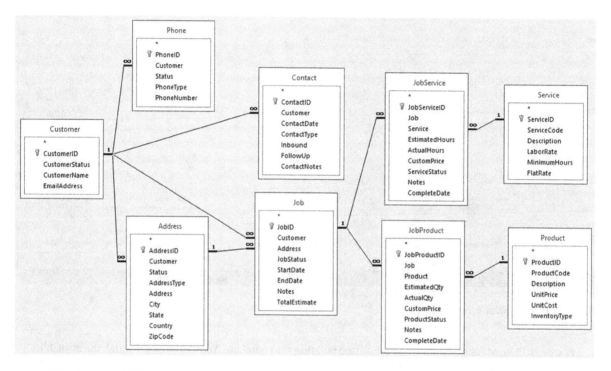

Figure 5-3. *Data model diagram*

Addresses and phone numbers are stored in separate tables, Address and Phone, which allows each customer to have more than one. The Job table also references the Address table to indicate the location of a particular job. The Contact table records correspondence with a customer.

A job is a collection of products and services. The Product and Service tables provide static information about each product or service such as description and price. The JobProduct and JobService tables are used to indicate when these are included in a specific job and provide job-specific details as well.

Creating the Customer Table

You'll start by creating the Customer table. Click the Add a new blank table link in the initial Table page, shown previously in Figure 5-2. This will create a blank table as shown in Figure 5-4.

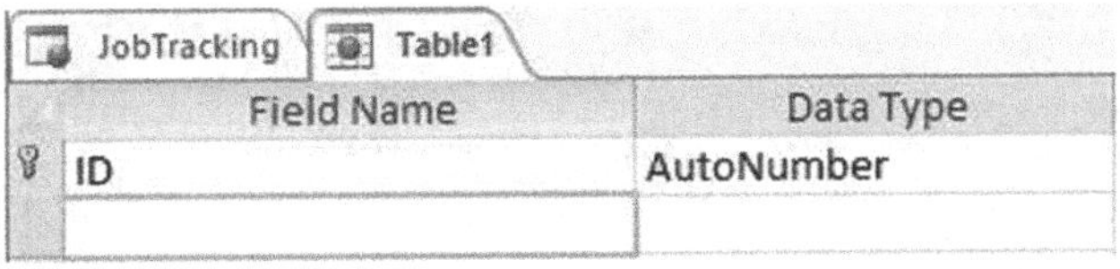

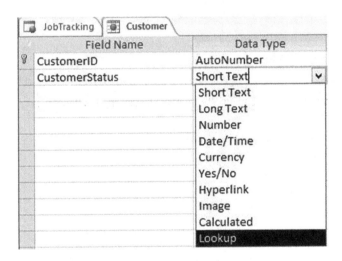

Figure 5-4. *Starting with a blank table*

■ **Note** In Access, the terms `column` and `field` can be used interchangeably. You will see field being used most often so we will follow that convention and refer to both columns in a table and fields on a form as fields.

Click the ID field and change the field name to **CustomerID**. The next field will indicate the current status of this customer, such as `Prospect` or `Active`. To add another field, click in the first empty cell and enter the field name, **CustomerStatus**. In the `Data Type` field, select the `Lookup` link as shown in Figure 5-5.

Figure 5-5. *Adding a Lookup field*

Defining Static Lookup Values

The Lookup Wizard will then appear and it has two options for providing values for a lookup field. The first is to get the values from another table. This will create a foreign key relationship between the tables. The second option is to specify a static list of allowed values. For this field, you will use the second option; select this in the dialog box.

Then, enter the following values as illustrated in Figure 5-6:

- **Prospect**
- **Active**
- **Inactive**
- **Removed**

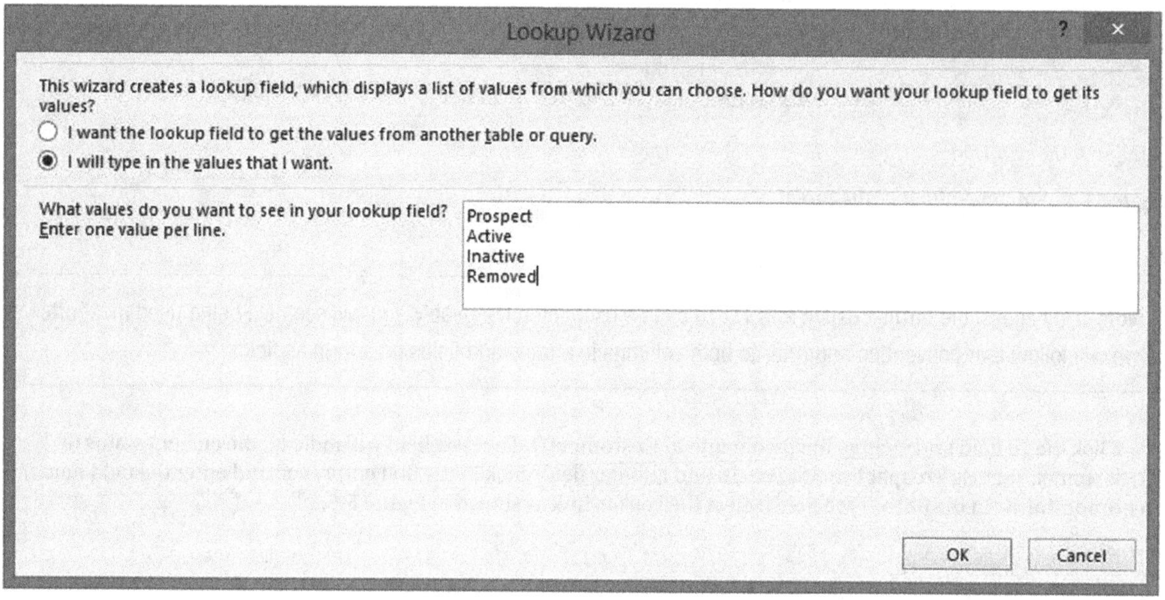

Figure 5-6. *Specifying the CustomerStatus values*

■ **Tip** If you need to later adjust this list of values, you can display the Lookup Wizard again by clicking the Modify Lookups button in the DESIGN tab of the ribbon.

Creating the Remaining Fields

Add the following additional fields to the Customer table:

- CustomerName – Text
- EmailAddress – Text

Click the Save button in the title bar to save the table design. Enter the table name **Customer** when prompted. The completed table should look like Figure 5-7.

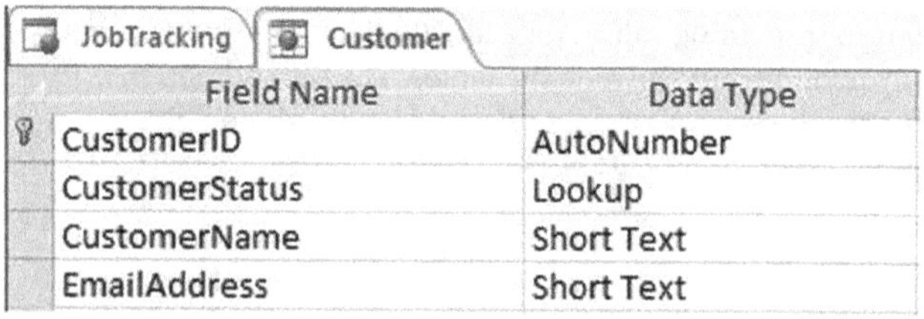

Field Name	Data Type
CustomerID	AutoNumber
CustomerStatus	Lookup
CustomerName	Short Text
EmailAddress	Short Text

Figure 5-7. *The completed Customer table*

Creating the Phone Table

The Phone table contains customer phone numbers. By placing these in a separate table, each customer can have more than one. The Phone table will have the following fields:

- PhoneID – primary key
- Customer – a lookup field using the Customer table as its source
- Status – a lookup field with a static list
- PhoneType – a lookup field indicating the type of phone (cell, home, fax, etc.)
- PhoneNumber – the actual phone number

To add a new table, go to the HOME tab of the ribbon and click the Table button. This will take you to the initial page that was displayed when you first created the Access database. Click the add a new blank table link again to create a new blank table just like you did for the Customer table and rename the ID field to **PhoneID**.

Creating a Foreign Key Relationship

For the next field, enter the name **Customer**, and then select the Lookup data type. This time, in the Lookup Wizard, select the first option, to get the values from another table. The dialog box will then list the existing tables and views for you to select the source. The Customer table should be the only one listed; select it.

You'll then have several other options for configuring the table relationship. First, when displaying a record from the Phone table, you need to select which field in the related Customer record should be displayed. Select the CustomerName field.

Then you need to decide how deletes are handled. The first option is to prevent a delete from a table if there are other records referencing it. The second option is to cascade the delete, which means that when a Customer record is deleted, all related Phone records are also deleted. The third option will allow these orphaned Phone records. Select the first option. The completed dialog box will look like Figure 5-8.

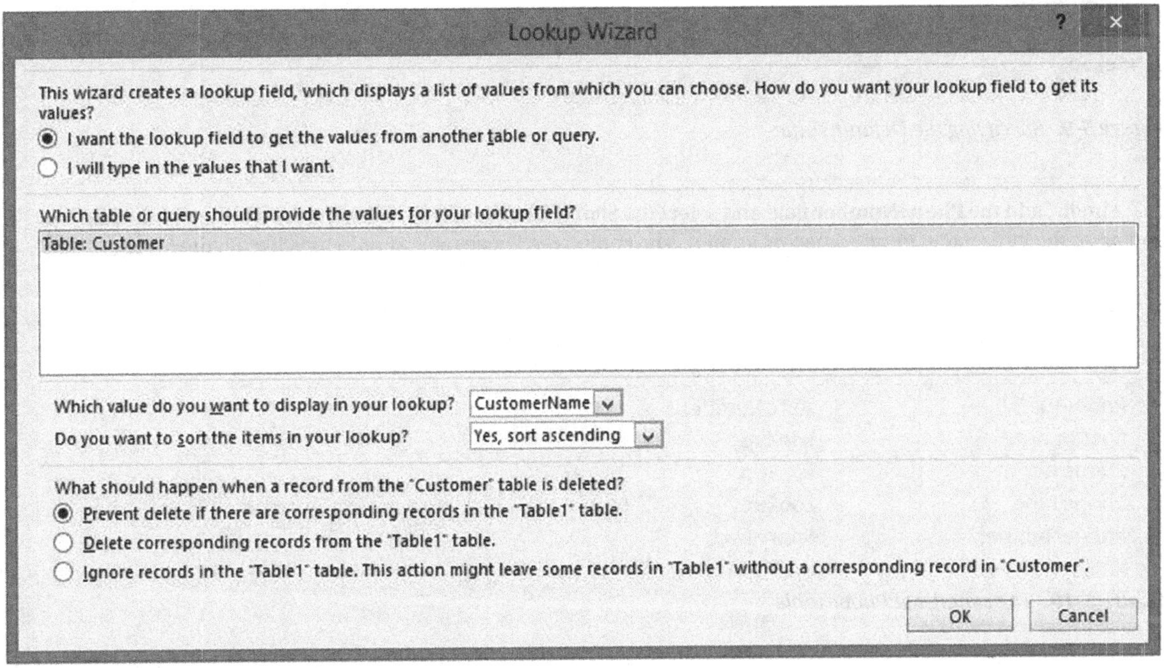

Figure 5-8. *Setting up a foreign key relationship*

Creating the Remaining Fields

Add a new field named **Status** and select the Lookup data type. Select the first option and enter the following list of values:

- **Active**
- **Inactive**

Then add a **PhoneType** field using the Lookup data type with the following list of values.

- **Home**
- **Cell**
- **Business**
- **Fax**
- **Job**

After creating the Status field, you should provide a default value. Select this field and enter **"Active"** in the Default Value property as shown in Figure 5-9. This will default all new records to the Active status.

General	
Limit Length	Yes
Character Limit	220
Label Text	
Default Value	"Active"
Validation Rule	
Validation Text	
Required	No
Indexed	No

Figure 5-9. *Specifying the Default Value*

Finally, add the **PhoneNumber** field and select the Short Text data type. Click the Save button in the title bar and enter the table name **Phone** when prompted. The completed Phone table should look like Figure 5-10.

JobTracking	Customer	Phone
Field Name		**Data Type**
PhoneID		AutoNumber
Customer		Lookup
Status		Lookup
PhoneType		Lookup
PhoneNumber		Short Text

Figure 5-10. *The completed Phone table*

Viewing the App in SharePoint

When you created the Access database, the template automatically created the app in your Team Site. Also, a SQL Server database was provisioned in Azure. As you defined tables, these were created in SQL Server. All of this happens behind the scenes as you edit your Access database. (This is why saving may seem a little slow.)

To demonstrate the integration, let's go to your Team Site and look at the JobTracking app. You'll find this in your Apps in Testing list. The initial page will look like Figure 5-11.

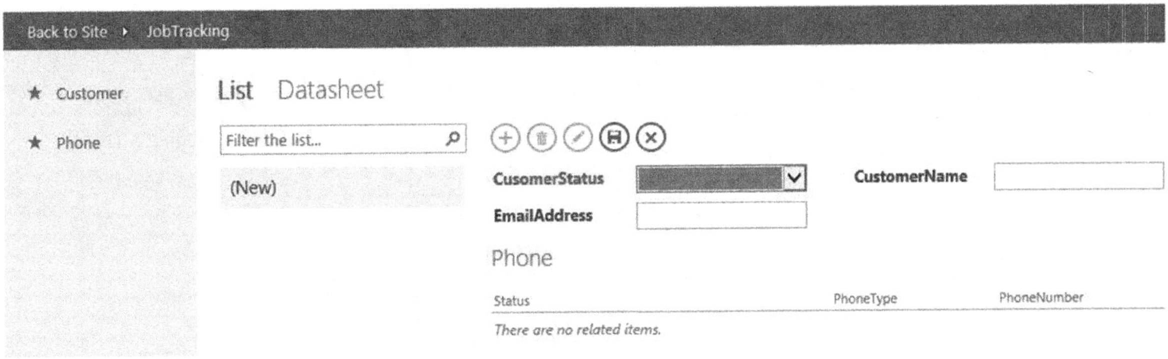

Figure 5-11. *The initial app page*

At this point the tables are empty so let's insert some data. Select a CustomerStatus from the dropdown list and enter a name and e-mail address. Then click the Add Phone link, which is underneath the empty list of phones. A pop-up window, shown in Figure 5-12, will appear for you to enter the phone details.

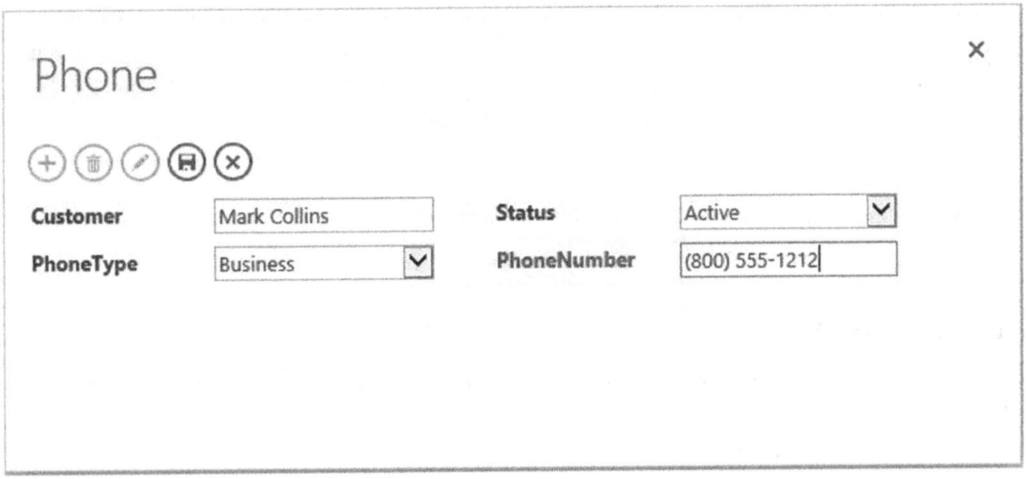

Figure 5-12. *Adding a Phone record*

Notice that the `Customer` field is already pre-filled using the `CustomerName` field from the `Customer` table and the `Status` was defaulted to `Active`. Enter some data, click the Save icon and close the dialog box. The completed `Customer` record will look similar to Figure 5-13.

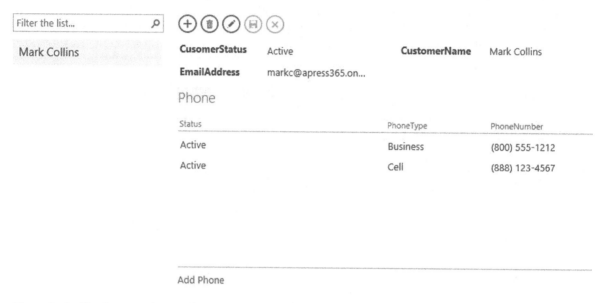

Figure 5-13. *The Customer form with Phone records*

▪ **Tip** In previous versions of Access, even with web databases, Access was used to edit a local (`.accdb`, or `.mdb`) file. With web databases, this could be later published to a SharePoint site and also downloaded from SharePoint. With Web apps in Access 2013, there is no local file, Access is communicating directly with SharePoint and SQL Server. When you close Access and then want to later make additional changes, you'll need to go to the SharePoint site. From the `Settings` menu, select the `Customize in Access` link. This will launch Access 2013 and open your app.

Now you'll define the remaining tables. To add a new table, you'll need to go to the `HOME` tab on the ribbon and click the `Table` button.

Creating the Address Table

The `Address` table is similar to the `Phone` table with a foreign key relationship with the `Customer` table. Create a new table with the following fields:

- **AddressID** – AutoNumber, primary key
- **Customer** – Lookup, a lookup field using the `Customer` table
- **Status** – Lookup, a static list of values (**Active** and **Inactive**), set **Active** as Default
- **AddressType** – Lookup, a static list of values (**Billing**, **Job**, **Shipping**)
- **Address** – ShortText

- **City** – ShortText

- **State** – ShortText

- **Country** – ShortText

- **ZipCode** – ShortText

I added a default value for the Country field so the users would not have to enter this. You can choose to leave this without a default value or enter a different value as appropriate. Save the table and enter the name **Address** when prompted. The completed Address table should look like Figure 5-14.

Field Name	Data Type
AddressID	AutoNumber
Customer	Lookup
Status	Lookup
AddressType	Lookup
Address	Short Text
City	Short Text
State	Short Text
Country	Short Text
ZipCode	Short Text

Figure 5-14. *The completed Address table*

Creating the Product and Service Tables

Next you'll create the Product and Service tables that will store static information about the products and services that can be included in a job or job estimate. You'll create these much like the previous tables.

The Product table will contain the following fields:

- **ProductID** – AutoNumber, the primary key

- **ProductCode** – ShortText, a string containing a user-recognizable identifier such as a UPC code

- **Description** – LongText

- **UnitPrice** – Currency

- **UnitCost** – Currency

- **InventoryType** – Lookup, a static list of values (**Inventoried**, **Special Order**, **Custom Made**) that define if/how this item is maintained in inventory.

The Service table will have the following fields:

- **ServiceID** – AutoNumber, primary key

- **ServiceCode** – ShortText, a user recognizable identifier

- **Description** – LongText

- **LaborRate** – Currency, defines the hourly rate charged for this service

- **MinimumHours** – Number, a numeric field indicating the minimum hours that will be charged (0 indicates that there is no minimum), for the Subtype select Whole Number.

- **FlatRate** – Yes/No, a Boolean field that indicates if this service is charged at a flat rate. If it is, the LaborRate field specifies the flat rate instead of an hourly rate.

■ **Tip**   To define a default value for a boolean Yes/No field, enter the expression as **Yes** or **No**.

Creating the Job Table

The Job table will contain the proposed, active and completed jobs. It will generally start out as an estimate. When the job is completed, the actual values will replace the estimates and this will then be used for billing purposes.

Create the Job table as you have the previous tables. It will contain the following fields:

- **JobID** – AutoNumber, primary key

- **Customer** – Lookup, a lookup field using the Customer table

- **Address** – Lookup, a lookup field using the Address table (select the Address field to be displayed)

- **JobStatus** – Lookup, a static list of allowed values (**New, Proposed, Accepted, InProgress, Complete, Cancelled**) defaults to **"New"**

- **StartDate** – Date/Time, indicating the expected date the job will start (select Short Date for the display format)

- **EndDate** – Date/Time, indicating the expected or actual completion date (select Short Date for the display format)

- **Notes** – LongText

- **TotalEstimate** – Currency, field that will be computed by a data macro

Creating the JobProduct and JobService Tables

The JobProduct and JobService tables specify the products and services that are included in a job. The referenced tables, Product and Service, respectively, define the static properties such as price and description. The JobProduct and JobService tables supply the job-specific details such as quantity and status. These tables also allow for a custom price to be assigned that is applicable for this job only.

1.   Create the JobProduct table and include the following fields:

- **JobProductID** – AutoNumber, primary key

- **Job** – Lookup, a lookup field using the Job table, select JobID to be displayed

- **Product** – Lookup, a lookup field using the Product table, select ProductCode to be displayed

- **EstimatedQty** – Number, for the SubType select Whole Number

- **ActualQty** – Number, for the SubType select Whole Number

- **CustomPrice** – Currency, used to override the price for this job only

- **ProductStatus** – Lookup, a static list of allowed values (**New**, **Waiting**, **Delivered**, **Cancelled**), set default as **"New"**

- **Notes** – LongText

- **CompleteDate** – Date/Time, indicates when the product was delivered, select Short Date for the display format

2. Save the table and enter **JobProduct** for the name when prompted.

3. Create the JobService table and include the following fields:

- **JobServiceID** – AutoNumber, primary key

- **Job** – Lookup, a lookup field using the Job table, select JobID to be displayed

- **Service** – Lookup, a lookup field using the Service table, select ServiceCode to be displayed

- **EstimatedHours** – Number, for the SubType select Whole Number

- **ActualHours** – Number, for the SubType select Whole Number

- **CustomPrice** – Currency, used to override the price for this job only

- **ServiceStatus** – Lookup, a static list of allowed values (**Planned**, **Waiting**, **Completed**, **Cancelled**), set default as **"Planned"**

- **Notes** – LongText

- **CompleteDate** – Date/Time, indicates when the service was completed, select Short Date for the display format

4. Save the table and enter **JobService** for the name when prompted.

Creating the Contact Table

The Contact table is used to record correspondence with a customer, such as e-mails or phone calls. Create the Contact table and add the following fields:

- **ContactID** – AutoNumber, primary key

- **Customer** – Lookup, a lookup field using the Customer table

- **ContactDate** – Date/Time, when the contact occurred, for the Subtype select Date with Time, set default as =**Now()**

- **ContactType** – Lookup, a static list of allowed values (**Email**, **Phone**, **Mail**, **InPerson**, **Other**)

- **Inbound** – Yes/No, a Boolean field indicating if the customer initiated the contact

- **FollowUp** – Lookup, a static list of values (**None**, **Callback**, **Schedule Visit**, **Estimate Job**), specifying an appropriate action

- **ContactNotes** – LongText

Save the table and enter **Contact** for the name, when prompted.

Creating the Queries

A select query can be used to combine the fields of two or more tables into a single view. This technique is often used to simplify form development since a form can use a query just like it would a table. The form can then be developed from the query, which combines the fields from each table.

For example, the JobProduct table provides the job-specific details but the Product table contains some important static details such as product code and description. You'll combine these two tables into a single, de-normalized view (query). The form will use the query and can include fields from both tables.

You will create the following queries:

- qryJobProduct – combines the JobProduct and Product tables

- qryJobService – combines the JobService and Service tables

- qryJobSummary – combines the Job, Customer, and Address tables

Implementing the qryJobProduct Query

We'll start with the qryJobProduct query that combines the JobProduct and Product tables.

1. From the HOME tab of the ribbon, click the Advanced button and then select the Query link as shown in Figure 5-15.

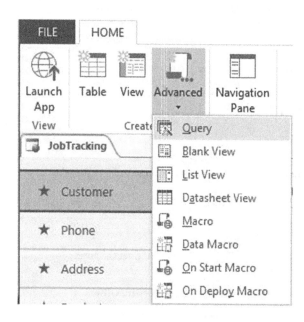

Figure 5-15. *Creating a new query*

2. This will display the Show Table dialog box that allows you to select the tables to be included in the query. Select the JobProduct table, hold down the Ctrl key, and select the Product table as shown in Figure 5-16. Click the Add button to add these tables and then click the Close button to close the dialog box.

Figure 5-16. *Adding the JobProduct and Product tables*

3. These tables will be displayed in the upper pane of the query window. Because of the foreign key relationship that exists between these two tables, there is already a join relationship shown.

■ **Tip** You can remove or edit these joins in the query window without affecting the table relationships.

---

4. Double-click the following fields, one at a time, to add them to the query definition:

    - `JobProduct.JobProductID`

    - `JobProduct.Job`

    - `JobProduct.Product`

    - `JobProduct.EstimatedQty`

    - `JobProduct.ActualQty`

    - `JobProduct.ProductStatus`

    - `JobProduct.CompleteDate`

    - `JobProduct.CustomPrice`

    - `Product.ProductCode`

- Product.Description

- Product.UnitPrice

- Product.UnitCost

- Product.InventoryType

- JobProduct.Notes

5.   Click the Save button in the title bar and enter the name **qryJobProduct** when prompted.
     The completed query should look like Figure 5-17.

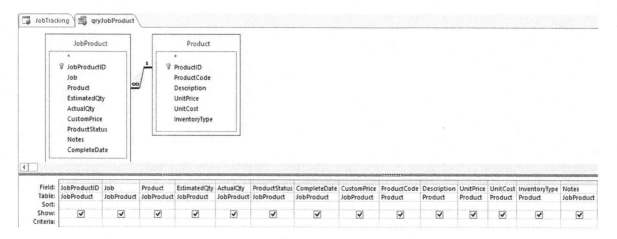

Figure 5-17. *The completed qryJobProduct query*

Implementing the qryJobService Query

Implement the qryJobService query the same way except use the JobService and Service tables. Include the following fields:

- JobService.JobServiceID

- JobService.Job

- JobService.Service

- JobService.EstimatedHours

- JobService.ActualHours

- JobService.ServiceStatus

- JobService.CompleteDate

- JobService.CustomPrice

- Service.ServiceCode
- Service.Description
- Service.LaborRate
- Service.MinimumHours
- Service.FlatRate
- JobService.Notes

Save the query and enter the name **qryJobService** when prompted. The completed query should look like Figure 5-18.

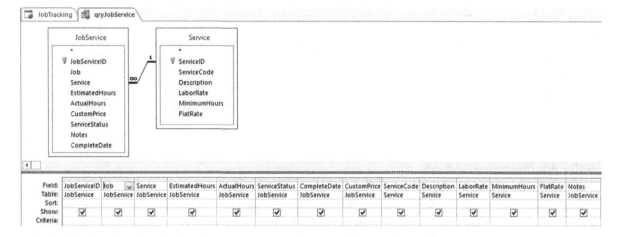

Figure 5-18. *The completed qryJobService query*

Creating the qryJobSummary Query

Create a new query and add the following tables:

- Customer
- Job
- Address

You may need to rearrange the tables but the initial query will look similar to Figure 5-19.

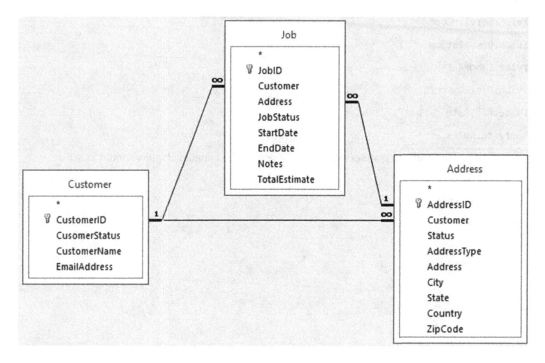

Figure 5-19. *The initial query design*

Notice that the Address table is linked to both the Customer and Job tables. A customer can have multiple addresses but a job can only have one address. For this query, the Job table is the main table and you'll want to keep the join between Job and Address but remove the one between Customer and Address. Click this join and then press the Delete key to remove it. This will have no effect on the table relationships.

Double-click the following fields to add them to the query:

- Job.JobID
- Customer.CustomerID
- Customer.CustomerName
- Customer.EmailAddress
- Job.TotalEstimate
- Address.Address
- Address.City
- Address.State
- Address.ZipCode
- Address.Country
- Job.Notes

The completed query should look like Figure 5-20.

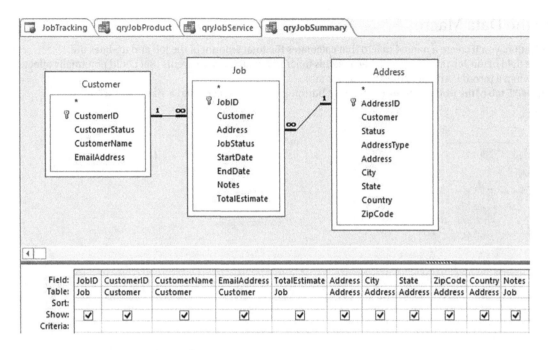

Figure 5-20. *The completed qryJobSummary query*

Implementing a Data Macro

Data macros are a handy place to implement data processing procedures. They can be automatically executed when certain data events occur, such as a record being added or modified. Because of this, they are particularly useful for keeping related tables in sync and enforcing business rules. A data macro can be assigned to a data event directly, or you can create a named macro that can be called by data events. Named macros can also be called manually from a form.

To add an event macro, edit the table that you want the macro to run on. Then, from the DESIGN tab of the ribbon, click either the On Insert, On Update, or On Delete button as shown in Figure 5-21, depending upon which event to want the macro to respond to.

Figure 5-21. *The DESIGN tab of the ribbon*

Creating the Data Macro

For this application, you'll create a named macro that calculates the total amount of the job and updates the TotalEstimate field of the Job table. You will then call this macro from all the data events that could potentially affect the total such when a record is added to the JobProduct table.

From the HOME tab of the ribbon, click the Advanced button and then select the Data Macro link as shown in Figure 5-22.

Figure 5-22. *Creating a data macro*

The macro will need to know which job should be updated so you'll create a parameter that will be passed in when the macro is called. Click the Create Parameter link in the upper right-hand corner of the macro editor. Enter the name **jobID**, select the Number (No Decimal) type, and enter a description as shown in Figure 5-23.

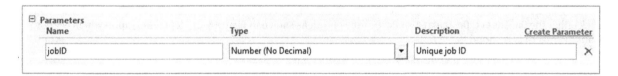

Figure 5-23. *Adding the jobID parameter*

Using the Macro Editor

The macro editor allows you to define the logic of your data macro. Data macros will typically perform actions such as reading data from a table, and updating or inserting a record. The Action Catalog, shown in Figure 5-24, illustrates the kinds of things you can do in a macro.

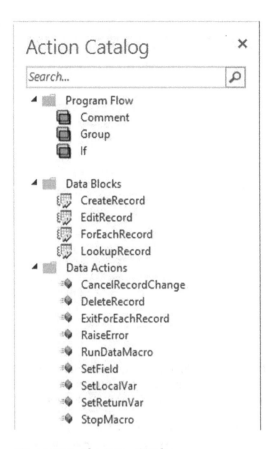

Figure 5-24. *The Action Catalog*

Actions are often nested inside other actions. For example, an EditRecord action specifies the record to be updated. Within this, you can add one or more SetField actions, which modify a single field within that record. Figure 5-25 shows a really simple macro that uses several of the most common actions. We will walk through this to explain how the individual actions are used.

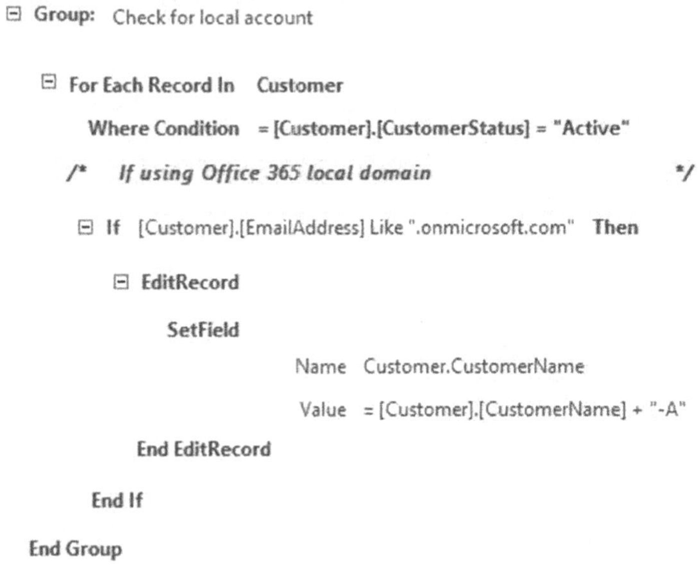

⊟ **Group:** Check for local account

　　⊟ **For Each Record In** Customer

　　　　Where Condition = [Customer].[CustomerStatus] = "Active"

　　　/* **If using Office 365 local domain** */

　　　　⊟ **If** [Customer].[EmailAddress] Like ".onmicrosoft.com" **Then**

　　　　　　⊟ **EditRecord**

　　　　　　　　SetField

　　　　　　　　　　Name Customer.CustomerName

　　　　　　　　　　Value = [Customer].[CustomerName] + "-A"

　　　　　　End EditRecord

　　　　End If

　　End Group

Figure 5-25. *Sample macro*

The Group action functions much like the #region directive in C#. You can include a set of related actions within it and collapse or expand the entire group, as necessary. For large, complex macros this will allow you to more easily follow the overall process and drill into the areas you need to focus on. A Group action can be nested inside another Group as well.

The ForEachRecord action returns data from a table or query and you can define a Where Condition to filter the rows that you want returned. In this case, we're using the Customer table and processing only Active accounts. All the actions nested inside this action are repeated for each record. You can break out of this loop by including the ExitForEachRecord action.

For each record returned, the If action checks to see if the e-mail address includes **.onmicrosoft.com**. We could have included that in the Where Condition but wanted to demonstrate the If action. You can also include an Else or an Else If section to define actions to be executed when the e-mail does not include this string. An EditRecord action is inside the If action, which means it will be executed only on records where the If condition is true.

The EditRecord action operates on a single record, which must be a record already read in through one of the read actions (either the ForEachRecord or LookupRecord action). By the default, it updates the current record; the record that was last accessed. In this case this will be the Customer record currently being evaluated by the ForEachRecord action. In a complex macro, you can have multiple nested read actions. In this situation, the "current" record may not be as obvious, or you may want to update a record that is not the current one. To deal with this, you can define an Alias on each of these actions. The EditRecord action will then operate on the record returned by the read action with the matching Alias. An Alias works much like they do when defining joins in an SQL statement. You specify an alias for each table in the query and then when selecting or updating a field, it is referenced using the table alias.

As we mentioned, you include one or more SetField actions inside the EditRecord action. Each one specifies the field name and the value it is to be updated to. In this macro, we're simply appending a **-A** to the CustomerName field.

■ **Tip** You'll notice that an Add New Action dropdown appears in various places in the macro. These are places where you can insert an action. The list of available actions in each location is limited based on its context. For example, you can only include a SetField action inside an EditRecord or CreateRecord action. You can also drag an action from the Action Catalog to the macro.

Computing the Job Total

Now you'll employ some of these actions to compute the total cost of a job. The macro will compute this by adding up the products and services included in the job. The macro is fairly long so we will describe it in pieces.

■ **Tip** To implement this macro, you'll probably find it easier to just use the figures that are shown. This will indicate exactly where each action should be placed and the specific expressions that you'll need to enter. The instructions that follow provide an overview of what the macro is doing.

1. The first macro action creates a local variable, jobTotal, and initializes it to 0. Add a SetLocalVar action with the name **JobTotal** and an expression of **0** as shown in Figure 5-26.

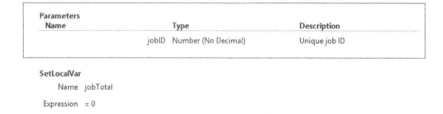

Parameters

Name	Type	Description
jobID	Number (No Decimal)	Unique job ID

SetLocalVar
    Name jobTotal
Expression = 0

Figure 5-26. *Adding a SetLocalVar action*

2. Then the macro iterates through all of the JobProduct records, accumulating the price multiplied by the quantity. Create a Group action named **Accumulate Product Costs**.

3. Inside of this add a ForEachRecord action that iterates through all the JobProduct records for this job, excluding the cancelled records. For each record, either accumulate the CustomPrice field or the UnitPrice times the quantity. Use the ActualQty field, if available, or the EstimtedQty if not. The completed Group action should look like Figure 5-27.

⊟ **Group:** Accumulate Product Costs

  ⊟ **For Each Record In** JobProduct

     Where Condition = [JobProduct].[Job]=[jobID] And [JobProduct].[ProductStatus] <>"Cancelled"

         Alias JobProduct

    ⊟ **If** [JobProduct].[CustomPrice]>0 **Then**

      SetLocalVar

            Name jobTotal

          Expression = [jobTotal] + [JobProduct].[CustomPrice]

    ⊟ **Else**

      ⊟ **Look Up A Record In** Product

        Where Condition = [Product].[ProductID]=[JobProduct].[Product]

            Alias Product

      SetLocalVar

            Name quantity

          Expression = [JobProduct].[ActualQty]

      ⊟ **If** Coalesce(quantity,0) <=0 **Then**

        SetLocalVar

              Name quantity

            Expression = [JobProduct].[EstimatedQty]

      End If

      SetLocalVar

            Name jobTotal

          Expression = [jobTotal] + [quantity]*[Product].[UnitPrice]

    End If

  End Group

Figure 5-27. *Designing the data macro – Product Costs*

■ **Note** The JobProduct table contains both an EstimatedQty field as well as an ActualQty field. If the actual value is populated, the formula will use that field instead of the estimated quantity. If a price has been specified in the CustomPrice field, this value is used instead of the UnitPrice. It is also assumed that this value will be an extended amount and does not need to be multiplied by the quantity to get the total amount for this product.

---

4.   The next step is to accumulate the JobService records. Add another Group action named **Accumulate Service Costs**, and within this, add a ForEachRecord action to iterate the JobService table.

5.   Just like you did for the product totals, add an If action inside the ForEachRecord to see if the CustomPrice field is populated. For the Else section, just add a Group action named **Compute Service Cost**. The macro should look like Figure 5-28.

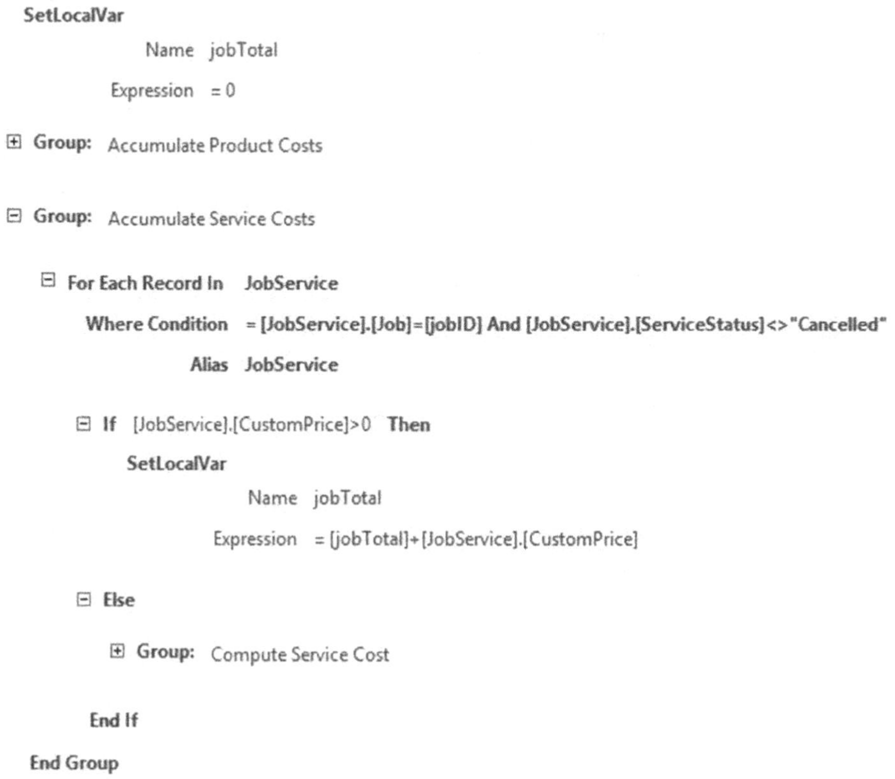

SetLocalVar

        Name jobTotal

      Expression = 0

⊞ **Group:** Accumulate Product Costs

⊟ **Group:** Accumulate Service Costs

    ⊟ **For Each Record In**   JobService

        Where Condition   = [JobService].[Job]=[jobID] And [JobService].[ServiceStatus]<>"Cancelled"

                Alias JobService

      ⊟ **If** [JobService].[CustomPrice]>0 **Then**

          SetLocalVar

                  Name jobTotal

                Expression = [jobTotal]+[JobService].[CustomPrice]

      ⊟ **Else**

        ⊞ **Group:** Compute Service Cost

      End If

End Group

Figure 5-28. Designing the data macro – Part 2

6.   Now you'll need to implement the Compute Service Cost group. Add a LookupRecord action to retrieve the Service record associated with this JobService record.

7.   If this is a flat rate service, the FlatRate amount from the Service record is used and the hours are ignored.

8.   For the Else section, you'll add a SetLocalVar action to define the hours variable. Through a series of If actions, you'll set this using either the ActualHours, EstimatedHours or MinimumHours fields.

9.   Finally, the hours variable is multiplied by the LaborRate and accumulated to the jobTotal variable. The Compute Service Cost group implementation should look like Figure 5-29.

⊟ **Group:** Compute Service Cost

   ⊟ **Look Up A Record In** Service

      Where Condition = [Service].[ServiceID]=[JobService].[Service]

    ⊟ **If** [Service].[FlatRate]= Yes **Then**

       SetLocalVar

            Name jobTotal

          Expression = [jobTotal]+[Service].[LaborRate]

    ⊟ **Else**

       SetLocalVar

            Name hours

          Expression = [JobService].[ActualHours]

      ⊟ **If** Coalesce([hours],0)<0 **Then**

        SetLocalVar

              Name hours

            Expression = [JobService].[EstimatedHours]

      End If

      ⊟ **If** Coalesce([hours],0)<=0 Or [hours]<[Service].[MinimumHours] **Then**

        SetLocalVar

              Name hours

            Expression = [Service].[MinimumHours]

      End If

      SetLocalVar

            Name hours

         Expression = Coalesce(hours,0)

      SetLocalVar

            Name jobTotal

         Expression = [jobTotal]+[hours]*[Service].[LaborRate]

    End If

  End Group

Figure 5-29. *Designing the data macro – Part 3*

    10.   The last step is to update the Job table, storing the computed jobTotal variable. You must first add a LookupRecord action to get the Job record. Then add an EditRecord action with a single SetField action as shown in Figure 5-30.

Updating the Job Table

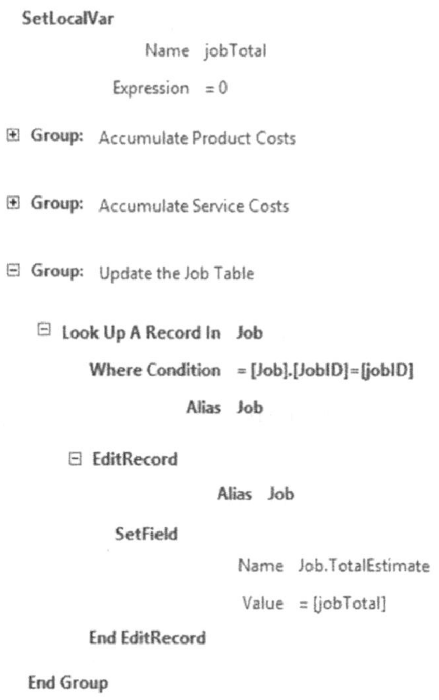

```
SetLocalVar
              Name    jobTotal
         Expression   = 0
⊞ Group:   Accumulate Product Costs


⊞ Group:   Accumulate Service Costs


⊟ Group:   Update the Job Table

     ⊟ Look Up A Record In   Job
          Where Condition   = [Job].[JobID]=[jobID]
                    Alias   Job

       ⊟ EditRecord
                      Alias   Job
           SetField
                      Name    Job.TotalEstimate
                      Value   = [jobTotal]
          End EditRecord

  End Group
```

Figure 5-30. *Designing the data macro – Part 4*

11. When you have entered all this logic, save the data macro. Enter the name **CalculateJobTotal** when prompted.

Entering Test Data

To test this macro, you'll need to first enter some data. For now, you'll just enter the data directly into the tables. To enter data, you can open a table in Datasheet View and key in the values for each field. From the Job Tracking tab, right-click the table and select the View Data link.

1. Start by defining some products and services. To test the various conditions that the macro supports, you'll need a variety of items with different values. Enter the values shown in Figures 5-31 and 5-32.

ProductID	ProductCode	Description	UnitPrice	UnitCost	InventoryType
1	1231	Widget	$15.00	$10.00	Inventoried
2	1232	Gadget	$20.00	$12.00	Special Order

Figure 5-31. Enter data into the Product table

ServiceID	ServiceCode	Description	LaborRate	MinimumHours	FlatRate
1	ABCD	Simple service item	$75.00	0	☐
2	ABCE	Flat rate service	$55.00	0	☑
3	ABCF	Minimum hour service	$30.00	2	☐

Figure 5-32. Entering data into the Service table

2. The Job table needs an address record so you'll create one now. You can enter whatever values you want here; our address looks like Figure 5-33.

AddressID	Customer	Status	AddressType	Address	City	State	Country	ZipCode
1		Active	Job	12 Maple Street	Anywhere	AZ	United States	96025

Figure 5-33. Setting up a job address

3. Next, you'll need to create a Job record. Use the Customer record that you created earlier and select the Address record that you just created. Set the JobStatus to **Proposed** and leave all the other fields with their default values. The TotalEstimate should be $0.00 as shown in Figure 5-34.

JobID	Customer	Address	JobStatus	StartDate	EndDate	Notes	TotalEstimate
1	Mark Collins	12 Maple Street	Proposed				$0.00

Figure 5-34. Adding a Job record

4. Now attach products to this job by adding JobProduct records. Enter the data shown in Figure 5-35; this will test all of the scenarios such as using a CustomPrice and overriding the EstimatedQty with the ActualQty.

JobProductID	Job	Product	EstimatedQty	ActualQty	CustomPrice	ProductStatus	Notes	CompleteDate
1	1	1231	3		$0.00	Waiting		
2	1	1232	4	5	$0.00	Delivered		
3	1	1231	3	0	$110.00	Delivered		
4	1	1232	0	6	$0.00	Cancelled		

Figure 5-35. Adding JobProduct records

5. Finally, enter records in the JobService table using the data shown in Figure 5-36.

JobServiceID	Job	Service	EstimatedHours	ActualHours	CustomPrice	ServiceStatus	Notes	CompleteDate
1	1	ABCD	3	0	$0.00	Planned		
2	1	ABCE	1	2	$0.00	Delivered		
3	1	ABCF	0	0	$0.00	Waiting		
4	1	ABCD	0	0	$95.00	Delivered		

Figure 5-36. *Adding JobService records*

Calling the Named Macro

The job total can change any time a record is added, changed, or deleted from either the JobProduct or JobService tables. So now you'll add an event-triggered macro for each of these events that simply calls your named macro.

Open the JobProduct table in Design View. In the DESIGN tab of the ribbon, you'll see a button for each of the three events as we showed earlier. Click the On Insert button, which will display the macro editor. Add a RunDataMacro action and select the CalculateJobTotal macro from the dropdown. Since this macro has a jobID parameter, the macro editor shows this and gives you a place to specify the value that should be passed in. Enter **Job** as shown in Figure 5-37. Click the Save button in the ribbon to save the change and then click the Close button.

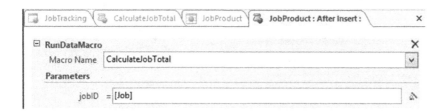

Figure 5-37. *Defining an Event Macro*

Repeat this process to define macros for the update and delete events. The macros will be identical to the On Insert macro. Then, create macros for all three events on the JobService table. Again, these will be identical to the On Insert macro shown in Figure 5-37.

Testing the Data Macro

Now you're ready to test your macro. You can invoke the macro by updating one of the JobProduct or JobService records. But first, we'll turn on the macro tracing facility. This is a really nice feature with Access 2013.

Open the CalculateJobTotal macro in the macro editor. If you don't have it already open, you can find it in the Navigator pane. Just double-click it to open it in Design View. Select the DESIGN tab of the ribbon. You'll see a Data Macro Tracing button as demonstrated in Figure 5-38. Click the Data Macro Tracing button to turn on tracing. This button acts like a toggle; if you click it again it will disable tracing.

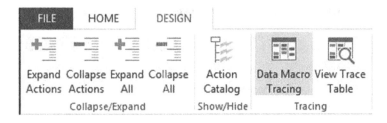

Figure 5-38. *Turning on the trace mode*

Now open the JobProduct table and change the ProductStatus field of one of the records. Then click off of this row to trigger the save operation, which will also invoke your macro. Go back to the CalculateJobTotal macro and click the View Trace Table button.

A portion of the trace information is shown in Figure 5-39.

ID	MacroName	ActionName	Operand	Output	TargetRow
1516	JobProduct:On Update	RunDataMacro	CalculateJobTotal		
1517	CalculateJobTotal	SetLocalVar	jobTotal	0.000000	
1518	CalculateJobTotal	ForEachRecord	JobProduct;WHERE [JobProd		
1519	CalculateJobTotal	ForEachRecord			[JobProductID] = 1 ; [Cust·
1520	CalculateJobTotal	Else			
1521	CalculateJobTotal	LookupRecord	Product;WHERE [Product].[I		
1522	CalculateJobTotal	LookupRecord			[ProductID] = 1 ; [UnitPric·
1523	CalculateJobTotal	SetLocalVar	quantity		
1564	CalculateJobTotal	If	[JobService].[CustomPrice]·		
1565	CalculateJobTotal	SetLocalVar	jobTotal	465.000000	
1566	CalculateJobTotal	LookupRecord	Job;WHERE [Job].[JobID]=[j		
1567	CalculateJobTotal	LookupRecord			[JobID] = 1 ; [TotalEstimat·
1568	CalculateJobTotal	EditRecord			
1569	CalculateJobTotal	SetField	Job.TotalEstimate	465.000000	

Figure 5-39. *The trace log*

The first entry is from the On Update event of the JobProduct table. You can see that it called the CalculateJobTotal macro. The remaining entries are from the CalculateJobTotal macro, starting with the initializing of the jobTotal variable to 0. At the end of the procedure, you can see where it looked up the Job record and set the TotalEstimate field to 465.00.

Now for a final check, open the Job table and verify the TotalEstimate field has the correct value.

Designing Forms

Now that you have the tables designed you can customize the forms that allow the users to view and edit the data contained in them. Generally, you will need a form for each table. In some cases you'll use a query that combines the data from multiple tables. When there is a parent-child relationship such as with the Customer and Phone tables, you use a Related Items control, which we'll demonstrate later.

There are three types of forms that you can create. If you click the Advanced button in the ribbon, you will see this listed as Blank View, List View, and Datasheet View, as demonstrated in Figure 5-40.

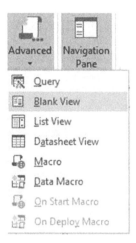

Figure 5-40. *The form options*

The blank view is pretty self-explanatory. Use this type if you want to setup the data binding manually. The name List View is somewhat misleading. A list view is just a form that displays a single record. In contrast, the datasheet view displays multiple records in a grid format. In Access 2010 these were called Form, and Multiple Items. Use a list view if you want to show a single record, and a datasheet view if you need to show multiple.

In Access 2013 the forms are automatically created for you. For every table, there will be a list view as well as a datasheet view. You can find these in the Navigation pane as demonstrated in Figure 5-41.

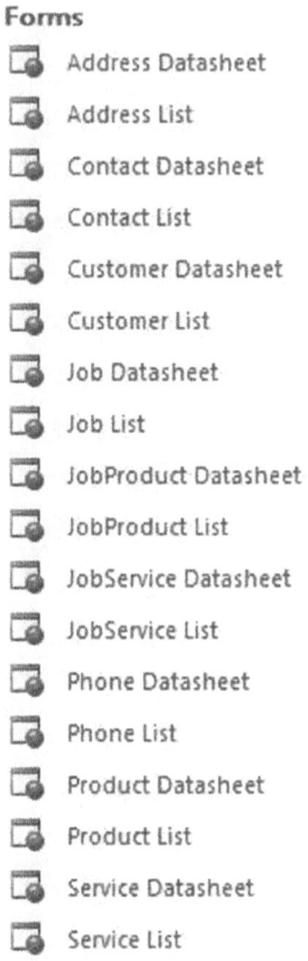

Forms

- Address Datasheet
- Address List
- Contact Datasheet
- Contact List
- Customer Datasheet
- Customer List
- Job Datasheet
- Job List
- JobProduct Datasheet
- JobProduct List
- JobService Datasheet
- JobService List
- Phone Datasheet
- Phone List
- Product Datasheet
- Product List
- Service Datasheet
- Service List

Figure 5-41. *Listing the existing forms*

The generated forms provide a good starting point and will save you some time. They attempt to deal with parent-child relationships by embedding a Related Items control within a form. We'll walk you through the changes that are needed. You'll also need to make some new forms.

■ **Caution**   You cannot use VBA in a web form as this is not supported with SharePoint. Instead you'll use macros to perform advanced features such as form manipulation.

Exploring the Form Designer

Open the Phone Datasheet form by double-clicking it in the Navigation pane. The form will be displayed in the Layout view shown in Figure 5-42.

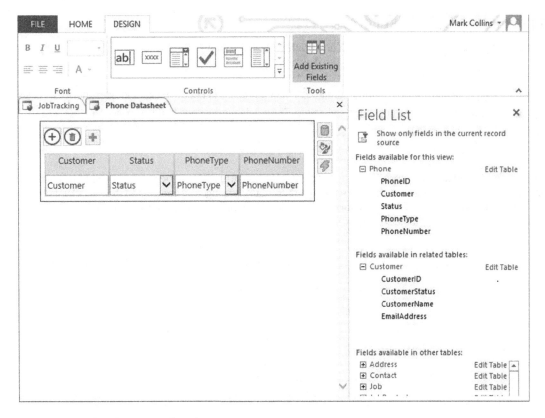

Figure 5-42. *The Phone Datasheet form*

The design experience in Access 2013 is very powerful and fairly intuitive. The first thing you'll generally need to do is adjust the fields included in the form. You can resize a field and drag it around to change the order. You can also include additional fields by dragging them from the Field List pane.

Because the Phone table has a foreign key to the Customer table, you can also include any of the fields from the Customer table on the form. All the other tables are listed in the Field List pane and you can include fields from these tables as well. However, you will need to define how the record should be selected because there is no database relationship that defines that.

To the right of the grid you'll find three small icons that are used to configure data, formatting, and action properties. One or more of these may be hidden depending on what element in the form is selected. The data properties allow you to configure the data source for the form or control. The formatting properties include defining the tooltip or caption or making the control visible or not. The actions properties allow you define custom actions for certain events such as On Click or On Load.

The action bar is shown above the grid and contains two default actions; a plus symbol for adding a new record and a trash can for deleting the selected row(s). You can also create your own custom actions, by clicking the green plus sign.

Creating the Phone and Address Forms

We'll start with the phone and address forms. Let's begin with the datasheet views.

Modifying the Phone Datasheet Form

The Phone Datasheet should already be displayed. If not, double-click it from the Navigation pane.

■ **Tip** The value of the primary key field is auto-generated and in many cases is not meaningful to the end users. These have been removed from the generated form to save real estate. The notable exceptions to this rule are the CustomerID and JobID fields. These are often used in documents such as invoices.

Delete the Customer field from the grid. Since the Phone Datasheet form will only be used as a child form of the Customer form, displaying the customer name here would be redundant. Arrange the controls so the PhoneNumber field is before Status and PhoneType. Also use the formatting properties icon to change the captions to **Phone Number** and **Type**. The form should look like Figure 5-43.

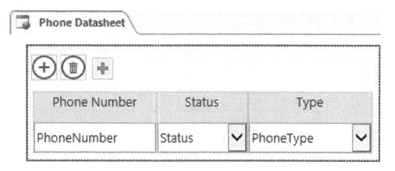

Figure 5-43. *The layout of the Phone form*

Modifying the Address Forms

Open the Address Datasheet form. Remove the Customer field from the grid and resize and rearrange the fields just like you did with the Phone Datasheet form. The completed form will look similar to Figure 5-44.

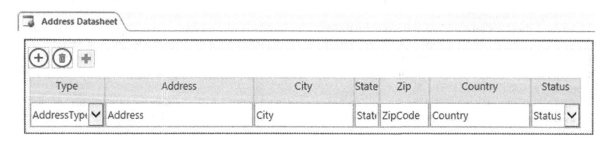

Figure 5-44. *The layout of the Address Datasheet form*

Now open the Address List form and remove the Customer field and caption. Re-arrange the controls to look like Figure 5-45.

Figure 5-45. *The Address List form*

Creating the Product and Service Forms

Next, you'll adjust the forms that will display the products and services that can be included in a job. First, you'll customize the Product Datasheet and Service Datasheet forms by resizing the fields and editing the field labels. These will be similar to the Phone and Address forms. Then you'll modify the list views to remove the related item information.

The Product Datasheet and Service Datasheet forms just need some resizing of fields and customizing the captions. Modify these so they look like Figures 5-46 and 5-47.

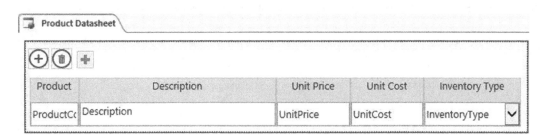

Figure 5-46. *The Product Datasheet form*

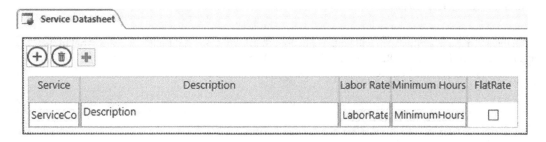

Figure 5-47. *The Service Datasheet form*

However, the list views have some related information that needs to be removed. For example, the Product List form, shown in Figure 5-48, includes a Related Items control to display related JobProduct records. This is here because there is a foreign key relationship defined between these tables. For this application you'll navigate from JobProduct to Product and not the other way around.

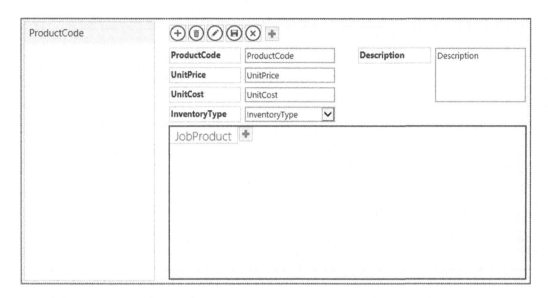

Figure 5-48. *The initial Product List form*

Delete the Related Items control and adjust some of the field labels so the form looks like Figure 5-49.

Figure 5-49. *The adjusted Product List form*

Save your changes. To see what this form will look like in your SharePoint site, right-click the view label in the Job Tracking tab and select the Open in Browser link as shown in Figure 5-50.

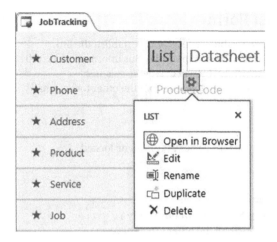

Figure 5-50. Opening a form in SharePoint

Click the edit icon and the form should look like Figure 5-51.

Figure 5-51. The Product List form in edit mode

■ **Tip**   When saving changes in the Access application, if you already have the SharePoint site open in your browser, the changes may not be immediately available. If you experience this, close all your browser windows and go back to the SharePoint site.

Make the same changes to the Service List form. The completed form should look like Figure 5-52.

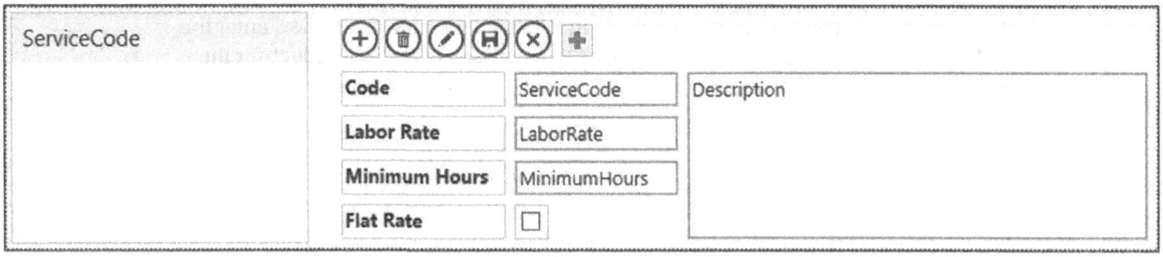

ServiceCode	⊕ 🗑 ✎ 💾 ⊗ ✚		
	Code	ServiceCode	Description
	Labor Rate	LaborRate	
	Minimum Hours	MinimumHours	
	Flat Rate	☐	

Figure 5-52. The final Service List from

Creating New JobProduct and JobService List Form

Now you'll create new list view forms for the JobProduct and JobService tables. These tables establish the link between a job and the product and services that are included. The forms will need to display this information as well as data from the associated product or service, such as description and price. You will delete the existing JobProduct List form and create new forms from scratch. These forms will be different from the other forms you have worked on so far because:

- You will use a query instead of a table as the data source

- The controls associated with fields from the linked tables (Product or Service) will be locked to prevent editing

1. Delete the JobProduct List form.

2. Go to the JobTracking tab and select the JobProduct table. Notice that there is only a Datasheet view listed as demonstrated in Figure 5-53, whereas all the other tables have both a List and Datasheet view.

Figure 5-53. *Displaying the JobProduct views*

3. Click the green plus icon to define a new view. In the Add New View dialog box, enter the name **JobProduct List**, select the List Details type and select qryJobProduct for the data source as shown in Figure 5-54.

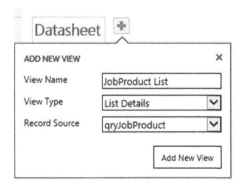

Figure 5-54. *Defining the list view*

4. The display name in the JobTracking tab is JobProduct List. Click the settings icon, select the Rename link, and enter **List**.

5. Since the form uses the qryJobProduct query, it will contain the fields from both the JobProduct as well as the Product table. The default form will look like Figure 5-55.

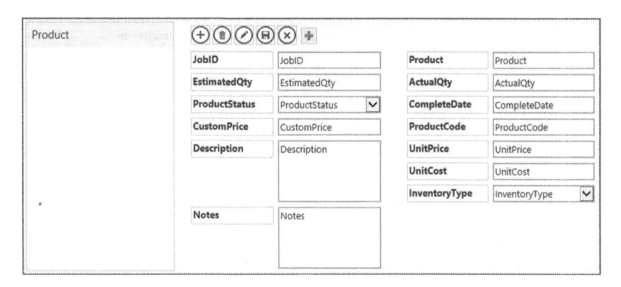

Figure 5-55. *The initial list form*

6. Click the Edit button, to put this form in edit mode. Remove the JobID and Product fields and their associated labels. Then rearrange the fields so the Product fields are at the bottom of the form, as shown in Figure 5-56.

Figure 5-56. *The final list form*

7. Select the ProductCode field and then click the formatting properties icon. Unselect the Enabled check box as shown in Figure 5-57. This will make this a read-only field.

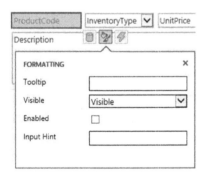

Figure 5-57. *Disabling the ProductCode field*

8. In the same way, disable the other fields from the Product table. This includes the InventoryType, UnitPrice, UnitCost, and Description fields.

9. Click the Save icon in the title bar.

10. Go to your SharePoint site and select the JobTracking app. Select the Job table and then select the List view, if not already selected. The form should look similar to Figure 5-58.

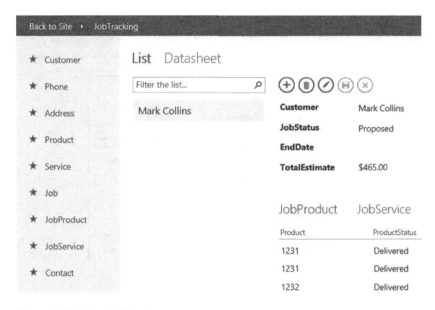

Figure 5-58. *The Job List form*

11. Click one of the products listed in the JobProduct tab. This will display the JobProduct List form that you just created. Click the edit icon to view this in edit mode. The form will look like Figure 5-59. Notice that the Product fields are disabled and cannot be modified.

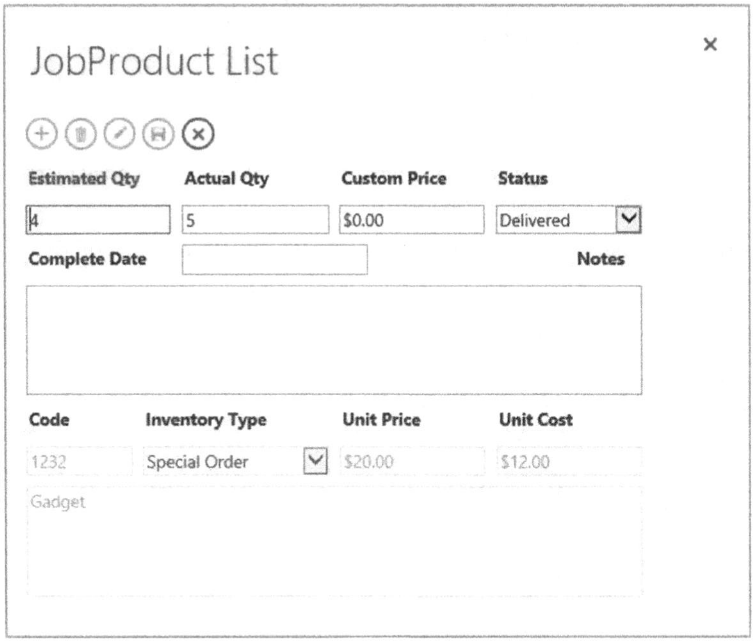

Figure 5-59. *The JobProduct List form*

12. Repeat these steps to re-create the JobService List form. Use the qryJobService query as the data source for the form, which should look like Figure 5-60 when you're done.

Figure 5-60. *The layout of the JobService form*

13. Just like you did with the JobProduct List form, unselect the Enabled check box on the ServiceCode, FlatRate, LaborRate, MinimumHours, and Description controls.

Modifying the Job Form

Next you'll customize the Job List form. First you'll do some basic re-arranging of controls like you have done with the other forms. Then we'll show you how to configure the Related Items control.

1. Open the Job List form in the Navigation pane to open in edit mode. Arrange the controls to look like Figure 5-61.

Figure 5-61. *The modified Job List form*

The bottom portion of this form contains a Related Items control. This is a handy way of way of displaying multiple one-to-many relationships. A job consists of products and services; the sample job that you created earlier to test the data macro had four of each. When displaying a job you'll need to show both lists. In Access 2010 this was done by including a subform for each list. In 2013 you'll use a Related Items control.

Each child list will be put into a different tab. Two tabs were created for you, JobProduct and JobService. As you configure each list, you can choose up to four fields of the child record that will be displayed in this control. You can also choose which form will be used as a pop-up form when one of the rows is selected. Click the JobProduct tab and then click the data properties icon.

2. In the dialog that is displayed, select qryJobProduct as the data source. Recall that you created this earlier in the chapter. It contains fields from both the JobProduct table as well as the related Product table. For the Related Field property, select Job. This defines the field in the child table that is used to link a record to the parent record.

3. Then you'll see four sets of fields and captions; these specify the fields that should be displayed in this control. Select the following four fields and enter an appropriate caption:

   - Product

   - ProductStatus

   - EstimatedQty

   - ActualQty

4. For the Popup View selection, choose the JobProduct List form. This is the custom form you created earlier that uses the qryJobProduct query. This form will be displayed as a pop-up dialog box when a row is selected.

5. Finally, select the field that you want the rows to be sorted by. Select JobProductID so they will be displayed in the order they were created. The completed dialog box should look like Figure 5-62.

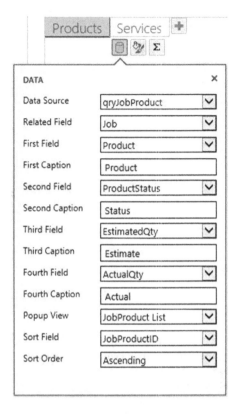

Figure 5-62. The initial layout of the Job form

6. Close the data properties dialog box and click the formatting properties icon. Enter the caption **Products** as shown in Figure 5-63.

Figure 5-63. Changing the tab caption

7. Then make similar changes to the JobService tab, configuring this as shown in Figure 5-64.

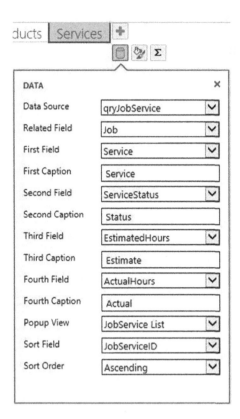

Figure 5-64. *Configuring the JobService tab*

8. Close the data properties dialog box and click the formatting properties icon. Change the caption to **Services**.

9. Click the Save button in the title bar to save your changes. Then go to the SharePoint site and your Job form should look similar to Figure 5-65.

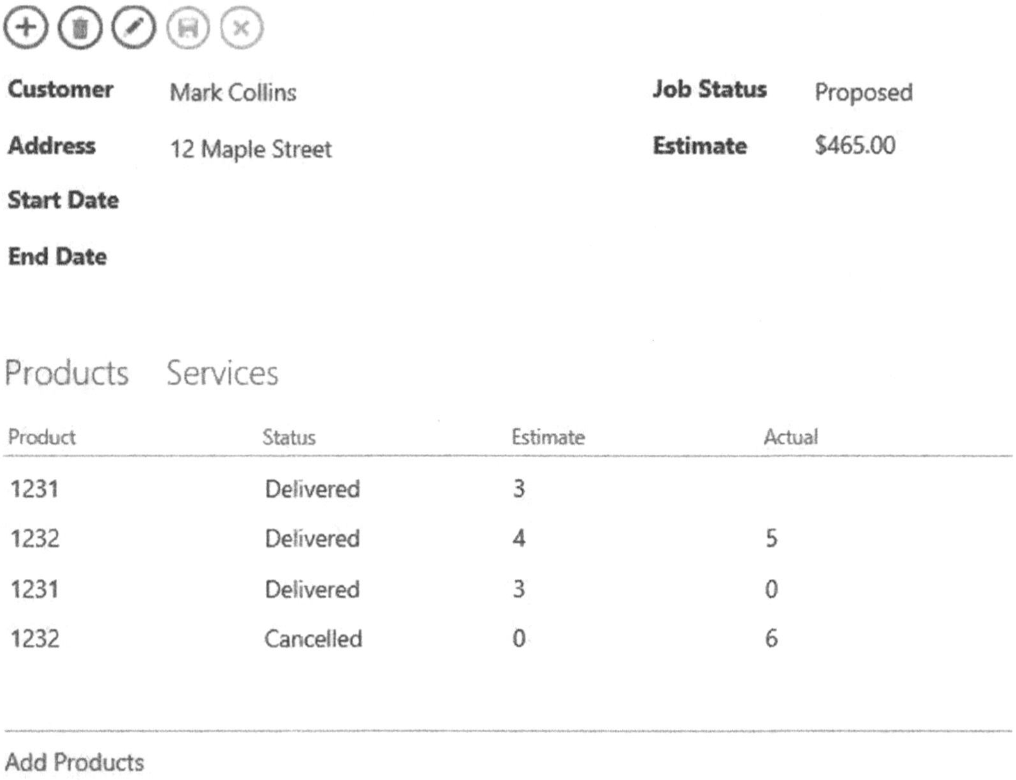

Customer	Mark Collins	**Job Status**	Proposed
Address	12 Maple Street	**Estimate**	$465.00
Start Date			
End Date			

Products Services

Product	Status	Estimate	Actual
1231	Delivered	3	
1232	Delivered	4	5
1231	Delivered	3	0
1232	Cancelled	0	6

Add Products

Figure 5-65. *The completed Job List form*

Modifying the Customer Form

The Customer form will be used to view and update customer information. This is where you'll view and add phone numbers and addresses for a customer. This form will also allow you to add and modify customer jobs. You'll also record correspondence (contacts) with a customer from here. This is the portal of your applications where you'll bring all of the other forms together.

1. Open the Customer List from in edit mode. There are just a few fields on this form and you just need to better arrange them.

2. Add the CustomerID field to this form. As we said earlier, this is one place where this will be meaningful to the users.

3. You can also re-arrange the tabs in the Related Items control. The completed form should look like Figure 5-66.

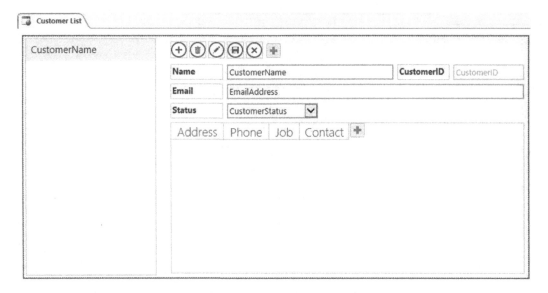

Figure 5-66. *The modified Customer List form*

The section on the left side of the form is used to search for a specific record. So far, we have been ignoring this. It is not used when the form is presented as a pop-up window. Most of the other forms will generally be used that way so this was not that important. However, since the Customer List form is the primary form the users will start with, we'll need to address it.

■ **Tip**   As you have seen, the users can go directly to any form. If you expect a form to be used directly, then you should consider how searching will be done.

You can display up to two fields in the search box. The primary field is shown on top and the secondary, if used, is displayed on a separate line underneath. So if you use two, keep in mind that you will be able to display about half as many results. Also, be aware that the searching logic will compare the input string to any of the fields in the main table; you don't have to display a field for it to be used in the search. You can also include an image on the search box, if the main table has a field that stores images.

4.   For this form, you'll include both the CustomerName and the CustomerID fields. Select the search window and then click the data properties icon next to it. Select CustomerID as the secondary source as shown in Figure 5-67. The sort field should already be set to CustomerName; this will display the results in alphabetical order.

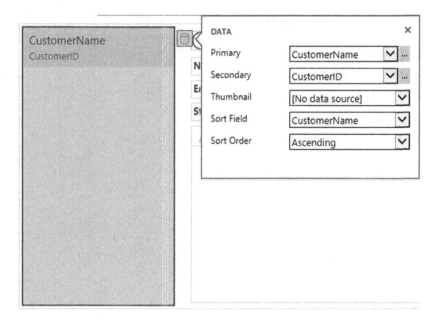

Figure 5-67. Configuring the search window

5.   Just like you did with the JobProduct and JobService forms, you'll need to configure the
     Related Items control. You can include up to four fields in each of these tabs. Configure
     the Address tab as shown in Figure 5-68.

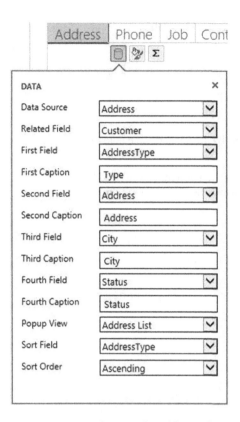

Figure 5-68. *Configuring the Address tab*

6. Then select the Phone tab and click the data properties icon. Select the following fields and enter the corresponding label:

   PhoneType - **Type**

   PhoneNumber - **Number**

   Status - **Status**

7. The pop-up view should be set to Phone List. Also, sort by the PhoneType field in ascending order.

8. In the Job tab, select the following fields and enter the corresponding label:

   JobStatus - **Status**

   StartDate - **Start**

   EndDate - **End**

   TotalEstimate - **Total**

9. The pop-up view should be set to the Job List. Also, sort by the StartDate field in descending order. This will show the most recent job at the top.

10. In the Contact tab, select the following fields and enter the corresponding label:

ContactDate - **Date**

ContactType - **Type**

Inbound - **Inbound?**

FollowUp - **Followup**

11. The pop-up view should be set to the Contact List. Also, sort by the ContactDate field in descending order.

12. Save your changes and go to the SharePoint site. To test out the filter you may need to add some more customers. The Customer List form with the Job tab selected, will look similar to Figure 5-69.

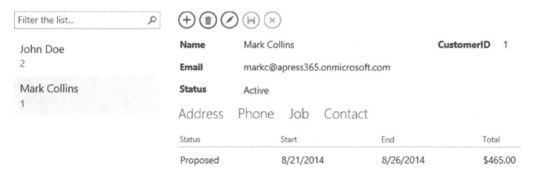

Figure 5-69. *The completed Customer List view*

Creating a Job Summary Form

Now you'll create a custom view for the Job table. The Summary form will list all of the jobs in the database using a datasheet view. This will use the qryJobSummary query that you created earlier in the chapter and will include fields from both the Customer and Job tables as well as details from the Address table. You will also create a macro that will display the job detail when a record is selected.

1. From the JobTracking tab, select the Job table. Buttons for the existing List and Datasheet views will be shown as well as a green plus symbol to the right of them. Click the green plus sign to define a new view. Enter the name **Summary**, select the Datasheet type, and select the qryJobSummary query as shown in Figure 5-70. Click the Add New View button to create the form.

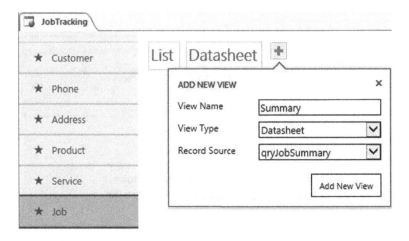

Figure 5-70. *Adding a new datasheet view*

2.   Click the Edit button open the new view in edit mode. The Field List pane, on the right-hand side, will list all of the fields in the referenced tables. To only show the fields that have been defined in this query, click the Show only fields in the current record source link. The resulting list is shown in Figure 5-71.

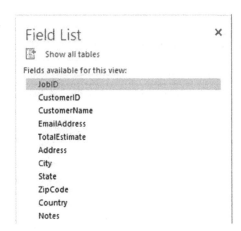

Figure 5-71. *Listing the available fields from the query*

3.   Drag the CustomerID and JobID fields to the grid and remove the Notes field. Re-arrange and resize the fields as shown in Figure 5-72.

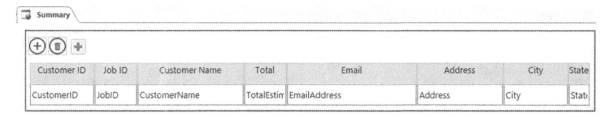

Figure 5-72. *Arranging the fields in the grid*

4.   Select the entire form and click the data properties icon. In the dialog box that is shown, select the Read Only check box as shown in Figure 5-73. This will disable the form so the data cannot be modified.

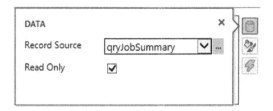

Figure 5-73. *Marking this as a read-only form*

5.   Save your changes and go to your SharePoint site. The completed form should look similar to Figure 5-74.

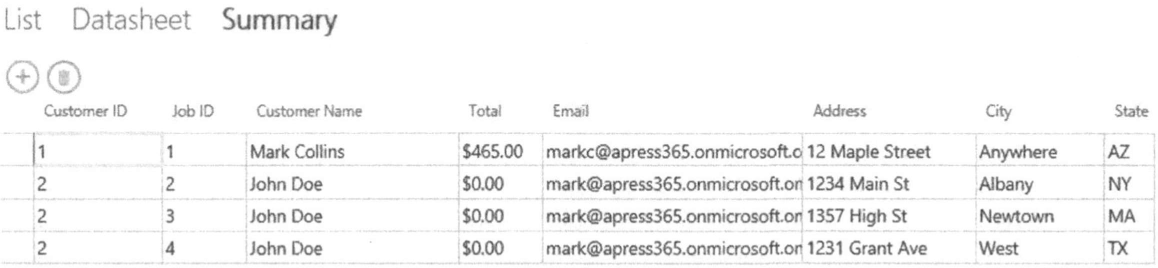

List   Datasheet   **Summary**

Customer ID	Job ID	Customer Name	Total	Email	Address	City	State
1	1	Mark Collins	$465.00	markc@apress365.onmicrosoft.c	12 Maple Street	Anywhere	AZ
2	2	John Doe	$0.00	mark@apress365.onmicrosoft.or	1234 Main St	Albany	NY
2	3	John Doe	$0.00	mark@apress365.onmicrosoft.or	1357 High St	Newtown	MA
2	4	John Doe	$0.00	mark@apress365.onmicrosoft.or	1231 Grant Ave	West	TX

Figure 5-74. *The completed Job Summary view*

6.   It would be really handy to be able to select one of these jobs and display all of the details for it. You'll accomplish that now by adding a simple macro. Edit the Summary form, select the JobID field, and click the actions icon. A dialog box will appear showing the available actions, as shown in Figure 5-75.

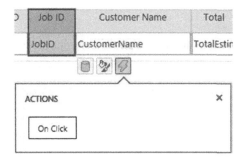

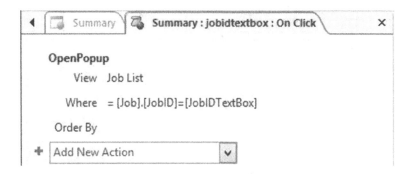

Figure 5-75. Adding an On Click action

7. Click the On Click button, which will open the macro editor that you have used earlier. You will use this to define the actions to be performed when this control is clicked. Add an OpenPopup action to the macro. This action is used to open a form.

8. Select the Job List view from the dropdown list. Then you'll need to specify a where clause to select the record that should be displayed. Enter **[Job].[JobID]=[JobIDTextBox]** in the Where parameter as shown in Figure 5-76.

Figure 5-76. Calling the OpenPopup macro action

9. Click the Save button in the ribbon to save the macro and then click the Close button to close the macro editor.

10. Click the Save button in the title bar to save the form changes. Then go to your SharePoint site and open the Summary view. Click the JobID column on one of the rows and the Job List form should be displayed, showing the details of the selected job.

Summary

In this chapter, I took you on a whirlwind tour of Access web databases and you built a fairly sophisticated application, which is now hosted on your Office 365 account. The application consists of:

- Tables

- Queries

- A data macro for calculating the job total

- Web forms, including Related Items controls

- A custom view that invokes another form through a UI macro

With relative ease and essentially no coding, you have created a cloud-based web application.

CHAPTER 6

■ ■ ■

Developing Exchange Online Solutions

In this chapter you'll create a client application that accesses the Exchange Online server in your Office 365 account. Exchange Online 2013 exposes a lot of features through Exchange Web Services (EWS) to client applications such as Outlook and Outlook Web App. Your custom application can use these same features as well. I will show you how to

- Connect to the Exchange Online server using the autodiscover process. The actual server that is hosting your Exchange instance can change, so you should always use the autodiscover process instead of hard-coding the connection string.

- Access the mailbox items stored in Exchange. Think of Exchange as a specialized database containing objects such as e-mails, appointments, tasks, and contacts, which are organized in a hierarchy of folders. You can view, modify, and create these objects programmatically.

- Determine the availability of someone or a group of people. Exchange provides a feature that allows you to see when people will be available based on their calendars. You can also use this feature to suggest windows of time when the specified group of people and resources will be available.

- Subscribe to notifications when certain events occur, such as the arrival of a new message. Your custom application can receive these notifications and take appropriate actions. I will show you both push- and pull-type subscriptions.

You'll create a Windows Presentation Foundation (WPF) application that will communicate with Exchange. To save you some time in designing the form, you can download the XAML file from www.apress.com and paste it into your project. This simply defines the visual controls that are used on the form. We will explain how to write the code-behind for each of the functions that you'll implement. Along the way, we'll explain how each works.

Creating the Visual Studio Project

Launch Visual Studio 2013 and create a new project and solution. Enter the project name **ExchangeApp**, as shown in Figure 6-1.

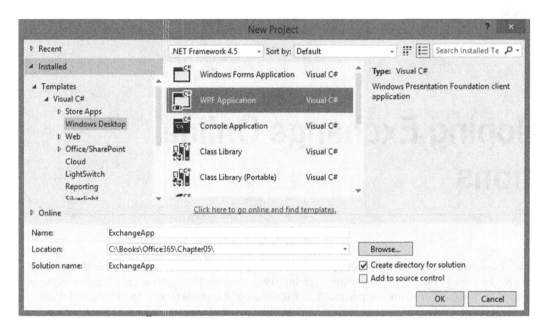

Figure 6-1. *Creating a Visual Studio project*

Click the OK button to create the project and solution. The MainWindow.xaml file will be opened and show a blank form.

Designing the Form

Select the XAML tab to see all of the code. Download the MainWindow.xaml file from www.apress.com and paste the XAML code from it into your local file. Switch to the Design tab, and the form should look like Figure 6-2.

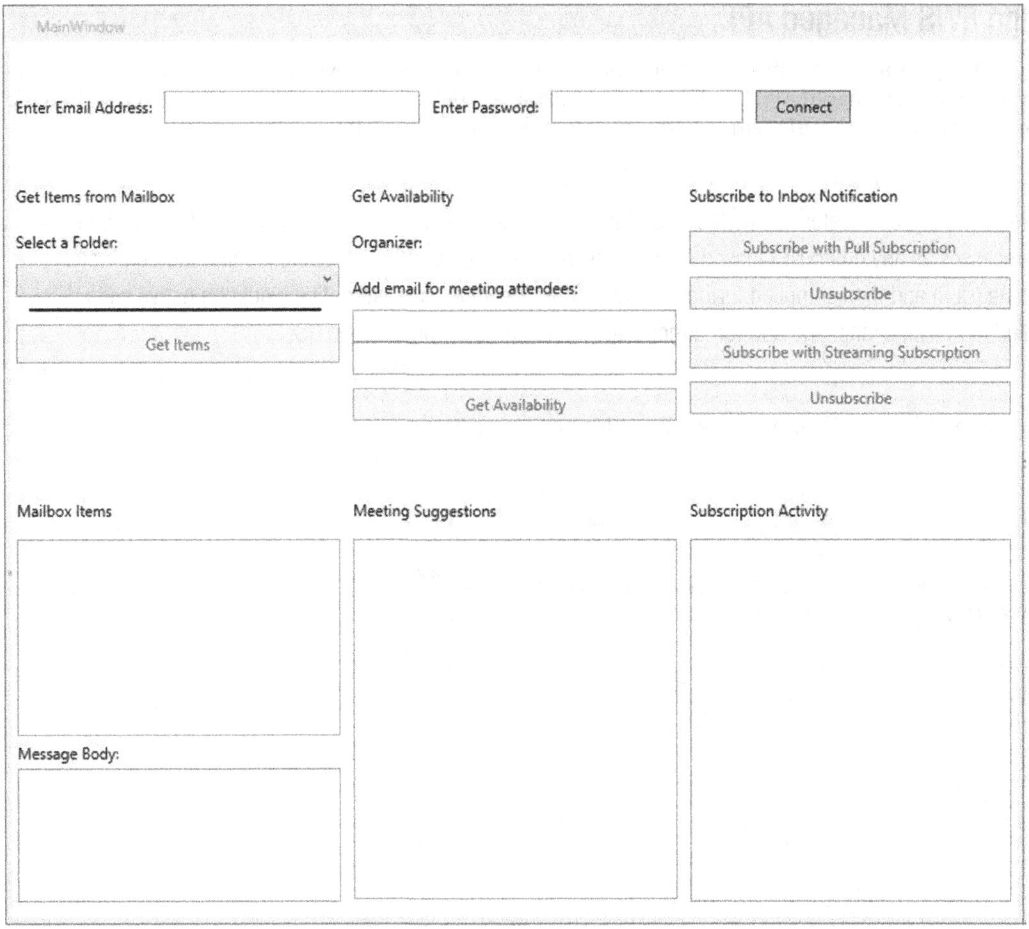

Figure 6-2. *The main window form design*

The form is divided into four areas that correspond to the four basic functions that you will implement in this chapter. The section across the top contains the controls you'll use to connect to the Exchange server. The other areas of the form consist of three columns that will be used to implement the remaining functions. From left to right the columns are for:

- Querying the mailbox contents

- Checking for availability

- Subscribing to inbox notifications

Preparing the Visual Studio Project

Before we explain the coding that is required, you'll first make some changes in the project's environment. You'll install the managed API and add the necessary reference in your project.

Installing the EWS Managed API

The features in Exchange Online are exposed to client applications through EWS. However, instead of calling the web service directly, you'll use a managed API. You'll need to install the API on your client machine. You can download the installation file (.msi) at www.microsoft.com/download/en/details.aspx?id=13480.

■ **Note**　The term managed API refers to the fact that the assemblies are written in .NET and run under the same management processes as any other .NET-based coding. This results in the code being compiled into the Common Language Runtime (CLR) and then compiled further upon the first execution. The alternative would be native code, which is compiled to machine language and run directly against the core services of the OS.

When you run this installation file, you'll see the dialog box shown in Figure 6-3.

Figure 6-3. Installing the EWS Managed API

You'll be presented with several more dialog boxes; you can use all the default values to complete the installation.

Adding a Reference

When it has finished, you'll need to add a reference to your project.

1. Right-click the ExchangeApp project in Solution Explorer and click the Add Reference link.

2. Select the Browse tab and browse to the C:\Program Files\Microsoft\Exchange\Web Services\2.2 folder shown in Figure 6-4.

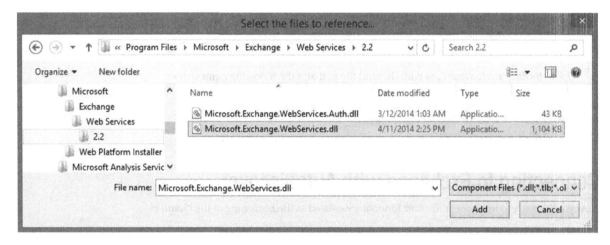

Figure 6-4. *Browsing for the Managed API*

3. Select the Microsoft.Exchange.WebServices.dll file, as shown in Figure 6-5. Click the OK button to create the reference.

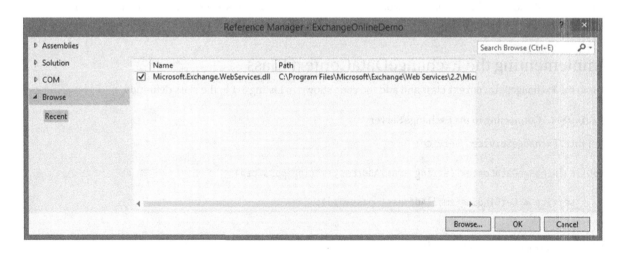

Figure 6-5. *Adding a reference to the EWS Managed API*

Creating the Data Class

To help organize the code, you'll create a separate class that contains the code used to communicate with Exchange via the managed API. The logic in the code-behind class, `MainWindow.xaml.cs`, provides the glue for moving the Exchange data to the form controls.

Right-click the ExchangeApp project in Solution Explorer and select the Add and then Class links. In the Add New Item dialog box, enter the class name **ExchangeDataContext.cs**. Then click the Add button to create the class. Add the following namespaces to this file:

```
using Microsoft.Exchange.WebServices.Data;
using Microsoft.Exchange.WebServices.Autodiscover;
using System.Windows;
```

Open the `MainWindow.xaml.cs` code-behind file and add the following namespaces:

```
using System.Web;
using Microsoft.Exchange.WebServices.Data;
using System.Windows.Threading;
```

Connecting to Exchange with Autodiscover

Now you're ready to implement the four functions we listed at the beginning of the chapter:

- Connecting to the Exchange Online server

- Accessing mailbox items

- Determining availability

- Subscribing to notifications

Before you can do anything else, you'll need to connect to the Exchange server. We'll start with that feature. You will first add the logic in the `ExchangeDataContext` class that calls the autodiscover process. Then you'll implement the click event in the code-behind class.

Implementing the ExchangeDataContext Class

Go to the `ExchangeDataContext` class and add the code shown in Listing 6-1 to the class definition.

Listing 6-1. Connecting to the Exchange Server

```
private ExchangeService _service;

public ExchangeDataContext(string emailAddress, string password)
{
    _service = GetBinding(emailAddress, password);
}

public ExchangeService GetService()
{
    return _service;
}
```

```
static ExchangeService GetBinding(string emailAddress, string password)
{
    // Create the binding.
    ExchangeService service =
        new ExchangeService(ExchangeVersion.Exchange2013_SP1);

    // Define credentials.
    service.Credentials = new WebCredentials(emailAddress, password);

    // Use the AutodiscoverUrl method to locate the service endpoint.
    try
    {
        service.AutodiscoverUrl(emailAddress, RedirectionUrlValidationCallback);
    }
    catch (AutodiscoverRemoteException ex)
    {
        MessageBox.Show("Autodiscover error: " + ex.Message);
    }
    catch (Exception ex)
    {
        MessageBox.Show("Error: " + ex.Message);
    }

    return service;
}

static bool RedirectionUrlValidationCallback(String redirectionUrl)
{
    // Perform validation.
    // Validation is developer dependent to ensure a safe redirect.
    return true;
}
```

This code is used to return an ExchangeService class. This defines a private _service member that is created by the class constructor. The GetService() method simply returns this private member.

The real work is done in the GetBinding() method. This method first creates an instance of the ExchangeService class. Notice that the constructor takes a version parameter. The managed API allows you to specify which version of Exchange you want to use. It then supplies the credentials, which consist of the e-mail address associated with the inbox and a password.

Finally, the AutodiscoverUrl() method is called. This is where the API does the work of finding the appropriate Exchange server and setting up the connection. This method takes a few seconds to complete. The code also handles exceptions. Finally, a callback is created to validate any redirects that may be configured for this inbox.

Modifying the Code-Behind Class

Add the following methods to the MainWindow.xaml.cs code-behind file:

```
private ExchangeDataContext _context;
private void btnConnect_Click(object sender, RoutedEventArgs e)
{
    _context = new ExchangeDataContext(txtEmailAddress.Text, txtPassword.Password);
    EnableButtons();
}

protected void EnableButtons()
{
    btnGetAvailability.IsEnabled = true;
    btnGetItems.IsEnabled = true;
    btnPullSubscribe.IsEnabled = true;
    btnStreamSubscribe.IsEnabled = true;
}
```

When the Connect button is clicked, this code will create an instance of the ExchangeDataContext class, passing in the credentials that were specified on the form. Now that the application is connected to the Exchange server, the EnableButtons() method enables the other buttons that you will implement shortly.

Accessing the Folder Contents

The next function that you will implement is displaying the contents of the selected folder.

Retrieving Items from Exchange

Add the methods shown in Listing 6-2 to the ExchangeDataContext class.

Listing 6-2. Reading the Mailbox Items

```
public List<Folder> GetFolders(FolderId parentFolderID)
{
    return _service.FindFolders(parentFolderID, null).ToList();
}

public List<Item> GetMailboxItems(WellKnownFolderName folder)
{
    return _service.FindItems(folder, new ItemView(30)).ToList();
}
```

```
public Item GetItem(ItemId itemId)
{
    List<ItemId> items = new List<ItemId>() { itemId };

    PropertySet properties = new PropertySet(BasePropertySet.IdOnly,
        EmailMessageSchema.Body, EmailMessageSchema.Sender,
        EmailMessageSchema.Subject);
    properties.RequestedBodyType = BodyType.Text;
    ServiceResponseCollection<GetItemResponse> response =
        _service.BindToItems(items, properties);

    return response[0].Item;
}
```

These methods retrieve the various Exchange objects from the service.

- GetFolders() returns all child folders for the given parent.

- GetMailboxItems() returns all items within the given folder.

- GetItem() returns an item for the given ItemId. This method uses the BindToItems() method to populate only the properties specified in the PropertySet type parameter.

- The RequestedBodyType attribute is set to BodyType.Text since the application will display the information in a TextBox. HTML is returned by default.

Displaying the Mailbox Items

Add this code to the MainWindow class constructor, which will set up the event handler for the OnLoaded event:

```
this.Loaded += MainWindow_Loaded;
```

Then add the methods shown in Listing 6-3 to the MainWindow.xaml.cs code-behind class.

Listing 6-3. Displaying the Mailbox Contents

```
void MainWindow_Loaded(object sender, RoutedEventArgs e)
{
    BindWellKnownFolderList();
}

protected void BindWellKnownFolderList()
{
    //bind the known folders to the list box
    foreach(WellKnownFolderName folderName in
        Enum.GetValues(typeof(WellKnownFolderName)))
    {
        cboWellKnownFolders.Items.Add(folderName);
    }
}
```

```
private void btnGetItems_Click(object sender, RoutedEventArgs e)
{
    //check for given values
    if (string.IsNullOrWhiteSpace(txtEmailAddress.Text))
    {
        MessageBox.Show("You must enter an email address to proceed.");
        return;
    }

    if (cboWellKnownFolders.SelectedIndex < 0)
    {
        MessageBox.Show("You must select a folder to proceed");
        return;
    }

    //get items for the given folder and bind them to the list box
    lstItems.ItemsSource = _context.GetMailboxItems
        ((WellKnownFolderName)cboWellKnownFolders.SelectedItem);
}

private void lstItems_SelectionChanged(object sender, SelectionChangedEventArgs e)
{
    Item email = _context.GetItem(((Item)lstItems.SelectedItem).Id);

    txtMessageBody.Text = "From:" + ((EmailMessage)email).Sender
                              + Environment.NewLine;
    txtMessageBody.Text += Environment.NewLine;
    txtMessageBody.Text += email.Body;
}

private void btnGetAvailability_Click(object sender, RoutedEventArgs e)
{
}

private void btnPullSubscribe_Click(object sender, RoutedEventArgs e)
{
}

private void btnPullUnsubscribe_Click(object sender, RoutedEventArgs e)
{
}

private void btnStreamSubscribe_Click(object sender, RoutedEventArgs e)
{
}

private void btnStreamUnsubscribe_Click(object sender, RoutedEventArgs e)
{
}
```

A ComboBox is populated when the application is loaded through the BindWellKnownFolderList() method. This ComboBox displays the default folders for Exchange. This method simply iterates through the WellKnownFolders enum and adds each item.

When the GetItems button is clicked, the GetMailboxItems() method is called from the DataContext class, and the results are bound to the lstItems ListBox. When an item is selected from the ListBox, the GetItem() method is called, and the results are used to populate the TextBox to display the sender and the body.

■ **Note**   The last five methods provide an empty event handler for each of the remaining command buttons on the form. You will need these to prevent compiler errors. You will provide the implementation later.

Testing the Application

Now is a good time to pause and test the functions that you have already implemented. Press F5 to compile and launch the application. Enter the e-mail address for a mailbox that is hosted on Office 365 and the corresponding password, and then click the Connect button, as shown in Figure 6-6. It will take a few seconds for the autodiscover process to obtain the correct address.

Figure 6-6. *Connecting to Exchange Online*

When the application has connected, most of the command buttons will be enabled. Select a folder and click the Get Items button. The items in that folder should be shown in the Mailbox Items list. Select one of these items and the message box will be displayed below it. The form will look similar to Figure 6-7.

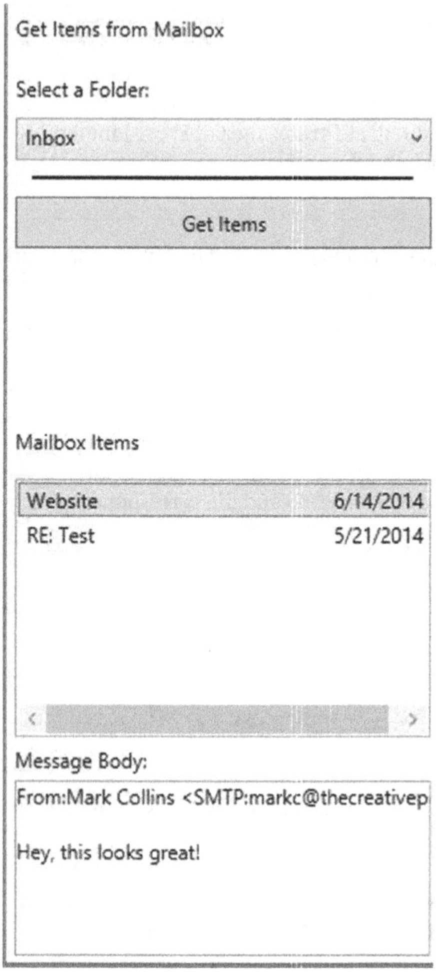

Figure 6-7. *Displaying the mailbox items*

Checking Availability

Exchange Online provides the ability to query the server for the availability of accounts based on their calendars. This provides the information necessary to schedule meetings when the desired participants are free. The meeting parameters, including the attendees, the time, and the duration of the meeting, are sent to the server. The service returns a list of possible meeting times with a quality setting based on the settings of the query.

■ **Note** Availability is only provided for users with accounts on the Exchange Online server. This service does not query calendars outside of the Exchange server.

Retrieving the Availability Results

Add the method shown in Listing 6-4 to the ExchangeDataContext class.

Listing 6-4. Querying Availability from Exchange

```
public GetUserAvailabilityResults GetAvailability
    (string organizer,
     List<string> requiredAttendees,
     int meetingDuration,
     int timeWindowDays)
{
    List<AttendeeInfo> attendees = new List<AttendeeInfo>();

    //add organizer
    attendees.Add(new AttendeeInfo()
    {
        SmtpAddress = organizer,
        AttendeeType = MeetingAttendeeType.Organizer
    });

    //add required attendees
    foreach(string attendee in requiredAttendees)
    {
        attendees.Add(new AttendeeInfo()
        {
            SmtpAddress = attendee,
            AttendeeType = MeetingAttendeeType.Required
        });
    }

    //setup options
    AvailabilityOptions options = new AvailabilityOptions()
    {
        MeetingDuration = meetingDuration,
        MaximumNonWorkHoursSuggestionsPerDay = 4,
        MinimumSuggestionQuality = SuggestionQuality.Good,
        RequestedFreeBusyView = FreeBusyViewType.FreeBusy
    };

    GetUserAvailabilityResults results = _service.GetUserAvailability
        (attendees,
         new TimeWindow(DateTime.Now, DateTime.Now.AddDays(timeWindowDays)),
         AvailabilityData.FreeBusyAndSuggestions,
         options);

    return results;
}
```

This code provides the method for getting the availability suggestions for the given e-mail addresses. The attendees are added using the `AttendeeInfo` object. The account used to connect to the Exchange service is used as the organizer. The e-mail addresses added in the form are added as required attendees. The `AttendeeOptions` object is used to set the options for the search against the service, setting the following properties:

- `MeetingDuration`: How long the open window needs to be

- `MaximumNonWorkingHoursSuggestionsPerDay`: Whether the search should include suggestions during non-working hours

- `MinimumSuggestionQuality`: Only returns items of this value and above

- `RequestedFreeBusyView`: What type of data is returned

The attendees' options are passed into the `GetUserAvailabilityResults()` service call along with the `AvailabilityData` setting. This property indicates whether to include suggestions in the result data.

Displaying the Results

Add the following code to the `btnConnect_Click()` method. This simply defaults the meeting organizer to the same inbox that you connected to.

```
lblOrganizer.Text += " " + txtEmailAddress.Text;
```

Replace the blank implementation of the `btnGetAvailability_Click` method with the code shown in Listing 6-5.

Listing 6-5. Implementing the Get Availability Button

```
private void btnGetAvailability_Click(object sender, RoutedEventArgs e)
{
    List<string> attendees = new List<string>();
    if (!string.IsNullOrWhiteSpace(txtAttendee1.Text))
    {
        attendees.Add(txtAttendee1.Text);
    }

    if (!string.IsNullOrWhiteSpace(txtAttendee2.Text))
    {
        attendees.Add(txtAttendee2.Text);
    }

    if (attendees.Count == 0)
    {
        MessageBox.Show("You must add at least one attendee to proceed.");
        return;
    }

    GetUserAvailabilityResults results =
        _context.GetAvailability(txtEmailAddress.Text, attendees, 30, 2);
```

```
    foreach (Suggestion suggestion in results.Suggestions)
    {
        foreach (TimeSuggestion time in suggestion.TimeSuggestions)
        {
            lstSuggestions.Items.Add(time);
        }
    }
}
```

When the Get Availability button is clicked, the attendees are added and passed into the GetUserAvailabilityResults() method in the DataContext. The returned suggestions are added to the lstSuggestions ListBox for display.

Testing the Availability Feature

Let's test the availability feature:

1. Press F5 to compile and start the application.

2. Enter an e-mail address and password, and click the Connect button as you did before. Once the buttons are enabled, the meeting organizer will be set using the e-mail address that was used to log in.

3. Specify another user or two and click the Get Availability button. The available time slots will be displayed in the suggestions list, as shown in Figure 6-8.

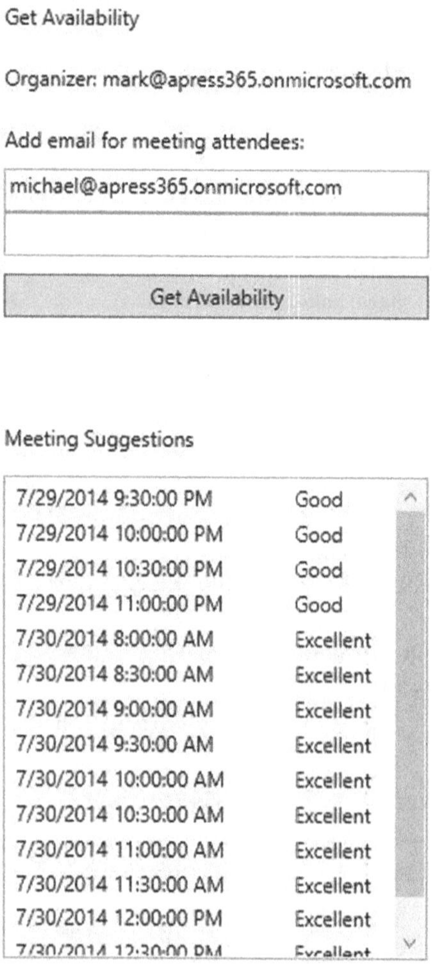

Get Availability

Organizer: mark@apress365.onmicrosoft.com

Add email for meeting attendees:

michael@apress365.onmicrosoft.com

Get Availability

Meeting Suggestions

7/29/2014 9:30:00 PM	Good
7/29/2014 10:00:00 PM	Good
7/29/2014 10:30:00 PM	Good
7/29/2014 11:00:00 PM	Good
7/30/2014 8:00:00 AM	Excellent
7/30/2014 8:30:00 AM	Excellent
7/30/2014 9:00:00 AM	Excellent
7/30/2014 9:30:00 AM	Excellent
7/30/2014 10:00:00 AM	Excellent
7/30/2014 10:30:00 AM	Excellent
7/30/2014 11:00:00 AM	Excellent
7/30/2014 11:30:00 AM	Excellent
7/30/2014 12:00:00 PM	Excellent
7/30/2014 12:30:00 PM	Excellent

Figure 6-8. *Displaying the availability results*

Subscribing to Notifications

For the final function, you will set up a subscription to be notified when a new item is added to the inbox. There are three types of subscriptions:

- The first, called a pull notification, happens when the client makes periodic calls to check for updates since the last call. This works by subscribing to the notification service and then polling that service for changes. A watermark is set each time the service is polled. Any changes that occurred since the last watermark are returned. This can easily be done in application code, but it does require polling the service. Notifications are not sent back to the subscription object automatically. Either some type of user event must be used to trigger the application to check the service or some sort of timer must be used.

- The second is called streaming notification. With this type of notification, an event is raised automatically. This works by opening a constant connection with the Exchange service. Notifications occur automatically. An event handler is used to respond to any notifications that are received from the subscription. A streaming subscription can only be open for 30 minutes or less. Any application designed to be open longer than this must either restart a streaming subscription after 30 minutes or use another type of subscription.

- The third is called push notification. Push notification works by subscribing to a notification service, similarly to a pull notification, except that a listener service is set up to receive notification events. This typically involves a WCF service, or some other type of web service that can receive the online event. This requirement for a listening service means that our WPF application does not demonstrate push notification.

Setting Up Pull Notification

Replace the blank implementations of the btnPullSubscribe_Click and btnPullUnsubscribe_Click methods with the code shown in Listing 6-6.

Listing 6-6. Implementing Pull Notification

```
private PullSubscription _pullSubscription;
private StreamingSubscription _streamSubscription;
DispatcherTimer _timer;

private void btnPullSubscribe_Click(object sender, RoutedEventArgs e)
{
    ExchangeService service = _context.GetService();

    _pullSubscription = service.SubscribeToPullNotifications
        (new FolderId[] {WellKnownFolderName.Inbox}, 10, null, EventType.NewMail);
    txtSubscriptionActivity.Text
        += "Pull Subscription Created" + Environment.NewLine;

    //set up polling
    _timer = new DispatcherTimer();
    _timer.Interval = TimeSpan.FromSeconds(10);
    _timer.Tick += timer_Tick;
    _timer.Start();

    btnPullSubscribe.IsEnabled = false;
    btnPullUnsubscribe.IsEnabled = true;
}

void timer_Tick(object sender, EventArgs e)
{
    GetEventsResults results = _pullSubscription.GetEvents();

    txtSubscriptionActivity.Text
        += "Pull Subscription checked for new items" + Environment.NewLine;
```

```
        foreach (ItemEvent itemEvent in results.ItemEvents)
        {
            switch (itemEvent.EventType)
            {
                case EventType.NewMail:
                    txtSubscriptionActivity.Text
                        += "Pull Subscription: New email received"
                        + Environment.NewLine;
                    break;
            }
        }
    }
}

private void btnPullUnsubscribe_Click(object sender, RoutedEventArgs e)
{
    _timer.Stop();

    _pullSubscription.Unsubscribe();

    txtSubscriptionActivity.Text
        += "Pull Subscription Unsubscribed" + Environment.NewLine;

    btnPullSubscribe.IsEnabled = true;
    btnPullUnsubscribe.IsEnabled = false;
}
```

When the Pull Subscribe button is clicked, a PullSubscription object is created. The WellKnownFolderName. Inbox enum is passed, along with a timeout of 10 (minutes) and the EventType.NewMail enum to send the subscription to be notified of any new items that are received in the inbox. The 10-minute timeout allows the subscription to expire if it is not polled within 10 minutes.

A DispatchTimer is set up to poll the PullSubscription object every 10 seconds. It uses the timer_Tick() method. This code calls the GetEvents() method, which checks for notifications and sets a new watermark. An event is recorded in the txtSubsctiptionActivity TextBox, and any notifications are processed. Each notification is recorded in the txtSubscriptionActivity TextBox as well.

The Pull Unsubscribe button stops the timer and calls the Unsubscribe() method, which ends the subscription. An event is recorded in the activity TextBox.

Using Streaming Notification

Replace the blank implementations of the btnStreamSubscribe_Click and btntreamUnsubscribe_Click methods with the code shown in Listing 6-7.

Listing 6-7. Implementing Streaming Notification

```
private void btnStreamSubscribe_Click(object sender, RoutedEventArgs e)
{
    ExchangeService service = _context.GetService();

    _streamSubscription = service.SubscribeToStreamingNotifications
        (new FolderId[] { WellKnownFolderName.Inbox }, EventType.NewMail);

    StreamingSubscriptionConnection connection =
        new StreamingSubscriptionConnection(service, 10);
```

```
        connection.AddSubscription(_streamSubscription);
        connection.OnNotificationEvent += connection_OnNotificationEvent;

        connection.Open();

        txtSubscriptionActivity.Text
            += "Stream Subscription Created" + Environment.NewLine;

        btnStreamSubscribe.IsEnabled = false;
        btnStreamUnsubscribe.IsEnabled = true;
}

void connection_OnNotificationEvent(object sender, NotificationEventArgs args)
{
    foreach(NotificationEvent notification in args.Events)
    {
        switch (notification.EventType)
        {
            case EventType.NewMail:
                Dispatcher.Invoke(new Action(
                    delegate()
                    {
                        txtSubscriptionActivity.Text
                            += "Stream Subscription: New email received"
                            + Environment.NewLine;
                    }));
                break;
        }
    }
}

private void btnStreamUnsubscribe_Click(object sender, RoutedEventArgs e)
{
    _streamSubscription.Unsubscribe();

    txtSubscriptionActivity.Text
        += "Stream Subscription Unsubscribed" + Environment.NewLine;

    btnStreamSubscribe.IsEnabled = true;
    btnStreamUnsubscribe.IsEnabled = false;
}
```

When the Stream Subscribe button is clicked, a streaming subscription is created using WellKnownFolderName.Inbox and EventType.NewMail parameter values to set up the service to notify the subscription object when a new item is received in the inbox. A StreamingSubscriptionConnection object is created and set to use the connection_OnNotificationEvent() method as its even handler. The connection is opened and the event is recorded in the activity TextBox.

Since this is a streaming subscription, it will receive notifications automatically from the service. It will then call the specified event handler. In this case, that is the connection_OnNotification() method. This method simply records the event into the activity TextBox. The Dispatcher.Invoke() method is used because the event handler is running on a different thread than the UI. To manipulate UI objects, the dispatcher must be used.

When the Stream Unsubscribe button is clicked, the Unsubscribe() method is called, which ends the subscription. The event is recorded in the activity TextBox.

Testing the Subscription Functions

Start the application and connect to the Exchange server as you have done before:

1. After it has connected, click the Subscribe with Pull Subscription button.

2. Then send an e-mail to this inbox (the one you just connected with).

3. After a few minutes you should see the "New e-mail received" text appear in the Subscription Activity list, as shown in Figure 6-9. Click the Unsubscribe button to stop the polling.

Subscribe to Inbox Notification

| Subscribe with Pull Subscription |
| Unsubscribe |

| Subscribe with Streaming Subscription |
| Unsubscribe |

Subscription Activity

Pull Subscription Created
Pull Subscription checked for new items
Pull Subscription checked for new items
Pull Subscription checked for new items
Pull Subscription checked for new items
Pull Subscription: New email received

Figure 6-9. *Testing the pull notification*

4.   Now click the `Subscribe with Streaming Subscription` button and send another e-mail to this inbox.

5.   You should see the "New e-mail received" text appear shortly after the e-mail arrives. The form will look like Figure 6-10. Click the `Unsubscribe` button to stop the polling.

Figure 6-10. *Testing the stream notification*

Summary

In this chapter, you created a WPF application that does the following, for the purposes of demonstrating the features offered by EWS:

- Uses the autodiscover service to dynamically connect to Exchange Online by determining which service is currently used to host the specified mailbox

- Queries a mailbox and returns all items within a specified folder

- Checks availability of accounts for a requested meeting, displaying suggested times returned by the service

- Subscribes to notification services to respond programmatically to events occurring within the Exchange service

This type of development allows features typically found in Outlook to be included in your custom applications. This type of functionality has been available for a long time, and could be used as long as Exchange server was hosted within your network. Now this powerful set of features is available to you through the cloud.

CHAPTER 7

■ ■ ■

Developing Lync Applications

The Lync features are provided to developers to make custom Lync applications or embed Lync features within an existing application. In this chapter I will show you how to build a custom Lync application. You'll start out with a simple application that includes a presence indicator in a WPF application. You'll then use more of the standard Lync controls to enhance the application by adding a contact search feature and a custom contact list. Finally, you'll use Lync automation to start a conversation and dock the conversation window in your custom application.

This was introduced in Chapter 1, but as a brief review, the Lync components that you'll use in this chapter are:

- Lync controls: You will add controls such as `PresenceIndicator` and `ContactSearch` to integrate Lync functionality directly into the WPF application.

- Lync automation: You will call Lync automation to control the running Lync client on the local machine and send conversation information.

These are shown in Figure 7-1.

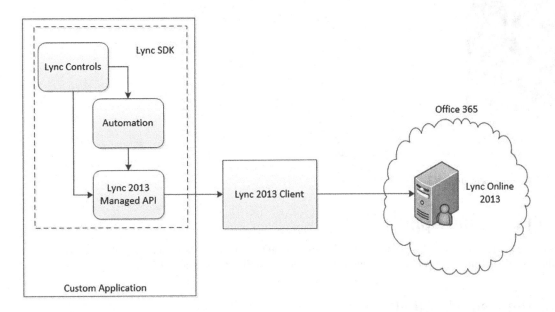

Figure 7-1. *Lync client architecture*

The Lync 2013 client application has a key role in the overall architecture. It manages the connection to the server component (Lync Online 2013). It also monitors client activity to report on presence such as Available or Idle.

■ **Caution**   Lync is the only Office 365 feature that requires a client installation. In order to use any of the Lync features, you must install the Lync 2013 client. A custom Lync application does not replace the need for the Lync client. Rather, the custom application will expect a running instance of the Lync client on the client machine.

If you have not already done so, you will need to download and install the Lync 2013 SDK. You can download this at www.microsoft.com/en-us/download/details.aspx?id=36824. This will download the LyncSdk.exe application. Run this applications and you'll see the installation screen shown in Figure 7-2. Follow the instructions using all of the default values to install the SDK on your machine. This will provide the necessary assemblies for Lync development.

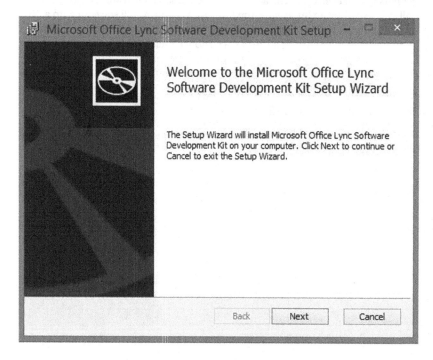

Figure 7-2. *Installing the Lync 2013 SDK*

Creating the Lync Application

You'll start by creating a standard WPF application and then add references to the assemblies included with the SDK. This will allow you to include the Lync controls, such as the presence indicator, in your application.

Creating the Visual Studio Project

Start Visual Studio 2013 and create a new project. Select the WPF Application project template, which you'll find in the Windows Desktop folder. Enter the project name **LyncApp** as shown in Figure 7-3 and click the OK button to create the project.

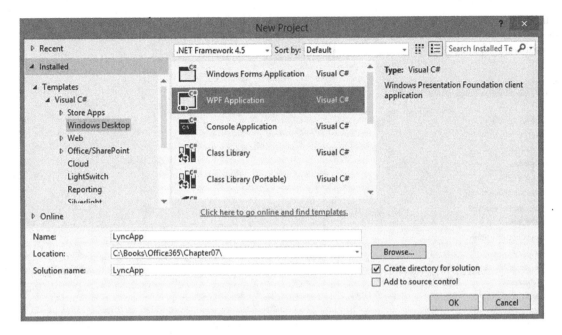

Figure 7-3. *Creating a WPF application project*

This project template creates a standard WPF application; now you'll need to add the Lync controls. In the Solution Explorer, right-click the `References` folder and select the `Add  Reference` link. Click the `Browse` button and navigate to the location where the Lync SDK was installed. This is normally `C:\Program Files (x86)\Microsoft Office 2013\LyncSDK`. Then go to the `Assemblies\Desktop` subfolder. Add the following DLLs as shown in Figure 7-4:

- `Microsoft.Lync.Controls`

- `Microsoft.Lync.Controls.Framework`

- `Microsoft.Lync.Model`

- `Microsoft.Lync.Utilities`

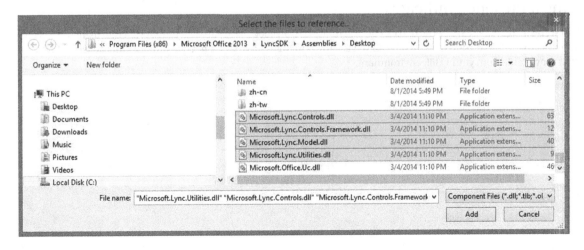

Figure 7-4. *Adding the Lync control assemblies*

By including these SDK assemblies, you can include any of the Lync controls in your application. We will demonstrate several of these controls in this chapter. If you expand the Toolbox, you can see the controls that are available, as shown in Figure 7-5.

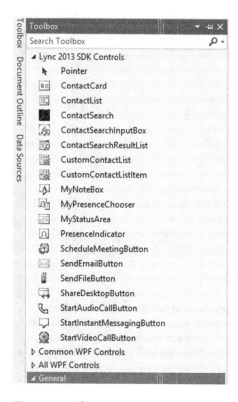

Figure 7-5. *The Lync 2013 SDK Controls available in the Toolbox*

Adding a Presence Indicator

You'll start by using the PresenceIndicator control. In the MainWindow.xaml file, edit the XAML code using the code shown in Listing 7-1. The code that must be added is shown in bold. Also, you'll need to enter a different sip address, one that is available from your O365 environment.

Listing 7-1. The Initial XAML Implementation

```xml
<Window x:Class="LyncApp.MainWindow"
        xmlns="http://schemas.microsoft.com/winfx/2006/xaml/presentation"
        xmlns:x="http://schemas.microsoft.com/winfx/2006/xaml"
        xmlns:controls
            ="clr-namespace:Microsoft.Lync.Controls;assembly=Microsoft.Lync.Controls"

        Title="MainWindow" Height="Auto" Width="Auto">
    <Grid>
        <StackPanel Orientation="Horizontal"
                    HorizontalAlignment="Center"
                    VerticalAlignment="Center">
            <controls:PresenceIndicator
                x:Name="Presence"
                Source="sip:mark@apress365.onmicrosoft.com"
                PhotoDisplayMode="Large"
                />
            <TextBlock
                Text="{Binding DisplayName, ElementName=Presence}"
                Margin="4,0,0,0"
                VerticalAlignment="Center"
                />
        </StackPanel>
    </Grid>
</Window>
```

The following line makes all of the Lync controls available to the application:

```xml
xmlns:controls
        ="clr-namespace:Microsoft.Lync.Controls;assembly=Microsoft.Lync.Controls"
```

And this line includes a presence indicator in the window:

```xml
<controls:PresenceIndicator
    x:Name="Presence"
    Source="mark@apress365.onmicrosoft.com "
    PhotoDisplayMode="Large"
    />
```

The TextBlock control is bound to the PresenceIndicator and will show the name of the person associated with the specified sip address.

Testing the Initial Application

This initial application does not require any implementation in the code-behind file, `Window1.xaml.cs`. Make sure the Lync client is installed and you are signed in to the Lync server.

Press F5 to build and run the application. The window will show the presence status of the specified address, as demonstrated in Figure 7-6.

Figure 7-6. *Running the initial application*

Hover over the presence indicator control to view the contact information and then click the expand button in the bottom-right corner. The expanded view may look similar to Figure 7-7, depending on how the user was set up in Office 365.

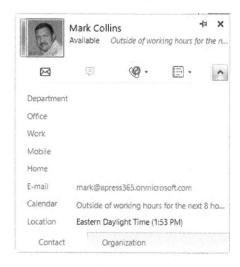

Figure 7-7. *Viewing the contact card*

While this application is still running, use the Lync client to change your status. Your WPF application should reflect the status change. Also try entering a note using the Lync client and then hover over the presence indicator in your custom application to see the new note, as shown in Figure 7-8.

Figure 7-8. *Displaying the status note*

Using Lync Controls

The Lync SDK provides several controls that you can drag and drop onto your application. This allows you to easily embed these Lync features into a custom application. You already used one of these, `PresenceIndicator`, in the initial implementation.

Dynamically Adjusting the Presence Indicator

Admittedly, displaying the presence of a hard-coded Lync address is not very useful. You'll extend the application to allow the user to select a contact from a drop-down list. The presence of the selected contact will then be displayed. The code-behind class will control the Lync address of the presence indicator based on the contact that was selected. You'll also provide an option to start a conversation with the selected contact.

Edit the `Window1.xaml` file and replace the entire contents with the code shown in Listing 7-2.

Listing 7-2. Revised XAML Implementation

```
<Window x:Class="LyncApp.Window1"
    xmlns="http://schemas.microsoft.com/winfx/2006/xaml/presentation"
    xmlns:x="http://schemas.microsoft.com/winfx/2006/xaml"
    xmlns:controls
        ="clr-namespace:Microsoft.Lync.Controls;assembly=Microsoft.Lync.Controls"
    Title="MainWindow" Height="Auto" Width="Auto">
    <Grid>
        <Grid.RowDefinitions>
            <RowDefinition Height="54" />
            <RowDefinition />
        </Grid.RowDefinitions>
        <StackPanel Orientation="Horizontal" Grid.Row="0">
            <TextBlock Margin="15" Text="View Presence of Selected Contact:" />
            <ComboBox x:Name="cboContacts" Width="200" Height="25" Margin="0,0,20,0"
                    SelectionChanged="cboContacts_SelectionChanged" />
            <!-- Presence Indicator -->
            <controls:PresenceIndicator PhotoDisplayMode="Large" x:Name="lyncPresence" />
            <!-- Start Instant Message -->
            <controls:StartInstantMessagingButton x:Name="lyncStartMessage" Height="25"
                                        Margin="20,10,10,10" />
        </StackPanel>
    </Grid>
</Window>
```

The Design tab should look like Figure 7-9.

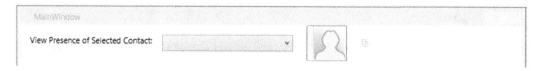

Figure 7-9. *The design of the revised window*

In addition to the PresenceIndicator control, the window now has a ComboBox that will contain the available contacts and a StartInstantMessagingButton control that will be used to start a conversation with the selected contact.

To populate the ComboBox, you'll need a class to represent the values of each contact. This simple class has two members, name and sipAddress. From the Solution Explorer, right-click the LyncApp project and select the New and then then Class links. Enter the class name **Contact.cs**. Then enter the following code for its implementation:

```
namespace LyncApp
{
    public class Contact
    {
        public string name { get; set; }
        public string sipAddress { get; set; }
    }
}
```

The initial application did not require any implementation in the code-behind class. However, now you'll need to provide code to update the presence indicator based on the selected contact. Enter the code shown in Listing 7-3.

Listing 7-3. Implementation of Window1.xaml.cs Code-Behind Class

```
using System;
using System.Collections.Generic;
using System.Linq;
using System.Text;
using System.Threading.Tasks;
using System.Windows;
using System.Windows.Controls;
using System.Windows.Data;
using System.Windows.Documents;
using System.Windows.Input;
using System.Windows.Media;
using System.Windows.Media.Imaging;
using System.Windows.Navigation;
using System.Windows.Shapes;

namespace LyncApp
{
    /// <summary>
    /// Interaction logic for MainWindow.xaml
    /// </summary>
```

```csharp
public partial class MainWindow : Window
{
    public MainWindow()
    {
        InitializeComponent();
        this.Loaded += MainWindow_Loaded;
    }

    void MainWindow_Loaded(object sender, RoutedEventArgs e)
    {
        BuildContactList();
        LoadContacts();
    }

    private List<Contact> _contacts = new List<Contact>();

    protected void BuildContactList()
    {
        // Build collection of valid contacts -- using Contact class
        _contacts.Add(new Contact()
        { name = "Mark Collins",
          sipAddress = "sip:mark@apress365.onmicrosoft.com" });
        _contacts.Add(new Contact()
        { name = "Michael Mayberry",
          sipAddress = "sip:michael@apress365.onmicrosoft.com" });
        _contacts.Add(new Contact()
        { name = "Sahil Malik",
          sipAddress = "sip:sahilmalik@winsmarts.com" });
    }

    protected void LoadContacts()
    {
        // Bind collection to combo box
        cboContacts.ItemsSource = _contacts;
        cboContacts.DisplayMemberPath = "name";
        cboContacts.SelectedValuePath = "sipAddress";
    }

    private void cboContacts_SelectionChanged
        (object sender, SelectionChangedEventArgs e)
    {
        // Set the sipAddress of the selected item as the
        // source for the presence indicator
        lyncPresence.Source = cboContacts.SelectedValue;

        // Set the start instant message button
        lyncStartMessage.Source = cboContacts.SelectedValue;
    }
}
```

This code creates a collection of `Contact` classes. The `BuildContactList()` method populates this collection using hard-coded values. You will need to change this implementation to use contacts that are reachable from your client. The `LoadContacts()` method binds this collection to the `ComboBox`.

The `cboContacts_SelectionChanged()` event handler is where the real work is done. This simply sets the `Source` property on both of the Lync controls. This will specify the Lync address used for determining the presence of the selected contact and the participant when starting a conversation.

Press F5 to build and run the application. Select a contact and their status will be displayed by the presence indicator, as shown in Figure 7-10.

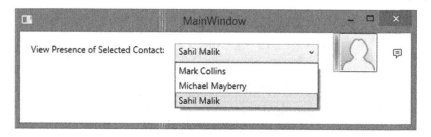

Figure 7-10. *Displaying the status of the selected contact*

Click the button next to the presence indicator and a new conversation window will appear. A sample conversation is shown in Figure 7-11.

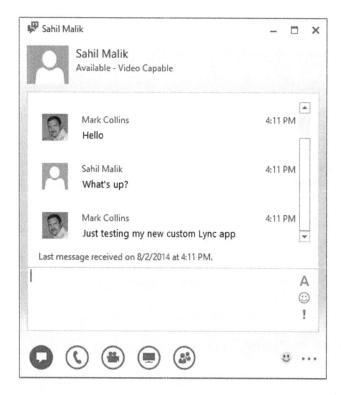

Figure 7-11. *A conversation window launched by the custom application*

Searching for Contacts

The Lync controls include a couple that are useful for searching for a contact:

- ContactSearch: Searches for contacts
- ContactList: Displays the standard Lync client contact lists

This functionality is identical to what you'll find on the standard Lync 2013 client. To include these controls in your application, add the following code to the Windows1.xaml file, just after the current StackPanel control:

```
<!-- Contact controls -->
<StackPanel Orientation="Horizontal" Grid.Row="1">
    <controls:ContactSearch Width="300" />
    <controls:ContactList Width="300" />
</StackPanel>
```

■ **Tip** The ContactSearch control is actually a combination of two controls. The ContactSearchInputBox control is used to receive the search criteria and the ContactSearchResultList control displays the contacts that were found. You can enter these as separate controls, which will allow you to configure where each is placed in the application. You would need to bind the two controls together so the results will be automatically displayed when the input is changed. The code would be similar to:

```
<controls:ContactSearchInputBox x:Name="search"/>
<controls:ContactSearchResultList
        ItemsSource="{Binding Results, ElementName=search, Mode=OneWay}"
        ResultsState="{Binding SearchState, ElementName=search, Mode=OneWay}" />
```

There is no need to include any additional implementation to the code-behind class. Press F5 to build and run the application. In the search box, start typing a contact's name, and the matching contacts will be displayed, as shown in Figure 7-12.

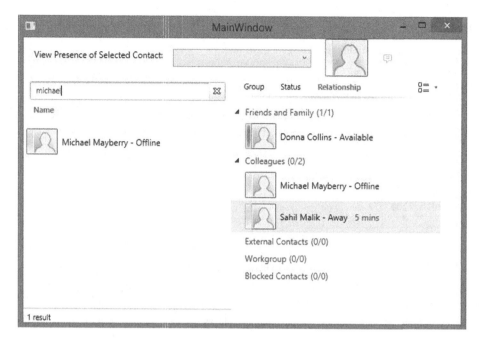

Figure 7-12. *Searching for a contact*

■ **Note**   The search feature looks for people in your contact list. It also searches for all other people in your organization. Generally this is limited to users defined in your Office 365 account. If you have configured federation, the search may be able to include these federated domains as well, depending on domain restrictions.

The second control you added displays your contact list, and this is identical to the way the Lync 2013 client displays these. There are several ways to organize the contacts. I chose to group by relationship, so friends and family are listed first, followed by colleagues. If you hover the mouse over a contact, the contact card is displayed. This provides links for starting a conversation.

Adding a Custom Contact List

In a custom application, you might need to control the contacts that are listed based on other application data and/or business rules. For example, you might want the user's immediate supervisor to be included, as well as other specific individuals for certain escalation rules. Whatever the reason may be, you'll want to provide a list of contacts that are application driven and not based on the user's contact list.

This is easy to do by using the CustomContactList control. You add this control to the application and then set its list of contacts in the code-behind class. In the Window1.xaml file, replace the ContactList control with the CustomContactList control, as shown here:

```
<StackPanel Orientation="Horizontal" Grid.Row="1">
    <controls:ContactSearch Width="300" />
    <!--<controls:ContactList Width="300" />-->
    <controls:CustomContactList x:Name="lyncCustomList" Width="300" />
</StackPanel>
```

In the code-behind class, `Window1.xaml.cs`, add the `LoadCustomContacts()` method using the following code:

```
protected void LoadCustomContacts()
{
    lyncCustomList.ItemsSource = (from C in _contacts select C.sipAddress);
}
```

This code simply loads the same contacts that you previously populated in the `ComboBox`. Then call the `LoadCustomContacts()` method in the `MainWindow_Loaded()` event handler, adding the line of code shown in bold.

```
void MainWindow_Loaded(object sender, RoutedEventArgs e)
{
    BuildContactList();
    LoadContacts();
    LoadCustomContacts();
}
```

Press F5 to build and run the application. Your custom contact list should include the same people that were included in the `ComboBox`, as shown in Figure 7-13.

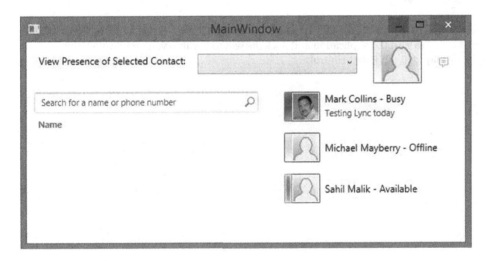

Figure 7-13. *Using the custom contact list*

Using Lync Automation

For the next exercise we'll show you how to use Lync automation to start a conversation and dock the window inside your custom application. This process requires interoperation between your custom WPF application and the Lync application.

Adding the Docking Host Location

Your application will need to include UI elements to interoperate with Lync. You will need to reference the classes in the XAML code needed for this and add a place for the Lync conversation to dock.

1. From the Solution Explorer, right-click the `Assemblies` folder and select the `Add Reference` link. Then select the `Assemblies` link and add `WindowsFormsIntegration`, `System.Windows.Forms` and `System.Drawing`. Then, in the `MainWindow.xaml` file, add the following namespaces:

    ```
    xmlns:interop="clr-namespace:System.Windows.Forms.Integration;assembly=
    WindowsFormsIntegration"
    xmlns:forms="clr-namespace:System.Windows.Forms;assembly=System.Windows.Forms"
    ```

2. Now you need to add the UI elements to accept the conversation window during docking. Add an additional row to the main grid by adding the following to the `Grid.RowDefinitions` section:

    ```
    <RowDefinition />
    ```

3. Just before the closing `Grid` tag (after the `StackPanel` controls), add the following XAML code:

    ```
    <interop:WindowsFormsHost x:Name="formHost" Grid.Row="2">
        <forms:Panel x:Name="formPanel"></forms:Panel>
    </interop:WindowsFormsHost>
    ```

This adds the host and panel elements for the docking process. The window layout should look like Figure 7-14. When the automation code is called to start the application and dock the window within your application, the conversation window will be displayed in this `Panel` control.

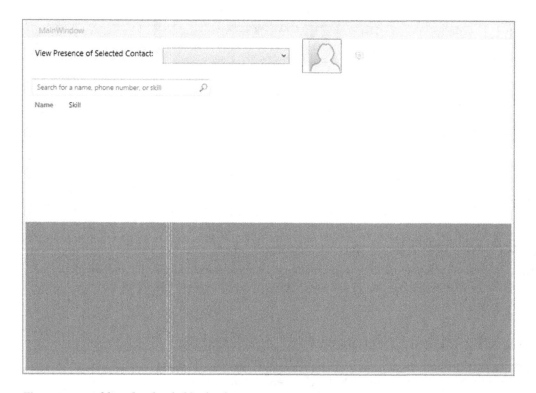

Figure 7-14. *Adding the placeholder for the conversation window*

Calling Lync Automation

Using Lync automation requires the application to respond to an event within the custom programming rather than the Lync controls. For this requirement, you will adjust the user interface to include a button to start the conversation.

1. In the MainWindow.xaml file and add the following code just after the StartInstantMessagingButton control. The Design tab should appear similar to Figure 7-15.

    ```
    <!-- Automation Button -->
    <Button x:Name="btnConversationStart" Content="Start Conversation" Margin="10"
    Click="btnConversationStart_Click" />
    ```

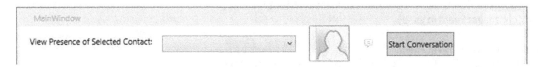

Figure 7-15. *Adding a custom button for Lync automation*

2. Now you'll implement the code-behind class. Open the MainWindow.xaml.cs file and add the following namespaces to the top of the file:

    ```
    using Microsoft.Lync.Model;
    using Microsoft.Lync.Model.Conversation;
    using Microsoft.Lync.Model.Extensibility;
    ```

3. Just inside the MainWindow class definition, add these private members, which will be used to manage the conversation window and the Lync objects that are needed.

    ```
    private LyncClient _client = null;
    private Automation _automation = null;
    private string _remoteUri = "";
    private ConversationWindow _conversationWindow = null;
    ```

4. Then add the following delegates, just after the private members. You'll need these later when managing the conversation window.

    ```
    private delegate void FocusWindow();
    private delegate void ResizeWindow(Size newSize);
    ```

5. The LyncClient and Automation objects should be initialized when the application starts. Add the following code to MainWindow constructor:

    ```
    _client = LyncClient.GetClient();
    _automation = LyncClient.GetAutomation();
    ```

6. Add all of the methods shown in Listing 7-4 to the end of the MainWindow class.

Listing 7-4. The automation event handlers

```
private void btnConversationStart_Click(object sender, RoutedEventArgs e)
{
    _remoteUri = cboContacts.SelectedValue.ToString();

    ConversationManager conversationManager = _client.ConversationManager;
    conversationManager.ConversationAdded
        += new EventHandler<ConversationManagerEventArgs>
            (conversationManager_ConversationAdded);
    Conversation conversation = conversationManager.AddConversation();
}

private void conversationManager_ConversationAdded(object sender,
    ConversationManagerEventArgs e)
{
    e.Conversation.ParticipantAdded
        += new EventHandler<ParticipantCollectionChangedEventArgs>
            (Conversation_ParticipantAdded);
    e.Conversation.AddParticipant
        (_client.ContactManager.GetContactByUri(_remoteUri));

    _conversationWindow = _automation.GetConversationWindow(e.Conversation);

    //wire up events
    _conversationWindow.NeedsSizeChange += _conversationWindow_NeedsSizeChange;
    _conversationWindow.NeedsAttention += _conversationWindow_NeedsAttention;

    //dock conversation window
    _conversationWindow.Dock(formHost.Handle);
}

void Conversation_ParticipantAdded(object sender,
    ParticipantCollectionChangedEventArgs e)
{
    // add event handlers for modalities of participants:
    if (e.Participant.IsSelf == false)
    {
        if (((Conversation)sender)
            .Modalities.ContainsKey(ModalityTypes.InstantMessage))
        {
            ((InstantMessageModality)e.Participant
                .Modalities[ModalityTypes.InstantMessage]).InstantMessageReceived
                += new EventHandler<MessageSentEventArgs>
                    (ConversationTest_InstantMessageReceived);

            ((InstantMessageModality)e.Participant
                .Modalities[ModalityTypes.InstantMessage]).IsTypingChanged
                += new EventHandler<IsTypingChangedEventArgs>
                    (ConversationTest_IsTypingChanged);
        }
```

```
        Conversation conversation = (Conversation)sender;

        InstantMessageModality imModality =
            (InstantMessageModality)conversation
            .Modalities[ModalityTypes.InstantMessage];

        IDictionary<InstantMessageContentType, string> textMessage =
            new Dictionary<InstantMessageContentType, string>();
        textMessage.Add(InstantMessageContentType.PlainText, "Hello, World!");

        if (imModality.CanInvoke(ModalityAction.SendInstantMessage))
        {
            IAsyncResult asyncResult = imModality.BeginSendMessage(
                textMessage,
                SendMessageCallback,
                 imModality);

        }
    }
}

private void SendMessageCallback(IAsyncResult ar)
{
    InstantMessageModality imModality = (InstantMessageModality)ar.AsyncState;

    try
    {
        imModality.EndSendMessage(ar);
    }
    catch (LyncClientException lce)
    {
        MessageBox.Show("Lync Client Exception on EndSendMessage " + lce.Message);
    }

}

private void ConversationTest_IsTypingChanged(object sender,
    IsTypingChangedEventArgs e)
{

}

private void ConversationTest_InstantMessageReceived(object sender,
    MessageSentEventArgs e)
{

}
```

```
private void _conversationWindow_NeedsAttention(object sender,
    ConversationWindowNeedsAttentionEventArgs e)
{
    FocusWindow focusWindow = new FocusWindow(GetWindowFocus);
    Dispatcher.Invoke(focusWindow, new object[] { });
}

private void _conversationWindow_NeedsSizeChange(object sender,
    ConversationWindowNeedsSizeChangeEventArgs e)
{
    Size windowSize = new Size();
    windowSize.Height = e.RecommendedWindowHeight;
    windowSize.Width = e.RecommendedWindowWidth;
    ResizeWindow resize = new ResizeWindow(SetWindowSize);
    Dispatcher.Invoke(resize, new object[] { windowSize });
}

private void SetWindowSize(Size newSize)
{
    formPanel.Size = new System.Drawing.Size(
    (int)newSize.Width, (int)newSize.Height);
}

private void GetWindowFocus()
{
    Focus();
}
```

When the Start Conversation button is clicked, the btnConversationStart_Click event handler is called. This gets the address of the selected contact and stores it in the _remoteUri class member. It then gets the ConversationManager from the Lync client and wires up an event handler for when a conversation is added. It then proceeds to add a conversation.

This invokes the conversationManager_ConversationAdded event handler. This then wires up an event handler for when a participant is added and adds a participant, using the address of the selected contact. In then gets the ConversationWindow using the Automation object associated to the Lync client. It then wires up the event handlers for the NeedsSizeChange and NeedsAttention events. Finally, it docks the window in the placeholder defined in the XAML file. This is what actually embeds the conversation window inside your custom application window.

The Conversation_ParticipantAdded event handler is then invoked. It is actually called twice because there are two participants, you, the sender or initiator, and the selected contact. This function checks the IsSelf property and effectively ignores this event if raised on behalf on the initiator. For the other participant, it sends a hard-coded message, "Hello, World!"

■ **Note** The modality defines the type of message that is being sent. In addition to instant messages (text), Lync supports audio and video messaging as well as application and screen sharing. A message can have more than one modality.

The `Conversation_ParticipantAdded` event handler wires up event handlers for the `InstantMessageReceived` and `IsTypingChanged` events. These event handlers allow your application to react to when these event occur. An `InstantMessageModality` object is obtained from the conversation. This is used to send the message asynchronously by calling its `BeginSendMessage` method. The `SendMessageCallback` method is then called when the message has been sent. It calls the `EndSendMessage` methods on the `InstantMessageModality` object.

The rest of the event handlers simply respond to events that are raised as messages are send back and forth. The `InstantMessageReceived` and `IsTypingChanged` event handlers have no implementation. This solution relies on the conversation window implemented by the Lync client. However, you could implement these events and display the received message in your own application controls.

Testing the Application

Press F5 to build and run the application. Select the desired contact from the drop-down list and click the `Start Conversation` button. The Lync client will begin the conversation and present the window within your custom application, as shown in Figure 7-16.

Figure 7-16. *Using Lync automation to dock a conversation window in a WPF application*

Summary

This chapter showed how to incorporate the functionality of the Lync client into a custom WPF application.

- You used the controls provided by the Lync SDK to easily provide communication functionality without much coding.

- You created a custom contact list, demonstrating how you can organize and present available contacts based on your own internal personnel data.

- You used Lync automation to provide access to the Lync communication window, presented within your custom application UI space.

Adding real-time communication functionality can greatly extend the usability of your custom applications. The techniques covered in this chapter provide you the ability to deliver a great experience to your users.

■ ■ ■

CHAPTER 8

Consuming Data with Office 365 APIs

Office 365 has provided a great set of products and services for the consumer from the beginning. By offering Office in the Cloud, business users have access to the best productivity tools available without the hassle of the infrastructure required to provide those tools.

However, the developer's experience might not have been as great. The data only exists in the Cloud, so any applications or websites that need to use that data also have to access it from the Cloud. It has been doable, but not easy.

This chapter introduces the Office 365 APIs. The following chapters will dive deeper to explain the details of how these services work, and any requirements developers need to know about. These chapters will include applications built in Visual Studio to demonstrate the ease of development and the power of the services.

Introducing Office 365 APIs

Microsoft improves the ability for the developer to build applications and websites using Office 365 data by providing REST APIs and a standard means of authentication. Web applications, native applications in Windows 8, iOS, and Android apps, along with virtually any device can consume Office 365 data over the wire.

■ **Note**   Microsoft declares the current release a Preview. As such, it is subject to change and evolution over time. The current release is only the beginning. The support is limited, yet powerful. In the future, limitations will be removed. Microsoft is dedicated to providing the ability to consume Office 365 data in web-enabled applications.

Before this release, developers had to rely on very different client libraries. Consuming data from SharePoint was a much different experience than consuming data from Exchange. Using client libraries inherently reduces the type of applications that could be developed.

Rather than separate libraries, Microsoft now provides unified REST APIs for the various types of data hosted in the cloud. This includes files, mail, and calendar data. To aid in accessing the cloud data, Microsoft has introduced a new Discovery Service. The current release offers a new File OData API for SharePoint 2013, an Exchange OData API, and expanded CSOM APIs along with the new Discovery Service.

More Unified Data Consumption

Now that data can be consumed using REST APIs, there is a more uniform process to development. The process to connect and consume data from the various sources has become a very similar process across the different options. Using web-based services tends to be similar regardless of the source. This places the process of using Office 365 data into more familiar territory for most developers.

Expanded Application Development

The new services also expand the options on what type of applications can consume Office 365 data. Nearly all types of applications have a means to call REST services. From native Windows 8 apps, to website, to iOS and Android apps, Office 365 is available over the wire. Authentication and authorization is handled using OAuth. Everything is done over the web, so any web-enabled application running on a web-enabled device can access Office 365 data.
Figure 8-1 demonstrates how a user could access Office 365 data from any device through the web using the Office 365 APIs. Developers can now make this a reality with much greater ease. This is a very powerful addition.

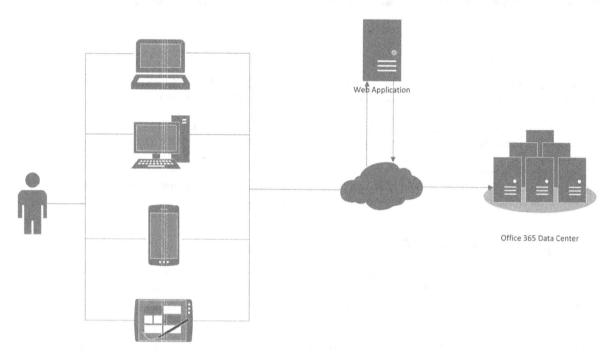

Figure 8-1. *Accessing Office 365 data over the wire through various devices*

A New Foundation

Office 365 is built on the foundation of Microsoft Azure Active Directory (AD). Developers may be familiar with Active Directory, the service running in Windows Server that manages identity within the network and other on-premise resources. In terms of identity and access management, Azure AD provides a similar role, only for the cloud. This service allows organizations to manage their cloud-based identities against their cloud-based applications.

Microsoft Azure AD can function on its own. Organizations that do not run full networks on-premise, or who desire to manage their cloud-based resources separately from their local ones, can use Azure AD as a separate service. For those organizations expanding their on-premise resources to the cloud, Azure AD can integrate with the existing Active Directory. However Azure AD is configured to work, it provides all users a single sign-on experience for applications that are integrated.

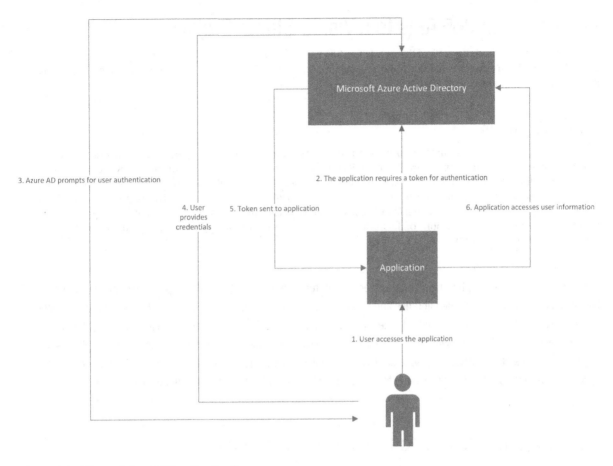

Figure 8-2. *Microsoft Azure AD authentication*

■ **Note** Microsoft Azure AD offers much more than is covered here. For more information on Microsoft Azure AD, visit http://azure.microsoft.com/en-us/documentation/services/active-directory/.

New Discovery Service

Consuming data through web services can greatly enhance application development and user experience. For the developer, accessing the hosted service is typically easy, as long as you can find where the service is hosted. Thinking about how Microsoft might host Office 365 data along with the services to access that data, might cause some concern for how particular applications will be able to find the necessary service endpoints to access the Office 365 data.

Microsoft introduced their new Discovery Service to allow organizations to determine the proper URL for the services that access their data. This service begins with a single URL for Office 365 services, and requires only the user's e-mail address to determine the proper endpoints. This allows the developer to begin at a common starting point and allows the application to determine the proper path for authorization and service endpoints to access the data desired for presentation and productivity. The Discovery Service will be discussed in detail in the next chapter.

Adding Office 365 APIs to a Visual Studio Project

Now that the overall fundamentals of the new Office 365 APIs have been presented, let's get started on actually accessing them in an application. Microsoft provides the Office 365 API Tools for Visual Studio 2013 to simplify the process of accessing the available services.

Client Libraries

The Office 365 API Tools for Visual Studio 2013 provide a set of client libraries to streamline the process of accessing the Office 365 services. The services are REST services, so the client libraries are not required. They are provided to enhance the development experience within Visual Studio. These libraries will speed up the process of developing against these services for applications built within Visual Studio 2013. These client libraries are portable .Net libraries, allowing developers to use them in their Windows and web applications along with iOS and Android applications through Xamarin. Javascript versions of the libraries are also included for the applications that target an HTML/JavaScript application.

▪ **Note** Earlier in the chapter, client libraries were presented as a negative to the development experience. In that case, the issue is that they are unrelated libraries and provided as the only means for accessing the hosted data. The Office 365 Tools for Visual Studio 2013 include libraries for a different purpose. These libraries are designed to speed up the development process. It is somewhat expected that most developers would build similar libraries around the REST services anyway, so Microsoft has provided these to solve the common problem. It is possible to bypass the client libraries and access the services directly. In development tools other than Visual Studio 2013, that is what would need to happen.

Installing the Office 365 API Tools for Visual Studio 2013

To setup Visual Studio 2013 to access Office 365 API, the Office 365 API Tools must be installed. This is an extension for Visual Studio, installed in a VSIX package. As of the writing of this book these tools are in Preview.

These tools extend Visual Studio 2013 to aid in development against the Office 365 APIs. They will work on any machine running Visual Studio 2013. They do not require SharePoint to be installed.

Take care where this is installed. As with any Visual Studio extension, these tools may be removed through the Extensions and Update dialog. This is found by clicking Tools, then Extensions and Update. Find the Officer 365 API Tools – Preview entry and click Uninstall.

Find the install package at http://aka.ms/Office365ApiToolsPreview.

1. Download the Office 365 API Tools - Preview. The download page should look similar to Figure 8-3.

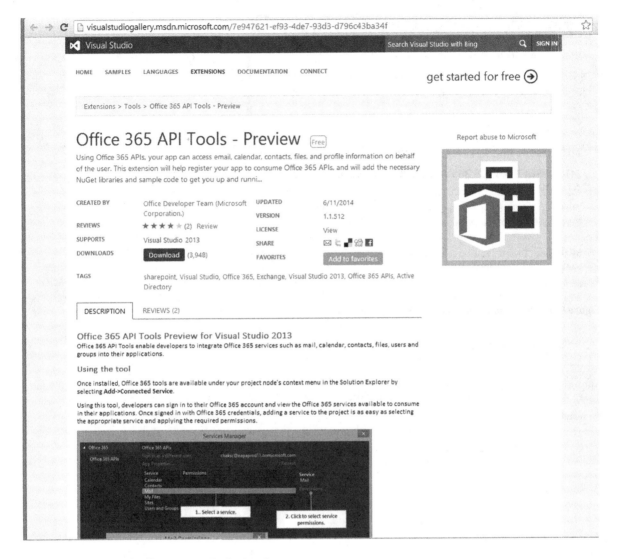

Figure 8-3. *Download Office 365 API Tools - Preview*

2. Download the .vsix file. The VSIX Installer dialog box, similar to Figure 8-4, will appear.

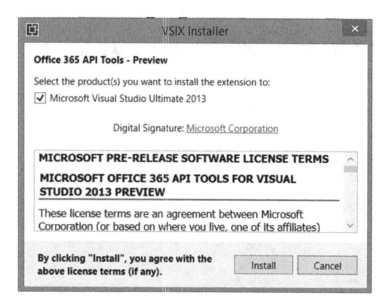

Figure 8-4. *VSIX Installer for Office 365 API Tools - Preview*

3.   Click the Install button

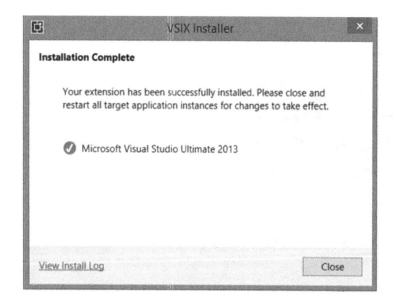

Figure 8-5. *VSIX Installation Complete*

■ **Note**   An Office 365 account is required to use the Office 365 APIs. If you do not have an account, visit
http://office.microsoft.com/en-us/tocreate one.

Now the Office 365 Tools for Visual Studio 2013 are installed on your machine and ready for development.

Adding Office 365 APIs to a Project

To enable any project to work with Office 365 APIs, they have to be configured using the Services Manager in Visual Studio. This includes signing into your Office 365 account. Once this is done, the proper assets will be added to your project along with sample code to demonstrate how to get started.

Choosing the Right Project Type

The Office 365 Tools for Visual Studio 2013 include client libraries. These are offered in .NET and JavaScript languages. Due to this, Office 365 APIs will only work with certain project types.

- ASP.NET MVC Web Applications
- ASP.NET Web Forms Applications
- .NET Windows Store Apps
- Windows Forms Applications
- WPF Applications
- Xamarin Android and iOS Applications
- Multi-device Hybrid Apps

While no one really likes to hear about limitations, this is not a small list. Developers can choose from a wide range of applications to build using these project types to offer functionality for their users.

Add Office APIs to the Project

For the example in this chapter, we will use an ASP.NET MVC Web Application. You can use any of the accepted projects types from the list above.

1. Create a new ASP.NET MVC Web Application in Visual Studio 2013

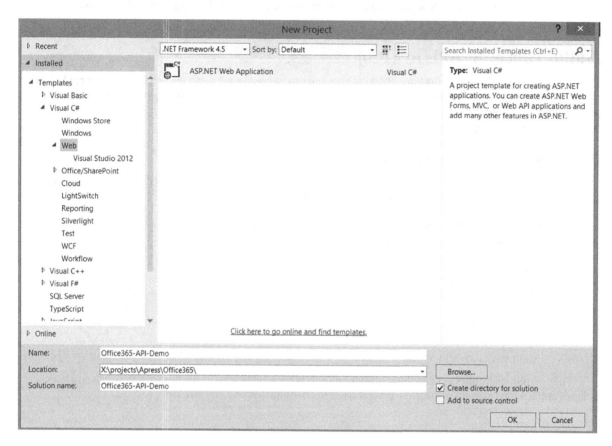

Figure 8-6. New ASP.NET MVC Web Application

2. Choose MVC options for the web application in the ASP.NET New Project dialog, as seen in Figure 8-7.

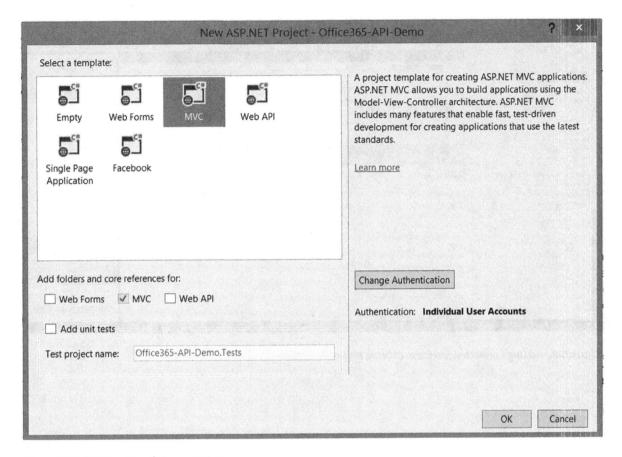

Figure 8-7. MVC options for new project

3. In the menu, click Project, then Add Connected Service. Figure 8-8 shows where this feature is found.

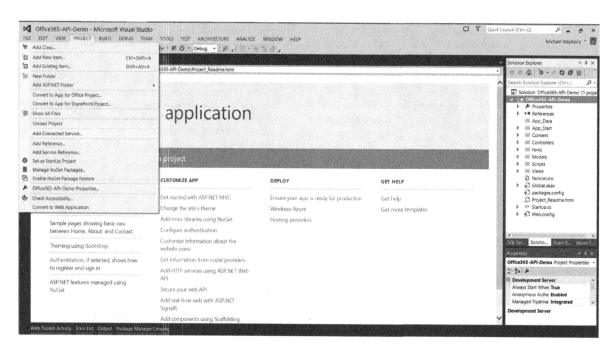

Figure 8-8. *Adding Connected Service to existing project*

4. Click the Sign In link in the Services Manager, under the Office 365 option. The screen
    should appear similar to Figure 8-9.

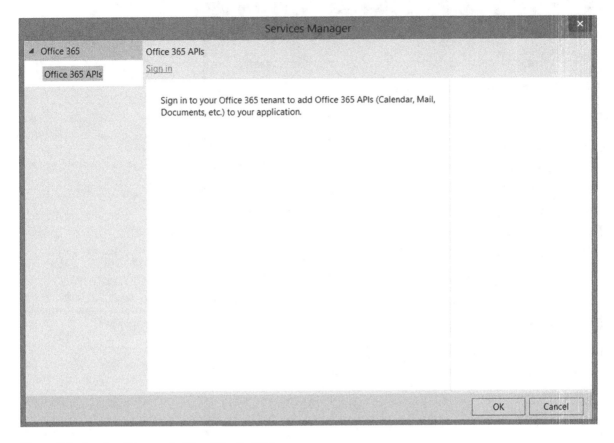

Figure 8-9. *Services Manager in Visual Studio 2013*

5. Sign into your Office 365 account. A dialog will appear similar to Figure 8-10.

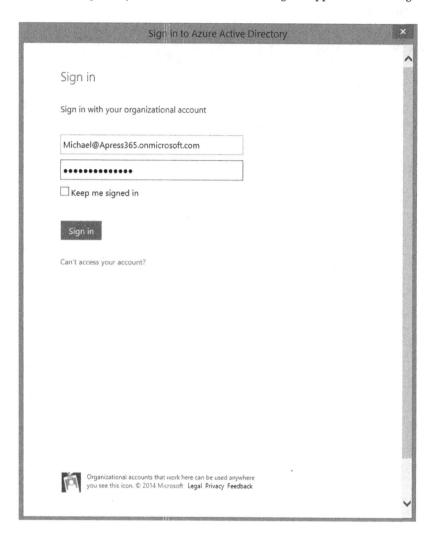

Figure 8-10. *Sign into Office 365*

6. Once connected to the Office 365 account, a list of available APIs will display, as shown in Figure 8-11.

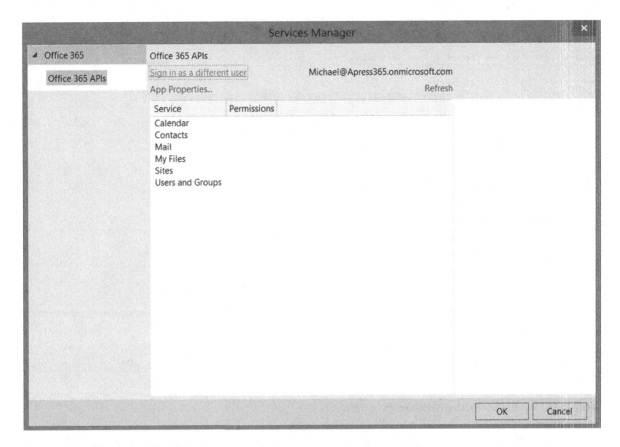

Figure 8-11. Available Office 365 APIs

7. Choose the API service for your project and click OK.

8. You may need to configure permissions for the service. If so, a dialog box, similar to Figure 8-12, will prompt you to make the appropriate choices.

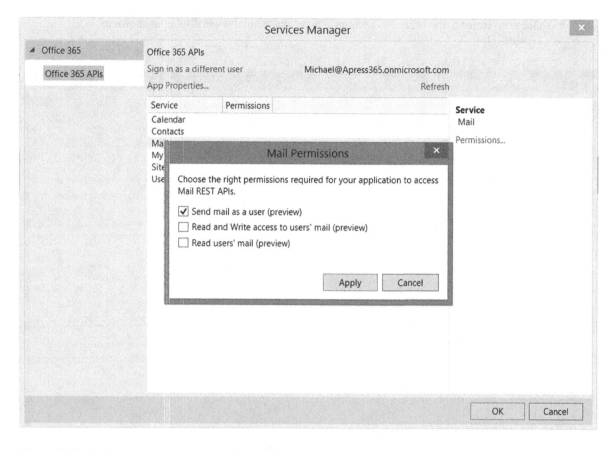

Figure 8-12. *Service Permissions requested from Office 365*

The proper libraries are added to the project, references are configured, and sample code is made available to help start development against the selected Office 365 API. The list of actions completed by the tools depends upon the type of project and service that were selected.

■ **Note** The Services Manager allows for permissions management throughout the development process. Simply revisit this area within Visual Studio to change or add permissions at any time.

Summary

The Office 365 APIs are a powerful addition to the services provided by Microsoft's productivity lineup. Office 365 opens a business or organization to the cloud and provides enhanced productivity without the infrastructure investment. The Office 365 APIs leverage the availability of that Office data and empowers developers to expand the productivity experience into custom websites and apps onto virtually any device.

The following chapters will demonstrate the ease and power of these APIs. You will see applications built in Visual Studio 2013 that consume data through the Office 365 APIs.

CHAPTER 9

■ ■ ■

Authentication, Authorization, and Discovery Service

Office 365 APIs allow for developers to write software that consumes business data from the Cloud. Microsoft hosts the data and provides the client software to access this data. However, Office 365 API allows for non-Microsoft developers to build the client software to access this business data. That can be wonderful, but is it safe (see Figure 9-1)?

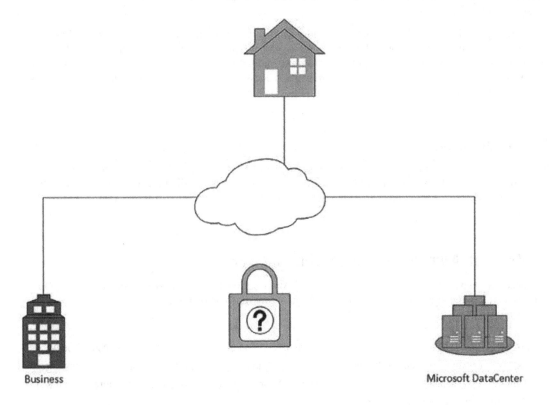

Figure 9-1. *Are Office 365 APIs safe?*

A business owner might be convinced that hosting their data on Microsoft servers on the internet is secure. When they use Outlook or Word or SharePoint, they are prompted for their Microsoft Account. They can trust that others cannot access their information.

Now, as a developer, we can provide custom applications and gain access through hand-crafted software using this Office 365 API "thing". Can business owners trust that their developer will protect their data properly? What about "hackers"? What stops them from building their own hand-crafted software to access this same data? Is this safe?

Business owners and developers alike can rest assured that Microsoft takes security very seriously. In fact, it is Microsoft that handles security for all Office 365 API traffic. Protection is not left to the individual developer. In fact, developers can also rest easy knowing they do not have to carry this burden.

This chapter will explain how Microsoft handles security issues through the Office 365 APIs. It will explain how to setup security within Azure Active Directory and utilize this configuration in Visual Studio. It will also connect these concepts to the new Discovery Service and demonstrate how that works as well.

Authentication and Authorization

Security for data breaks down into two concepts: authentication and authorization.

- **Authentication**: The process of confirming the identity of a user.

- **Authorization**: The process of confirming a particular user is allowed access to particular resources.

For a comparison, consider a security badge for a building with a photo. For proper security, there would need to be a process to assess whether the person holding the badge is indeed the person depicted on the badge. This would be the Authentication process. Once the person is authenticated, they would then swipe their badge against the security locks in various areas within the building. They may gain access to some areas and not gain access to others. This is the Authorization process.

Azure Active Directory

Microsoft handles authentication and authorization through the Azure Active Directory Service. Accounts are created and given roles. Apps are registered and given access to Office 365 assets. All of this is managed through the Azure Portal. Doing things this way does allow for a Single Sign-On experience. Microsoft uses OAuth for the authentication process.

Associate Microsoft Azure Subscription with Office 365

The Office 365 account needs to be associated with a Microsoft Azure subscription in order to manage security. Once these are connected, users and apps can be managed within the Azure Active Directory.

■ **Note**   A Microsoft Azure Trial subscription might be available, depending on the type of Office 365 account being used. If it's necessary to create a new Microsoft Azure subscription, try logging in with the Office 365 credentials to see if access is available. If this is available, the following process is not necessary. Otherwise, a separate subscription will need to be created and associated with the Office 365 account.

To associate your Office 365 account with your Azure subscription, complete the following steps:

1. Log in to the Microsoft Azure Management Portal (`http://manage.windowsazure.com`) with your existing Azure account.

2. Navigate to the Active Directory node.

3. Choose the Directory tab and click the Add at the bottom of the screen.

4. Select "Use existing directory" in the dialog box and check the box to sign out. Click the check mark in the bottom corner of the dialog.

5. Log in with your Office 365 credentials and continue through the screens that follow. Then choose, Sign out now. You will need to reaccess the Azure Portal with your Azure account, so you need to close your browser.

6. Open your browser again and reaccess the Azure Portal and login with your Azure account.

7. Navigate to the Active Directory node and you should see your Office 365 association under Directory.

Creating Users

The Single Sign-On process for Office 365 does not allow Microsoft Accounts for user authentication. For Office 365, organizational accounts must be created. These accounts are created directly within Azure Active Directory (see Figure 9-2) and managed within the Azure Portal.

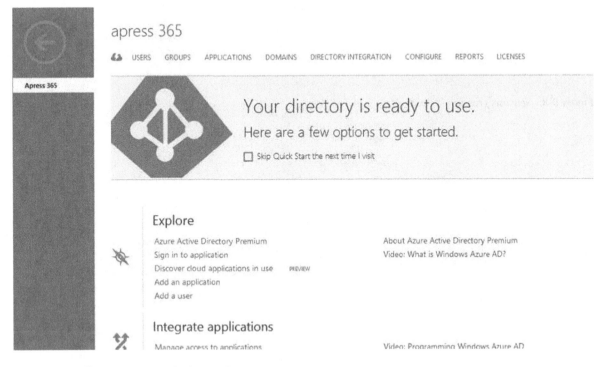

Figure 9-2. *Office 365 Directory in Azure AD*

1. Access your Azure Portal and navigate to the Active Directory node. Select your Office 365 Directory.

2. Click Add User and complete the dialog box that appears, as shown in Figure 9-3.

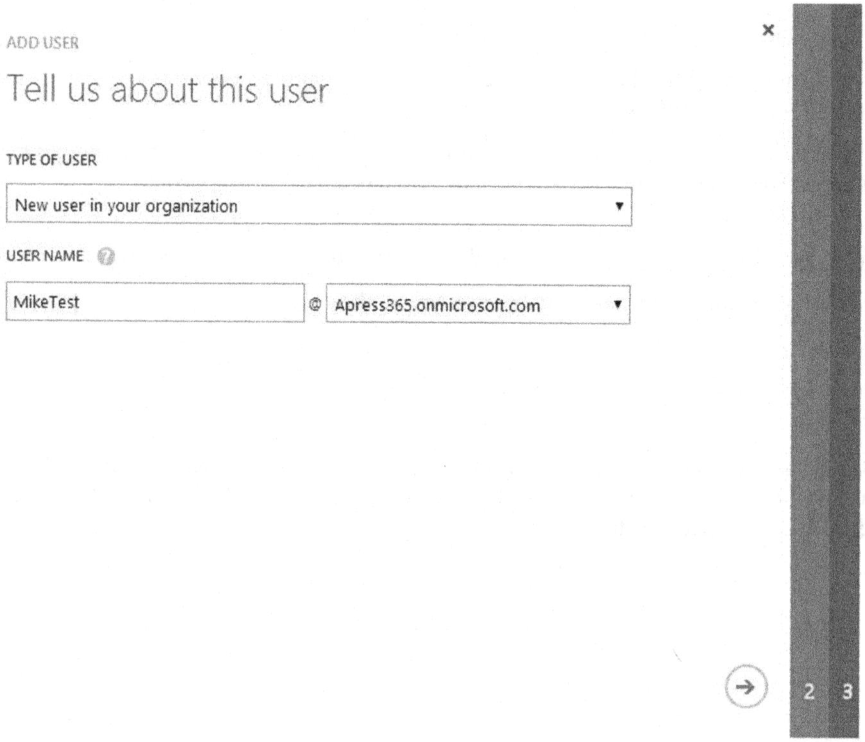

Figure 9-3. New user creation in Azure AD

3.   Enter the User Profile details (see Figure 9-4). This includes the first and last name, and a display name for the user. For this first account, choose the Global Administrator role. Also, enter an alternate e-mail address.

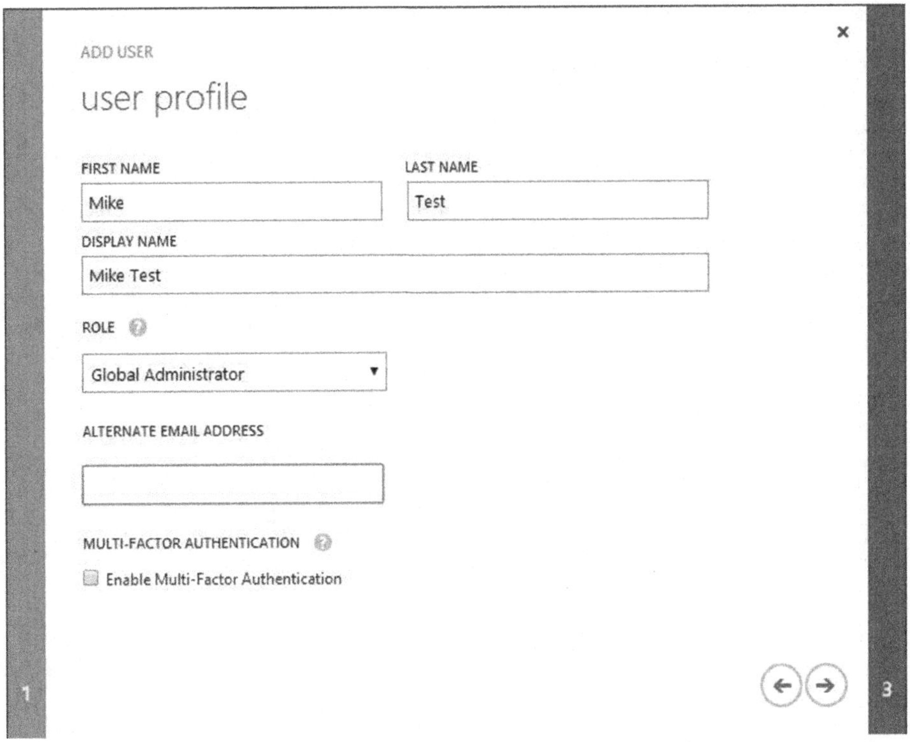

Figure 9-4. *User Profile details for Azure AD*

4.   Create a temporary password for initial account access. Click the large green button and a password will be generated (see Figure 9-5).

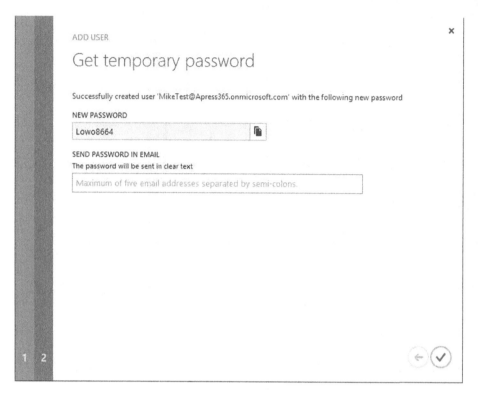

Figure 9-5. *Temporary password for new account*

5.   Enter e-mail addresses for notification of this new account.

6.   Click the check mark in the bottom corner of the screen. This will create the user.

Once the temporary password has been reset with a permanent one, this user can be used to access Office 365 assets. However, the user is not the only resource that requires management. It is important who accesses data, but it is also important how they access that data. The applications also have to be registered within Azure AD and managed.

Register App in Azure Portal

The Office 365 API Tools shown in the previous chapter will register the application when the service is connected to the project within Visual Studio. However, developers may also choose to manually register an application.

1.   In a browser, go to the Azure Management Portal (https://manage.windowsazure.com) and log in.

2.   Navigate to the Active Directory node and choose the Office 365 directory.

3.   Click the Applications tab at the top of the screen. Then choose the Add icon at the bottom of the screen. The dialog shown in Figure 9-6 should display.

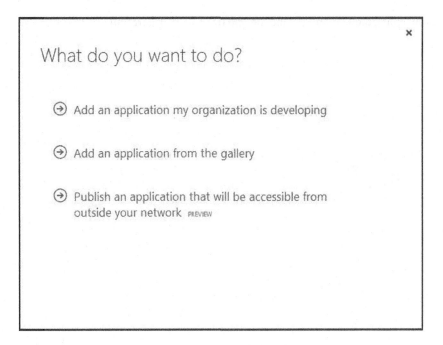

Figure 9-6. *Register new app in Azure AD*

4. Choose "Add an application my organization is developing" and enter the name of the application in the dialog (see Figure 9-7).

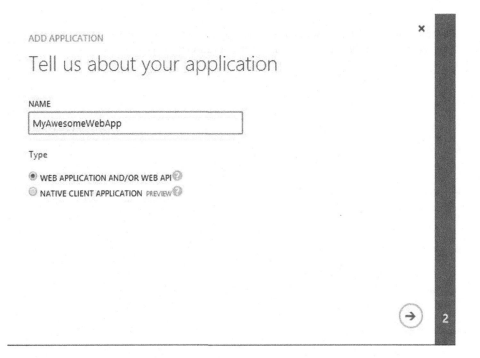

Figure 9-7. *Application name for new app in Azure AD*

5.   Add the App Properties, including the sign-on URL and the App ID URL (see Figure 9-8).

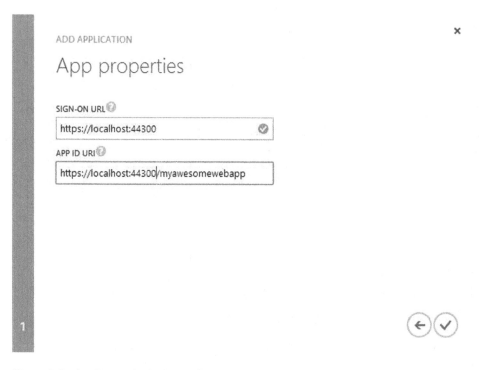

Figure 9-8. *App Properties in Azure AD*

6.   Click the Configure tab. Take note of the Client ID. For web applications, a key needs
     to be generated for access. Under the "keys" section, select a duration such as 1 Year
     (see Figure 9-9).

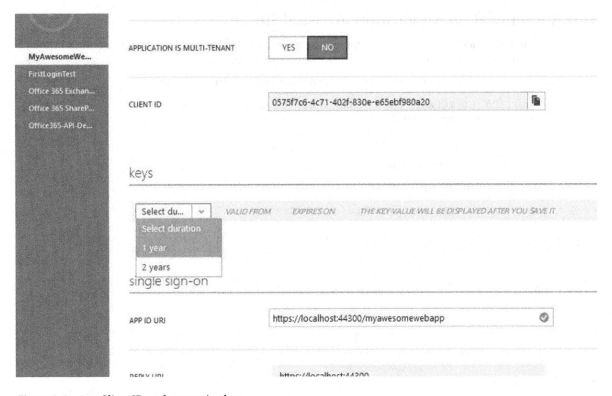

Figure 9-9. *App Client ID and generating keys*

7. Set the permissions for the app to access Office 365 APIs (see Figure 9-10).

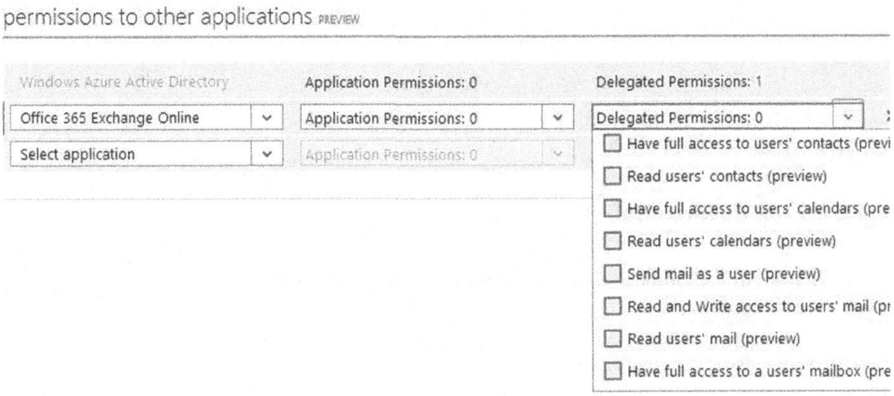

Figure 9-10. *Setting permissions for Office 365 APIs app registration*

Test Authentication Application in Visual Studio

Visual Studio and the Office 365 API Tools make things easy to get setup and handle authentication on their own. The developer simply has to enter the proper configuration to make things work.

1. Create a new Web Application in Visual Studio called TestAuthenticationApp.

2. Select MVC. Click Change Authentication to setup the project to use Office 365 authentication (see Figure 9-11).

    a. Select Organization Accounts

    b. Select Cloud - Single Organization

    c. Enter your Office 365 domain

    d. Set the Access Level to Single Sign On, Read directory data

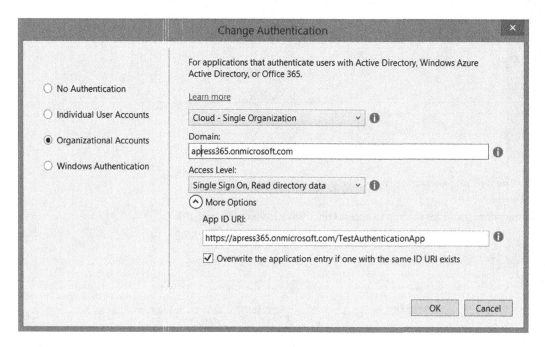

Figure 9-11. *Configure project to use Office 365 authentication*

3. Click OK. A prompt will appear for Office 365 credentials. Use the user account created earlier in this chapter (see Figure 9-12).

Sign in

Sign in with your organizational account

miketest@apress365.onmicrosoft.com

•••••••••••

☐ Keep me signed in

Sign in

Can't access your account?

Figure 9-12. Authenticate Office 365 setup for new project

4. The project should now be configured. The New Project dialog should appear similar to Figure 9-13. Note the Authentication setting. Click OK.

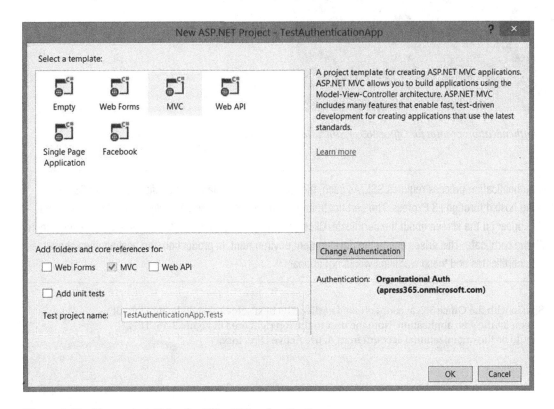

Figure 9-13. New project dialog for Office 365 authentication app

5. Multiple dialogs and progress screens may appear while the project is created and configured. Once Visual Studio stops processing, your application should be ready to authenticate through your Office 365 accounts. Run the web application. The first screen to appear should be a Microsoft login screen requesting an organizational account, as shown in Figure 9-14.

Figure 9-14. *Authentication prompt for Office 365 organizational account*

■ **Note**   The authentication process requires SSL. As such, the web application has been configured to use SSL, even if the site is being hosted through IIS Express. The certificate might not be fully trusted by the local machine, a warning message could appear on the screen about the certificate. Clicking continue anyway will allow the site to work and ignore the issues with the certificate. This arises due to the development environment. In production, the hosting sites should have proper SSL certificates and these warnings would not appear.

---

6. Sign in with the Office 365 account created earlier. The next screen should be the default screen for the web application. Note the user in the top right area in Figure 9-15. This should be the organizational account from Azure Active Directory.

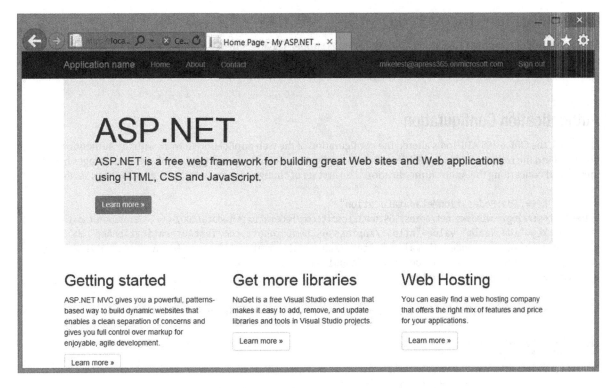

Figure 9-15. Web application screen with authenticated user

7. Click the logged-in user name and view the User Profile details of the current user. The screen should appear similar to Figure 9-16.

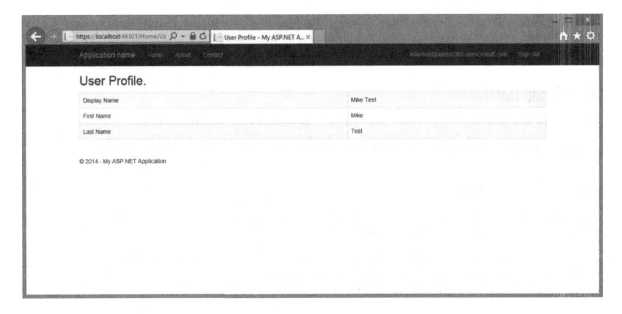

Figure 9-16. User Profile details after authentication

Authentication Uncovered

Setup and configuration for Office 365 authentication is simple. Developers like things simple so we can concentrate on the custom features of our apps. At the same time, it helps to know what is going on and how things work. Let's peel back the covers a bit and see what is going on here.

Authentication Configuration

First of all, the Office 365 API Tools altered the configuration of the web application to work with the authentication process. Find the web.config file in the Visual Studio application. Open it up and take a look. Several changes have been introduced concerning the Azure authentication. The first set of changes can be found in the appSettings section.

```
    <add key="ida:FederationMetadataLocation"
value="https://login.windows.net/apress365.onmicrosoft.com/FederationMetadata/2007-06/FederationMetadata.xml" />
    <add key="ida:Realm" value="https://apress365.onmicrosoft.com/TestAuthenticationApp" />
    <add key="ida:AudienceUri" value="https://apress365.onmicrosoft.com/TestAuthenticationApp" />
    <add key="ida:ClientID" value="eccfbefa-3613-4229-9d05-f134e05cb4f7" />
    <add key="ida:Password" value="" />
```

Another section added is the federationConfiguration section for the system.identityModel.services.

```
<system.identityModel.services>
    <federationConfiguration>
      <cookieHandler requireSsl="true" />
      <wsFederation passiveRedirectEnabled="true"
issuer="https://login.windows.net/apress365.onmicrosoft.com/wsfed"
realm="https://apress365.onmicrosoft.com/TestAuthenticationApp" requireHttps="true" />
    </federationConfiguration>
  </system.identityModel.services>
```

These configuration changes point the application to the proper URLs for login and supply the necessary information for accessing the Azure subscription and directory settings that enable the authentication flow to work properly.

User Profile Details

During the project setup, the Office 365 API Tools added a method to the Home controller called UserProfile. This method calls into Azure Active Directory and returns the user profile. This method demonstrates how to use the authenticated user to access resources in the cloud.

Home Controller Setup

Before looking at the UserProfile() method, take a look at the top of the HomeController.cs file within the project. A few constants and static properties have been added to the class.

```
private const string TenantIdClaimType = "http://schemas.microsoft.com/identity/claims/tenantid";
private const string LoginUrl = "https://login.windows.net/{0}";
private const string GraphUrl = "https://graph.windows.net";
```

```
private const string GraphUserUrl = "https://graph.windows.net/{0}/users/{1}?api-version=2013-04-05";
private static readonly string AppPrincipalId = ConfigurationManager.AppSettings["ida:ClientID"];
private static readonly string AppKey = ConfigurationManager.AppSettings["ida:Password"];
```

Note that most of these values are URLs to locations in the cloud where the application will need to access resources for authentication and information. A couple of the values, namely the AppPrincipalId and the AppKey, are pulled from the web.config file through the ConfigurationManager.

User Profile Method

Now take a look at the UserProfile() method.

```
[Authorize]
public async Task<ActionResult> UserProfile()
{
    string tenantId = ClaimsPrincipal.Current.FindFirst(TenantIdClaimType).Value;

    // Get a token for calling the Windows Azure Active Directory Graph
    AuthenticationContext authContext = new AuthenticationContext(String.Format(CultureInfo.
    InvariantCulture, LoginUrl, tenantId));
    ClientCredential credential = new ClientCredential(AppPrincipalId, AppKey);
    AuthenticationResult assertionCredential = authContext.AcquireToken(GraphUrl, credential);
    string authHeader = assertionCredential.CreateAuthorizationHeader();
    string requestUrl = String.Format(
        CultureInfo.InvariantCulture,
        GraphUserUrl,
        HttpUtility.UrlEncode(tenantId),
        HttpUtility.UrlEncode(User.Identity.Name));

    HttpClient client = new HttpClient();
    HttpRequestMessage request = new HttpRequestMessage(HttpMethod.Get, requestUrl);
    request.Headers.TryAddWithoutValidation("Authorization", authHeader);
    HttpResponseMessage response = await client.SendAsync(request);
    string responseString = await response.Content.ReadAsStringAsync();
    UserProfile profile = JsonConvert.DeserializeObject<UserProfile>(responseString);

    return View(profile);
}
```

This method accesses the Azure Active Directory and returns the User Profile details. This code is generated by the Office 365 API Tools. At this point, no code has been written. When first working with Office 365 APIs, it is helpful to look through this generated code to see what is being done and how information is passed between the application and the cloud in order to retrieve data from the web services.

The method is annotated with the [Authorize] attribute. This means that only authorized users will be allowed to run this method. If the user is not already authenticated, the application will send them through the authentication process. This is important because the method is written expecting an authenticated user.

The code then finds and sets the tenantId from the ClaimsPrincipal.Current set. This uses the constant TenantIdClaimType, set up during code generation. This claim exists as part of the data sent during the authentication process. The method simply searches through the set of claims sent during authentication to find the tenantId.

The `tenantId` is then used in the next few lines of code to call various pieces of data, including the `AuthenticationContext` and the `ClientCredential` that are needed to finally call the `authContext.AcquireToken(GraphUrl, credential)` method. This receives a token that is necessary for accessing protected resources using OAuth. This `AuthenticationResult` is then used to generate the authentication header for an HTTP request. Along with the header, the request URL is generated as well.

The `requestUrl` and the `authHeader` are used to send a request through HTTP and receive a JSON response. If successfully authenticated, the User Profile details will be returned as a JSON string. This string is deserialized into the UserProfile object and passed to the View for presentation.

It is important to remember this code is generated during the project setup process. This is not custom authentication code for any specific scenario. These changes are handled through the Office 365 API Tools. When the proper information is provided through the dialogs during setup, the application is automatically setup to handle authentication through Microsoft Azure AD. This is extremely convenient for the developer. Simplifying the process allows the application to remain the focus of the development process. Also, security handled by Microsoft provides a more consistent and secure experience for the end-user.

However, there are scenarios where the Office 365 API Tools cannot handle the configuration. For one, this is only available in Visual Studio. Other development tools do not have this available to them. iOS development and web-client app development requires programmers to handle the authentication configuration. Thankfully, Microsoft provides the Discovery service to help simplify these scenarios.

There are Azure SDKs for developers outside of Visual Studio. These are not specifically for Office 365, but they could help with authentication. These SDKs are not within the scope of this chapter. Many can be found at `http://azure.microsoft.com/en-us/downloads`.

Discovery Service

Microsoft's Discovery Service provides the single starting point for accessing online services, including Office 365 APIs. These are used for authentication, the primary hosting location for services as well as the specific service endpoints. Regardless of the need, it all starts at the Discover Service API Endpoint.

`https://api.office.com/discovery/me`

Overview

As with any application, the users must be created within Azure AD and the application must be registered. The proper permissions and access must be configured within the Azure Management Portal. Once that is complete, the application is ready to use the services.

Accessing these services will need to follow the proper flow. Office 365 resources are accessed using OAuth. The Discovery Service provides a consistent way to navigate through gaining the tokens needed for accessing resources.

1. First Sign-In

2. Authorization for Discovery

3. Discovery

4. Authorization for the Resource Service

5. Access the Service APIs

First Sign In

The application/user must begin the discovery process with an initial authorization. This allows the authentication process to complete and delivers the proper information to continue with discovery and authorization. Discovery begins with the FirstSignIn API.

GET /FirstSignIn

Parameters

scope: capability.operations tokens in space-delimited list;

redirect_uri: location to send user when authorization is complete

Response: The authentication process occurs within the browser. The user is taken to a sign-in page. Multiple calls are made between the browser and the services. After authorization is complete, the user is sent to the redirect_uri location. The following information is also sent to that URI.

```
user_email
account_type
authorization_service
token_service
scope
discovery_service
discovery_resource
```

The process can be as simple as sending the end-user to a URL similar to the following:

```
https://api.office.com/discovery/me/FirstSignIn?redirect_uri={appURI}&scope=MyFiles.Read
```

The screen will prompt for an e-mail address as seen in Figure 9-17.

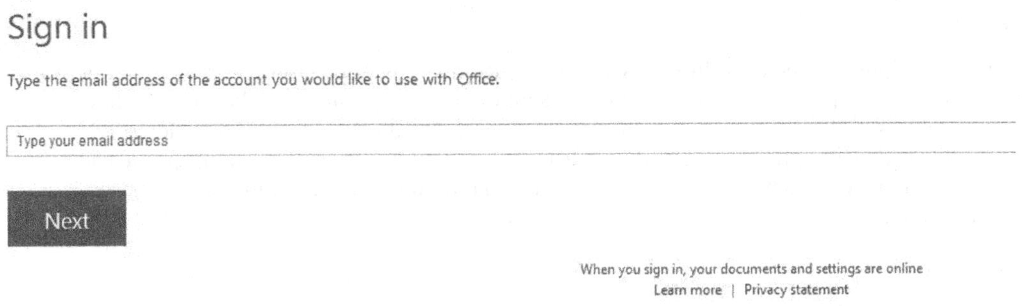

Figure 9-17. *Discovery service e-mail address prompt*

This prompt expects an Office 365 e-mail address. Once provided, the end-user is authenticated and sent to the redirect URL provided in the parameter. The response information is sent along to this location as well.

Authorization

The process for authorization will depend on whether the application needs access to more than one resource or not. For a single resource, the Authorization API can return an access token directly. The application would then use this token for authorization and access the necessary service. For the rest, the Token service and the Refresh Tokens are used for authorization.

Not every user has permission to every service. So, before Discovery can continue, authorization must occur.

GET /Authorization

Parameters

```
response_type: "code" or "token", depending on the desired response
client_id: unique client ID
client_secret: client's secret
scope: scope from the sign-in step
resource: the ID of the resource desired
redirect_uri: the location to send the user after authorization
```

Response

```
code OR token, depending on the request
```

Once /SignIn completes, the application then calls the /Authorization API and passes the discovery_resource, along with the other required application details, to gain either the access token or the authorization code. If the authorization code is requested, the application then needs to call the /Token API to request an access token. Otherwise, the application can call the /Services API using the access token returned from the /Authorization service.

Token

The remaining services all require an access token for authorization. The Token service provides these access tokens. The Token service also provides Refresh Tokens.

Refresh Tokens

Many, if not most, applications will need to gain access into more than one Office 365 resource. Custom development occurs often for that primary purpose: to consolidate Office 365 information into a single application. Authorization for this type of access follows a different path. Rather than requesting a token directly, the Authorization service returns an authorization code. The application uses this code to then call the Token service. This response will contain an access token along with a refresh token. The refresh token is used to gain access to subsequent service, after the initial authorization.

POST /Token

Headers

```
content-type: application/x-www-form-urlencoded
```

Parameters

```
grant_type: "authorization_code" is the only accepted value
client_id: the client ID used in the authorization API
client_secret: the client secret used in the authorization API
code: the authorization code returned from the authorization API
redirect_uri: the location to send the user after authorization
```

Response

```
access_token
refresh_token
```

The access token is used in the /Services API. If the application needs to access more than one service, the refresh token is passed into the /Token API to gain a new access token for additional services.

Services

Once authenticated, or signed in, the application is now ready to continue with the discovery process. The functionality of the application dictates which services or resources are needed. Discovery provides the location of those services. The Services APIs provides the service details.

■ **Note**   The /Services APIs follow the OData protocol. For more information on accessing OData resources, see http://www.odata.org/docs/.

GET /Services

Headers

```
authorization: access token obtained from the token service
accept: format of the response - application/json;odata=verbose
```

Parameters (standard OData operators)

```
$select: filters the properties that are returned
$filter: filters the services that are returned
```

Response

```
list of ServiceInfo items
```

ServiceInfo Fields

```
Capability
ServiceId
ServiceName
ServiceEndpointUri
ServiceResourceId
```

Calling the Services APIs will return the details matching the submitted criteria. The application now has the information it needs to access the needed resources. However, the application has only been authorized for Discovery, not for access to the given resource. The next step is to gain authorization for the desired service. The ServiceResourceId must be submitted into the /Authorization service to gain an access token. That token is then used to access the specified service.

Following this process, the application begins at the Discovery Service Endpoint. The application then follows the returned data through the process to gain access to the necessary services. The application does not store the specific URLs for the services it needs.

Summary

All applications attempting to gain access to Office 365 APIs must begin with Authorization and Authentication. Microsoft handles the security, but the application must guide the user through the process.

Microsoft provides the necessary services to authenticate users. They even make things simple by configuring and setting up application through the Visual Studio Office 365 API Tools. Specific development is often not necessary to get an application working with simple authentication.

Regarding service access, Microsoft also provides the Discovery Service help developers write applications against the Office 365 APIs without unnecessary concern with service locations and URIs. The Discovery Service provides the details for gaining access to the information and provides the necessary means for locating where these services are hosted.

The next chapter will dive into the details of the Office 365 APIs. A custom web application using ASP.NET MVC coded to access the Office 365 APIs will be the focus. As with any application, authentication, authorization, and discovery are necessary. However, the focus will be on the APIs themselves now that these other topics have been covered.

CHAPTER 10

■ ■ ■

Integrating Office 365 Technologies with REST APIs and MVC

Details are important. Background information is helpful. Visuals are nice. But as developers, we just want to learn by doing. In this chapter, we will build an ASP.NET MVC application that implements the Office 365 APIs.

The Plan

All good projects begin with a plan, or some problem to solve. For this project, we will create an application that simulates a Sales Lead Management system. The starting point will be Sales Lead e-mails, which would be generated from an external source. This could be directly from a website or from some internal system within a company. For our application, we will simply create them by hand and e-mail them to ourselves.

The application will present the e-mails to the user as a list of their sales leads. The user will be able to View their Leads, Assign Leads to another sales person, or Set an Appointment regarding the lead. As an addition to setting the appointment, the system will allow them to see the appointments already in their calendar.

Figure 10-1 illustrates the use cases for this system.

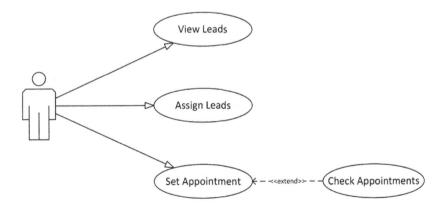

Figure 10-1. *Sales Lead System use case diagram*

The Setup

This application will simulate a sales lead system that integrates with other processes and workflows in an actual company. That being the case, this system depends on some external data. We will set up the data before building the application.

Products

If our system will process sales leads, we need something to sell. We will start by creating our own Subsite within Office 365 SharePoint. Then we will create a custom list of products.

1. First, create a new subsite from the Team Site in SharePoint Online. This is done by navigating to Site Contents from the Team Site, and clicking on New Subsite. The New Site form appears similar to Figure 10-2.

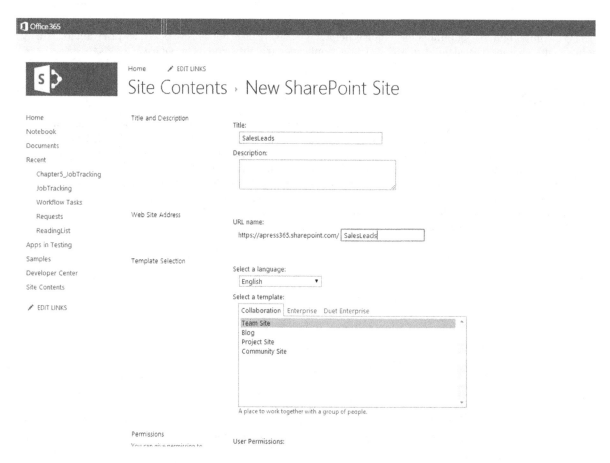

Figure 10-2. New SharePoint subsite form in Office 365

2. Use the form to create a new subsite. We will add the product list within this subsite.

■ **Note** For this code in this example, the Web Site Address is expected to end with SalesLeads. If you use something different, you will need to remember to adjust your code accordingly.

3. Navigate to the new subsite. Navigate to the Your Apps section and click on the Custom List. You should see a dialog similar to Figure 10-3.

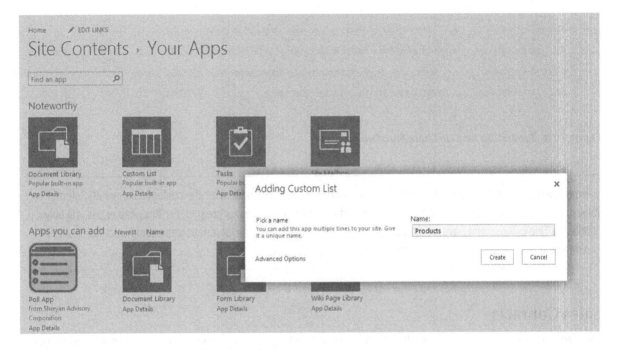

Figure 10-3. *Adding Custom List in SharePoint Online*

4. Add columns to the list.

5. Add items into the list. Your list should look similar to Figure 10-4.

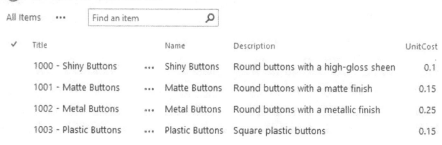

Home ✎ EDIT LINKS

Products

⊕ new item or edit this list

All Items ⋯ | Find an item 🔍

✓	Title		Name	Description	UnitCost
	1000 - Shiny Buttons	⋯	Shiny Buttons	Round buttons with a high-gloss sheen	0.1
	1001 - Matte Buttons	⋯	Matte Buttons	Round buttons with a matte finish	0.15
	1002 - Metal Buttons	⋯	Metal Buttons	Round buttons with a metallic finish	0.25
	1003 - Plastic Buttons	⋯	Plastic Buttons	Square plastic buttons	0.15

***Figure 10-4.** Product list items in SharePoint Online*

■ **Note** When accessing data from custom lists in SharePoint, the field names for the custom columns are internal values set by SharePoint. They are not the nice titles added when the column is created. For this chapter, we will only handle the Title column, and have structured the data accordingly. Other considerations and coding solutions would be implemented in an actual production environment.

Sales Contacts

The Use Case diagram includes the ability to assign a lead to another sales person. For this functionality, we will use Contacts as the sales personnel. To assign a lead, the application will forward the e-mail to the Contact. To control the full cycle, we will create users in Office 365, so that we have Exchange Mailboxes. Then we will create Contacts within Outlook.

1. Navigate to your Office 365 Portal at `https://portal.office.com`.

2. Navigate to the users & groups section within the portal.

3. Create a couple of users to use as Sales Contacts. The New User form is shown in Figure 10-5.

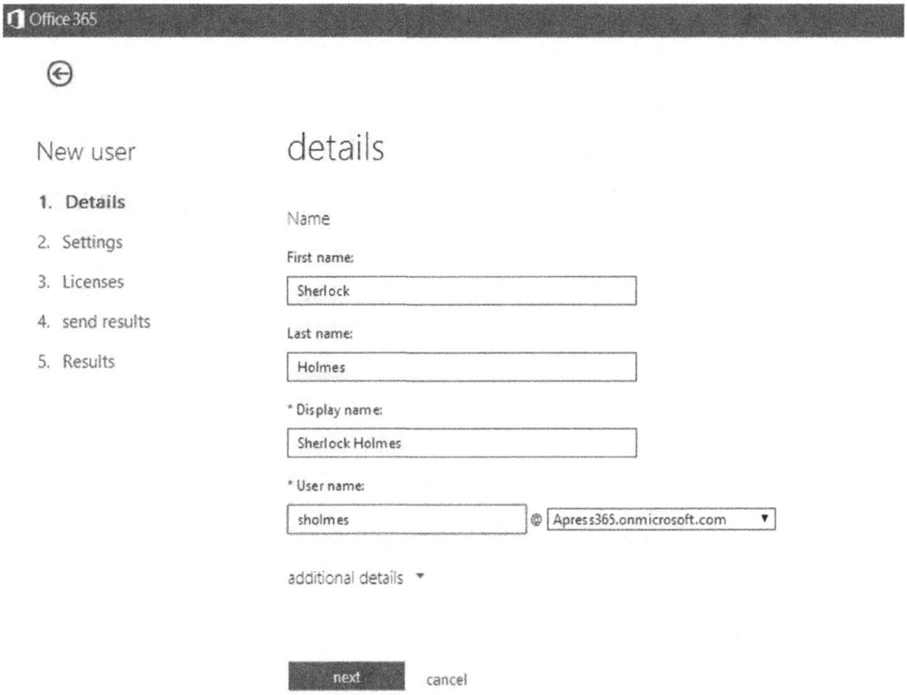

Figure 10-5. *New User details form in Office 365*

4. Navigate to Outlook Online.

■ **Note** Ensure the same account used to set up the Contacts and E-mails (later in the chapter) is the same account used during application testing.

---

5. Navigate to the People section of Office 365.

6. Create a new Contact for each user that was created in the previous steps. The new Contact form is shown in Figure 10-6. Make sure to enter the Office 365 e-mail addresses.

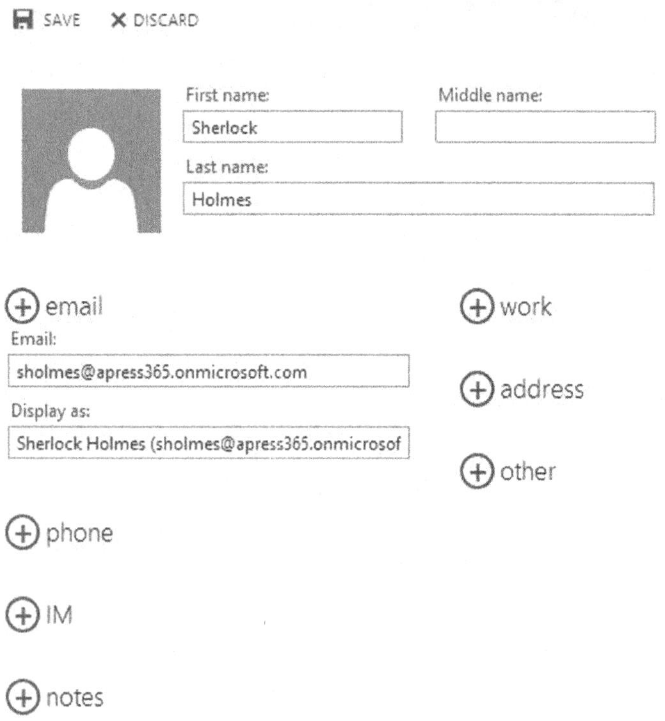

Figure 10-6. *New Contact form in Office 365*

Sales Leads

The application begins with the Sales Leads, which are specialized e-mails. To create the lead data, you will send these specialized e-mails to your Office 365 email. For this application, you can send these e-mails from any mailbox you choose.

The primary concern for this application is the Subject line. This application expects the subject line to include the SKU of the product for the potential customer. This information is expected to come in the format of "[SKU:####]". For the sales lead e-mails, make sure the subject includes that phrase with a SKU from the Products list. The rest of the e-mail is displayed, but is not expected in any specific format. Figure 10-7 displays a possible example.

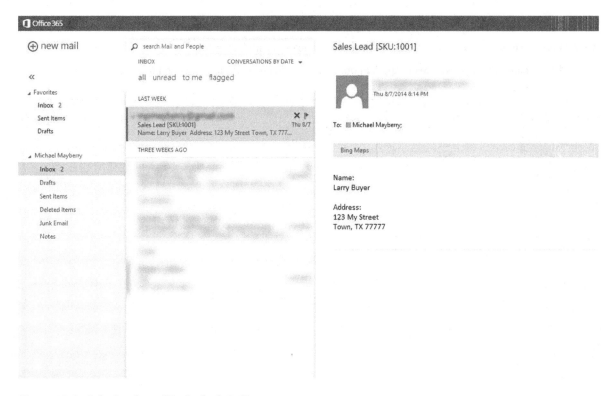

Figure 10-7. *Sales Lead email in Outlook Online*

The Sales Lead MVC Application

Now we will create the Sales Lead application using ASP.NET MVC. This application requires the Visual Studio Office 365 API Tools. Ensure this extension is installed. Installation of these tools is covered in Chapter 8.

Create a New ASP.NET MVC Application

We will begin by creating the new project and setup authentication with Office 365.

1. Create a new ASP.NET MVC Application named SalesLeadMVC, as shown in Figure 10-8.

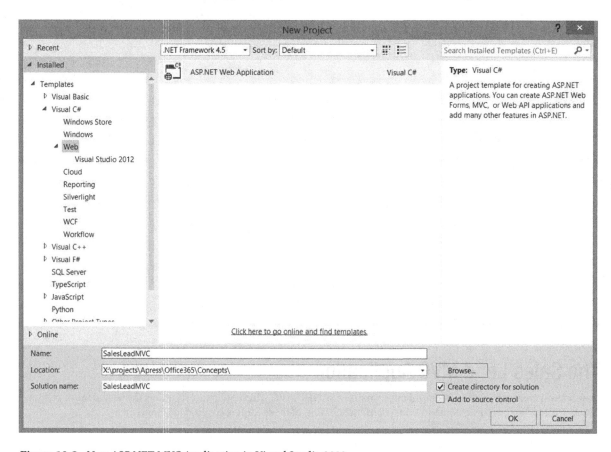

Figure 10-8. *New ASP.NET MVC Application in Visual Studio 2013*

2. Choose the MVC template and core references, as shown in Figure 10-9.

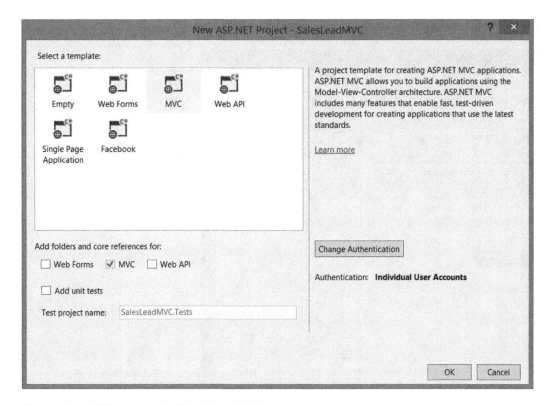

Figure 10-9. *MVC template in Visual Studio 2013*

3. This application will use Office 365 Authentication. To configure this, click the Change Authentication button. Enter your Office 365 domain and select the "Single Sign On, Read directory data" option for the Access Level. Your screen should appear similar to Figure 10-10.

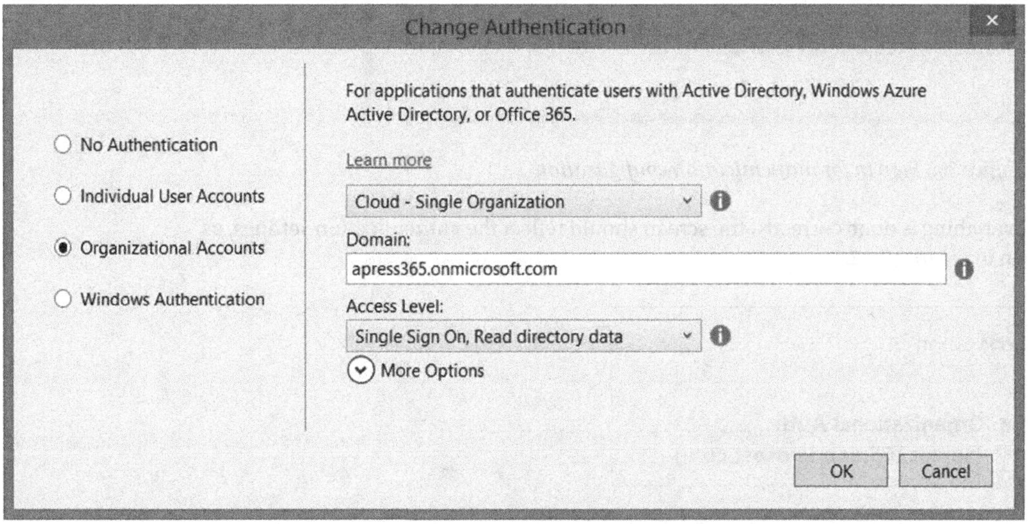

Figure 10-10. *Configure Office 365 Authentication for ASP.NET MVC project*

4. You will be prompted to enter your Office 365 credentials, as shown in Figure 10-11.

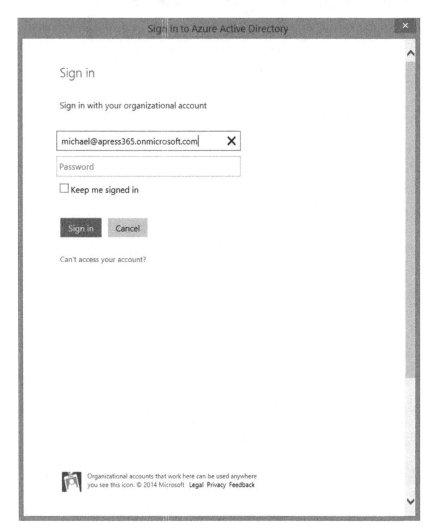

Figure 10-11. *Office 365 Sign in for authentication configuration*

5. If everything is done correctly, the screen should reflect the authentication settings, as seen in Figure 10-12.

Figure 10-12. *Authentication settings once configured for Office 365*

6.   Click OK. Visual Studio will create the solution and project files.

■ **Note**   The project needs to be configured to use Office 365 services. Office 365 also requires registration of every application. This can be done manually. However, the preferred method, and much easier method, is to use the Visual Studio Office 365 API Tools.

---

7.   Navigate to the Services Manager to configure the Office 365 services and register the application within Azure AD. This is done through the Add Connected Services option under the Project menu, as shown in Figure 10-13.

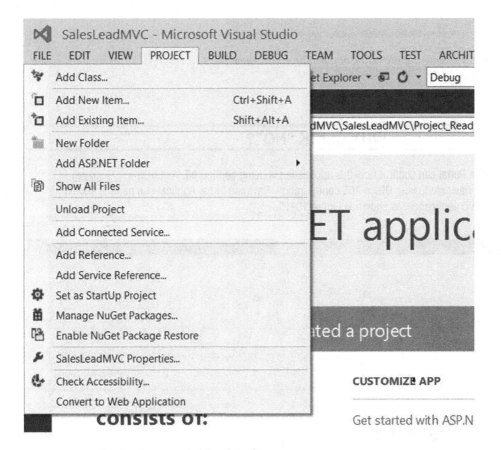

Figure 10-13. *Services Manager in Visual Studio 2013*

8.   You may need to sign in at this point. If so, click the sign in link and provide your Office 365 credentials.

Once authenticated, Visual Studio will register the application. As part of the registration process, the redirect URLs are added within the configuration information. The ASP.NET MVC application has been created with two local URLs. One for HTTP and one for HTTPS. The HTTPS local URL is automatically added as a redirect URL in the application registration. Visual Studio will then display a prompt before it adds the HTTP URL. This prompt appears similar to Figure 10-14.

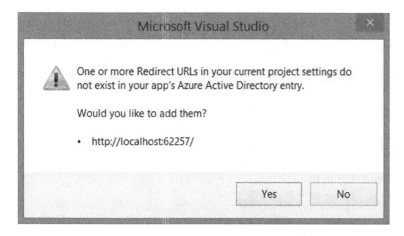

Figure 10-14. *Prompt for URL configuration during application registration*

9. Click "No".

WHY CLICK "NO"?

Navigating into the Azure Portal can confirm how this application is being configured. Visit https://manage.windowsazure.com and navigate to your Office 365 configuration. Navigate to the Applications page. It should include the SalesLeadMVC application, as shown in Figure 10-15.

Figure 10-15. *Azure Application configuration and registration*

Select the SalesLeadMVC application and navigate to the Configuration page. Find the "single sign-on" section. The local HTTPS URL should already be listed, similar to Figure 10-16.

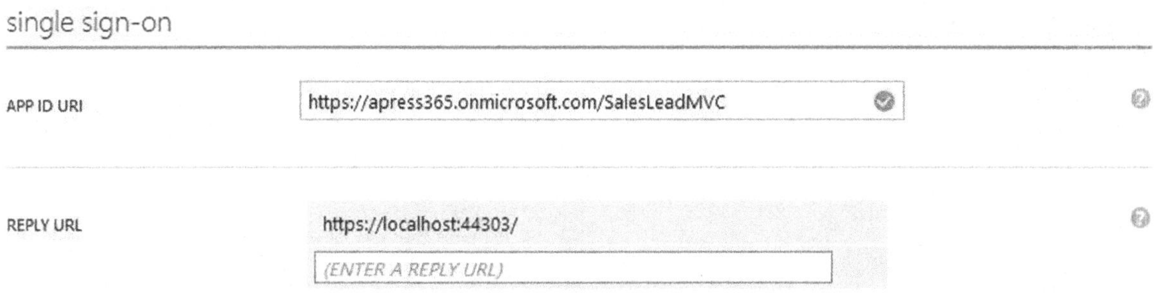

single sign-on

APP ID URI	https://apress365.onmicrosoft.com/SalesLeadMVC

REPLY URL	https://localhost:44303/
	(ENTER A REPLY URL)

Figure 10-16. *Single sign-on configuration for Office 365 applications*

If the local HTTP URL is also registered, then Azure will/may use the non-SSL URL to redirect traffic during the authentication process. However, this causes an error as SSL is required for the process. Therefore, in the prompt shown in Figure 10-14, click No.

After the services have been accessed and the application registered, Visual Studio will add necessary reference libraries. The installation process also adds sample code to help demonstrate how to use the client libraries for Office 365. Figure 10-17 shows how the solution should look once configuration is complete.

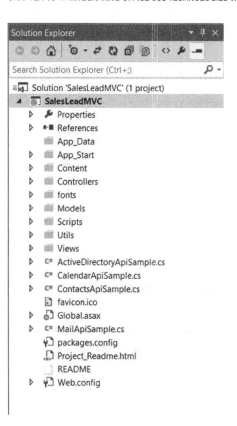

Figure 10-17. Solution Explorer with sample code files added after Office 365 configuration

Build MVC Application using Office 365 APIs

Now the project is ready to add code. The following steps will integrate Office 365 services into the MVC application. We will use the client libraries as well as access the Office 365 REST APIs directly.

10. Begin with adding the SalesLeadController. Right click the Controllers folder, click Add and choose the Controller option, as shown in Figure 10-18.

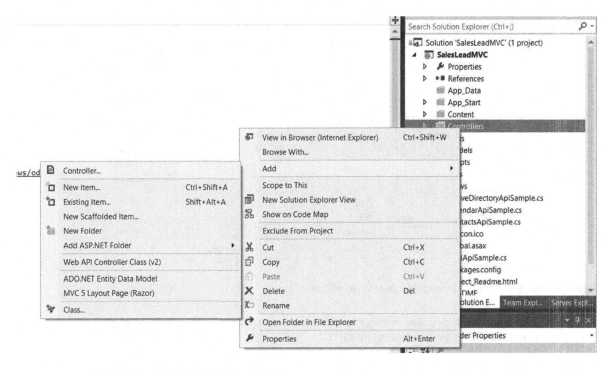

Figure 10-18. *Add new Controller to MVC application*

11. In the Add Controller prompt, type "SalesLeadController" as the controller name. Your screen should appear similar to Figure 10-19.

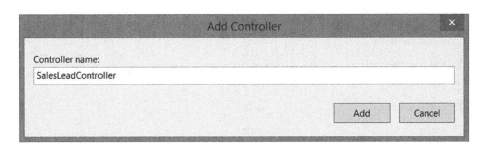

Figure 10-19. *Add SalesLeadController*

12. We will use a ModelView class in the controller, so we will add that now. Right click the Models folder, click Add and choose Class, as shown in Figure 10-20.

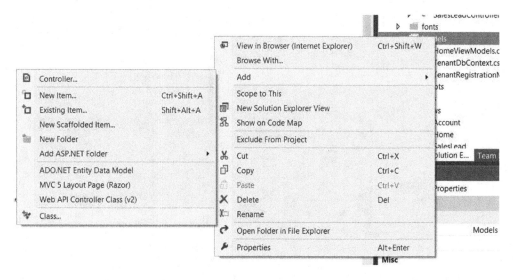

Figure 10-20. *Add Class to Models folder in MVC application*

13. In the Add New Item dialog, ensure Class is chosen and type in "LeadContactViewModel" in the Name field, as shown in Figure 10-21.

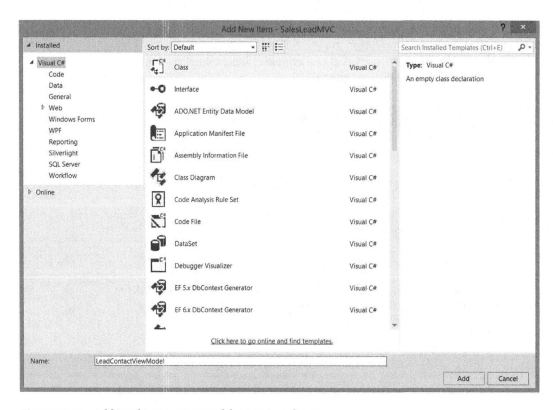

Figure 10-21. *Add LeadContactViewModel to MVC application*

14. Enter the code from Listing 10-1 as the LeadContactViewModel class.

Listing 10-1. LeadContactViewModel Class

```
public class LeadContactViewModel
{
    public LeadContactViewModel()
    {
        leads = new List<LeadInfo>();
        salesStaff = new List<SalesPerson>();
    }

    public List<LeadInfo> leads { get; set; }
    public List<SalesPerson> salesStaff { get; set; }

    public string selectedLeadID { get; set; }
    public string selectedSalesStaffID { get; set; }
}
```

15. The LeadContactViewModel class uses a couple of other custom classes, namely LeadInfo, SalesPerson, and Product. The code for these classes can be found in Listing 10-2. Add this code to the LeadContactViewModel.cs file.

Listing 10-2. Custom Classes LeadInfo, SalesPerson, and Product

```
public class LeadInfo
{
    public string ID { get; set; }
    public string sku { get; set; }
    public string email { get; set; }
    public string message { get; set; }
    public DateTime dateReceived { get; set; }
    public string productRequest { get; set; }
}

public class SalesPerson
{
    public string ID { get; set; }
    public string name { get; set; }
    public string email { get; set; }
}

public class Product
{
    public string Title { get; set; }
}
```

■ **Note**   For this demo application, the code for these custom classes is simply added to the same file as the ViewModel. These classes are only used by the ViewModel, so it works nicely.

---

16. Now we will build the SalesLeadController. To begin, add the constant values from Listing 10-3 to the beginning of the Controller class. The values of the Resource ID and Service Root URIs are found in the sample code that is generated in Visual Studio Office 365 Tools.

Listing 10-3. SalesLeadController Constants for Office 365 Services

```
const string ExchangeResourceId = "https://outlook.office365.com";
const string ExchangeServiceRoot = "https://outlook.office365.com/ews/odata";
const string SharePointResourceId = "https://apress365.sharepoint.com";
const string SharePointServiceRoot = "https://apress365.sharepoint.com/_api";
```

17. Add a method for creating an ExchangeClient to access the Exchange Services through the client library. The GetExchangeClient() method is in Listing 10-4.

Listing 10-4. GetExchangeClient() Method

```
private async Task<ExchangeClient> GetExchangeClient()
{
    Authenticator authenticator = new Authenticator();
    var authInfo = await authenticator.AuthenticateAsync(ExchangeResourceId);

    return new ExchangeClient(new Uri(ExchangeServiceRoot), authInfo.GetAccessToken);
}
```

■ **Note** The code in this chapter relies on multiple Namespaces added to the Controller. When a class is referenced in the code, but the Namespace is not found, Visual Studio will indicate the code. The Namespace can be resolved by either right clicking on the class name and clicking Resolve, or moving the cursor to the class name and using the Ctrl + "." shortcut key. Either method will add the proper using statement to the class file.

This method is essentially copied from the sample files installed by the Visual Studio Office 365 API Tools. This code handles authentication and returns an ExchangeClient for accessing the Office 365 services for Mail and Contacts.

Now we will move to build the first controller action for returning data from the Office 365 APIs. We will begin with the SaleLeadController.Index() action. This method accesses the Exchange service to query the user's inbox for any Sales Lead e-mails. Since the lead e-mail only includes the SKU of the product, the action also accesses the SharePoint service to query the product information from the custom list we setup. The resulting page will also present the option for assigning a lead to another sales person. This option requires a list of Contracts. The action method queries the Exchange service for the list of Contracts.

18. Add the Index() Controller Action. The code for this method is in Listing 10-5.

Listing 10-5. Index() Action for the SalesLeadController

```
//
// GET: /SalesLead/
public async Task<ActionResult> Index()
{
    LeadContactViewModel vm = new LeadContactViewModel();

    var client = await GetExchangeClient();
```

```
var messageResults = await (from i in client.Me.Inbox.Messages
                            where i.Subject.Contains("[SKU:")
                            orderby i.DateTimeSent descending
                            select i).ExecuteAsync();

foreach (var message in messageResults.CurrentPage)
{
    LeadInfo newContact = new LeadInfo();

    newContact.ID = message.Id;
    newContact.email = message.From.Address;
    newContact.message = message.BodyPreview;
    newContact.dateReceived = message.DateTimeReceived.Value.DateTime;

    //look up product from SKU
    var beginPos = message.Subject.IndexOf("[", 0) + 1;
    var endPos = message.Subject.IndexOf("]", beginPos);
    string skuLine = message.Subject.Substring(beginPos, endPos - beginPos);

    List<Product> products = await GetProducts();
    var product = products.Where(p => p.Title.Contains(skuLine.Split(':')[1])).SingleOrDefault();

    newContact.productRequest = product.Title;

    vm.leads.Add(newContact);
}

//get the sales staff from outlook
var contactsResults = await (from i in client.Me.Contacts
                             orderby i.DisplayName
                             select i).ExecuteAsync();

foreach (var contact in contactsResults.CurrentPage)
{
    SalesPerson person = new SalesPerson();

    person.ID = contact.Id;
    person.name = contact.DisplayName;
    person.email = contact.EmailAddress1;

    vm.salesStaff.Add(person);
}

return View(vm);
}
```

HOW THE CODE WORKS

The first thing to notice is that the action is an `async` method and returns a `Task<ActionResult>`. The method needs to handle asynchronous calls to the Office 365 services, so it will need to be asynchronous itself.

Once the `ExchangeClient` is created through our private method, the Inbox is queried for Sales Lead e-mails, using the following code:

```
var messageResults = await (from i in client.Me.Inbox.Messages
                            where i.Subject.Contains("[SKU:")
                            orderby i.DateTimeSent descending
                            select i).ExecuteAsync();
```

This code uses LINQ to query the `Inbox.Messages` collection, looking for any item with the phrase "[SKU:" in the subject. The ExchangeClient object handles the request anc creates all of the necessary HTTPS traffic for sending the request to the Office 365 services and receiving the data back. As the developer, this "plumbing" is hidden. Querying the Office 365 Inbox follows the same methodology as querying any other data source. This allows for rapid development and ease of maintenance. Although, this also requires a dependency on the functionality of the client libraries. This is a factor we will address later in this chapter.

The method then loops through the results to populate new `LeadInfo` objects for display on the screen. The data from the `Message` items are simply copied into the `LeadInfo` objects.

The subject line contains the SKU. This value is used to get the product information from the custom list in the SharePoint site. This is done through the following code section:

```
//look up product from SKU
var beginPos = message.Subject.IndexOf("[", 0) + 1;
var endPos = message.Subject.IndexOf("]", beginPos);
string skuLine = message.Subject.Substring(beginPos, endPos - beginPos);

List<Product> products = await GetProducts();
var product = products.Where(p => p.Title.Contains(skuLine.Split(':')[1])).SingleOrDefault();

newContact.productRequest = product.Title;
```

First, the SKU value is parsed from the subject line. The full list of products is queried from SharePoint through the private `GetProducts()` method. The code for the GetProducts() method is in Listing 10-5, found later in this chapter. Then the products are queried for any item that has the SKU value as part of the title. The found product item is then used to populate the productRequest property on the `ClientInfo` object.

■ **Note** When the custom list was created, the formula of <SKU>-<Name> was used for the Title field. Since the Title field is the only field returned with a known property name, this was chosen to make searching for a specific product easier.

The ClientInfo item is then added to the collection property of the ViewModel object.

The next section of code queries the ExchangeClient. This time, a list of Contacts is returned.

```
//get the sales staff from outlook
var contactsResults = await (from i in client.Me.Contacts
                             orderby i.DisplayName
                             select i).ExecuteAsync();
```

Again, LINQ is used to query the Clients collection and return the items. The list of Contacts is used to populate the salesStaff collection property of the ViewModel.

The ViewModel is then passed to the View for display.

The GetProducts() method, used to query the SharePoint services, needs to be added to the Controller.

19.   Add the code from Listing 10-6 to the Controller class.

Listing 10-6. GetProducts() Private Method for Querying SharePoint Custom List

```
private async Task<List<Product>>GetProducts()
{
    //get authorization token
    Authenticator authenticator = new Authenticator();
    var authInfo = await authenticator.AuthenticateAsync(SharePointResourceId);

    HttpClient httpClient = new HttpClient();
    httpClient.BaseAddress = new Uri(SharePointResourceId);
    httpClient.DefaultRequestHeaders.Authorization = new AuthenticationHeaderValue("Bearer", await
    authInfo.GetAccessToken());
    httpClient.DefaultRequestHeaders.Add("Accept", "application/json;odata=nometadata");

    var listResponse = httpClient.GetAsync("/SalesLeads/_api/web/lists/getbytitle('Products')/
                                           items").Result;

    var responseContent = await listResponse.Content.ReadAsStringAsync();

    var json = JObject.Parse(responseContent);

    List<Product> products = json["value"].ToObject<List<Product>>();

    return products;
}
```

HOW THE CODE WORKS

So far, the code has only used the Office 365 client libraries for accessing the online services. This method needs to access SharePoint lists, which is not currently available through the client libraries. In fact, this functionality is not yet available through the Office 365 APIs. However, there are SharePoint APIs we can use. Thankfully, authentication is the same for both, so we can still use the client libraries to make authentication easier.

To access the SharePoint REST APIs, we use the HttpClient object. We start with authorization. We copy the code from the sample files for authentication. This will get us an access token. Once we create the HttpClient object, we have to add this access token to the Headers, using the following line:

```
httpClient.DefaultRequestHeaders.Authorization = new AuthenticationHeaderValue("Bearer",
await authInfo.GetAccessToken());
```

For processing, we want to ensure the data is returned in JSON. We also do not need the extra OData metadata included, so we use the following code to add the "Accept" header and control the data type returned from the service:

```
httpClient.DefaultRequestHeaders.Add("Accept", "application/json;odata=nometadata");
```

Now the request is ready. The API for the ListItems is a GET method. We will use the GetByTitle API to access the list, and the items endpoint to return the data elements. This is achieved in the following line:

```
var listResponse = httpClient.GetAsync("/SalesLeads/_api/web/lists/getbytitle('Products')/
                                items").Result;
```

The rest of the code receives the JSON response and parses the data into the proper object for processing in the Action method. The list of products is returned.

The Controller Action code is complete, but the View is not available. Now we are ready to add the View.

20.   Right click the method name (Index) and click on Add View. In the Add View dialog, set the View Name to Index, the Template to Empty and select the LeadContactViewModel as the Model class. Leave the other default options. When your screen appears similar to Figure 10-22, click Add.

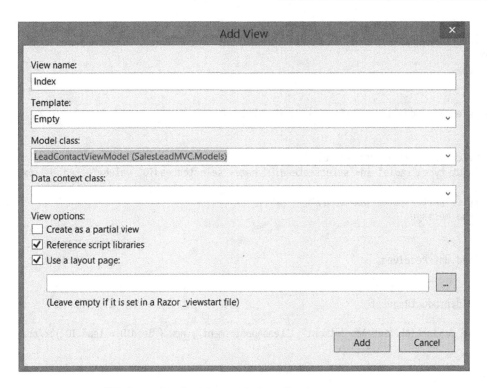

Figure 10-22. *Add SalesLead.Index View to MVC application*

21. Once the file has been created, use the code from Listing 10-7 to complete the View.

Listing 10-7. Index( ) View for SalesLead Controller

```
@model SalesLeadMVC.Models.LeadContactViewModel

<h2>Leads</h2>

@using (Html.BeginForm("Index"))
{
    <table width="800">
        <thead>
            <tr>
                <th>Select Lead</th>
                <th>
                    Lead Information
                </th>
                <th>
                    Date Received
                </th>
```

```
            <th>
                Product Request
            </th>
            <th></th>
        </tr>
    </thead>
    @foreach (SalesLeadMVC.Models.LeadInfo lead in Model.leads)
    {
        <tr>
            <td style="vertical-align:middle;">
                <input type="radio" id="selectedLeadID" name="selectedLeadID" value="@lead.ID" />
            </td>
            <td style="white-space: pre-line;">
                @lead.message
            </td>
            <td>
                @lead.dateReceived
            </td>
            <td>
                @lead.productRequest
            </td>
            <td>@Html.ActionLink("Set Appointment", "LeadAppointment", new { leadID = lead.ID })</td>
        </tr>
    }
</table>
<fieldset>
    <legend>Assign Lead</legend>

    <label>Sales Person:</label>
    @Html.DropDownListFor(x => x.selectedSalesStaffID, new SelectList(Model.salesStaff,
    "ID", "name"), "Select a Contact")

    <label></label>
    <input type="submit" value="Submit" />
</fieldset>
}
```

This View is simple MVC razor syntax for creating the Sales Lead page. A table is created for the lead information. The page loops through the leads property of the Model class to build the rows of the table. The final column contains an ActionLink to the LeadAppointment Action, which we will set up later in this chapter.

A form is set up to allow the user to reassign the lead to another sales person. The salesStaff collection property of the Model class is used to populate a drop list control. A radio button in each row allows the user to select a lead. They can then choose a Contact from the drop list. The Submit button then posts the form to the SalesLead Controller.

The Controller and View are ready. Now we simply need a way to call the Action. For this application, we will simply add a menu item to access this page.

22.   Add the code below to the Views\Shared_Layout.cshtml file, just after the other menu items.

```
<li>@Html.ActionLink("Sales Leads", "Index", "SalesLead")</li>
```

The necessary action methods for the links and submit button are not available yet. Clicking on those items will result in errors. Knowing this, run the application to view the Sales Leads page.

The first thing you will encounter is the Office 365 authentication process, which results in a Sign In screen hosted from Microsoft. As long as everything builds properly, your screen should appear similar to Figure 10-23.

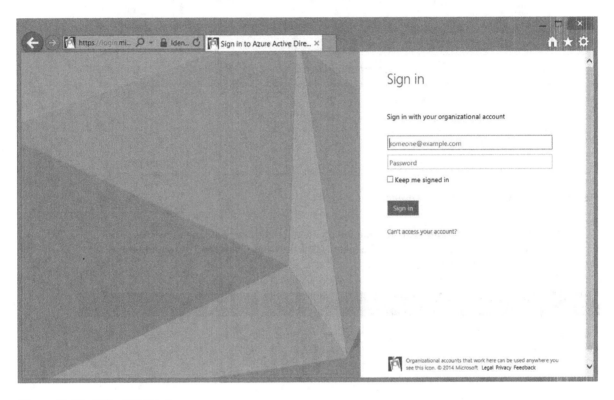

Figure 10-23. *Office 365 Sign In*

23.   Enter your Office 365 credentials and click Sign in. This should redirect you back to your localhost URL and display your application in the browser. You should see something similar to Figure 10-24.

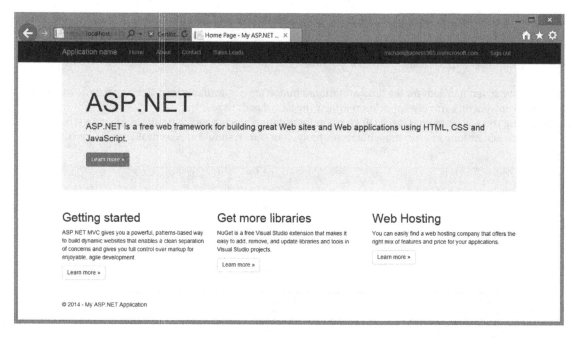

Figure 10-24. *First Run of Sales Lead Application*

24. You should notice your login information on the top right side of the menu bar. Also, you should have a Sales Leads link in the menu. Click the Sales Leads link. You should then view a page similar to Figure 10-25.

Figure 10-25. *Sales Leads Page Displaying Office 365 Data*

25. Confirm the list of leads is the e-mails you sent into your Office 365 mailbox. Confirm the drop list contains the Contacts you created in Office 365.

26. Return to Visual Studio to continue building the rest of the application. Begin with adding the POST method to accept the submit from the Sales Lead page. This method will forward the message to the chosen Contact and remove the message from the current Inbox. This code is in Listing 10-8

Listing 10-8. HttpPost Index( ) Action

```
[HttpPost]
public async Task<ActionResult> Index(LeadContactViewModel vm)
{
    var client = await GetExchangeClient();

    var contactResults = await (from i in client.Me.Contacts
                                select i).ExecuteAsync();

    var contact = contactResults.CurrentPage.Where(c => c.Id ==
    vm.selectedSalesStaffID).SingleOrDefault();

    //USE HTTPCLIENT
    //get authorization token
    Authenticator authenticator = new Authenticator();
    var authInfo = await authenticator.AuthenticateAsync(ExchangeResourceId);

    //send request through HttpClient
    HttpClient httpClient = new HttpClient();
    httpClient.BaseAddress = new Uri(ExchangeResourceId);

    //add authorization header
    httpClient.DefaultRequestHeaders.Authorization =
    new AuthenticationHeaderValue("Bearer", await authInfo.GetAccessToken());

    //prepare POST content for forward request
    ForwardMessage forwardContent = new Models.ForwardMessage();
    forwardContent.Comment = "This lead has been reassigned to you";
    forwardContent.ToRecipients.Add(new Recipient() { Address = contact.EmailAddress1,
    Name = contact.DisplayName });

    //convert POST content to JSON
    StringContent postContent = new StringContent(JsonConvert.SerializeObject(forwardContent));
    postContent.Headers.ContentType = new MediaTypeHeaderValue("application/json");

    //send forward request
    var forwardResponse = httpClient.PostAsync("/ews/odata/Me/Inbox/Messages('" +
    vm.selectedLeadID + "')/Forward", postContent).Result;

    //delete message to remove from INBOX/Lead List
    //send delete request
    var deleteResponse = httpClient.DeleteAsync("/ews/odata/Me/Inbox/Messages('" +
    vm.selectedLeadID + "')").Result;
```

```
//refresh leads
vm.leads.Clear();
var messageResults = await (from i in client.Me.Inbox.Messages
                            where i.Subject.Contains("[SKU:")
                            orderby i.DateTimeSent descending
                            select i).ExecuteAsync();

foreach (var message in messageResults.CurrentPage)
{
    LeadInfo newContact = new LeadInfo();

    newContact.ID = message.Id;
    newContact.email = message.From.Address;
    newContact.message = message.BodyPreview;
    newContact.dateReceived = message.DateTimeReceived.Value.DateTime;

    vm.leads.Add(newContact);
}

return View(vm);
}
```

HOW THE CODE WORKS

This Action begins similar to the GET version. An ExchangeClient is created and used to query a list of contacts. This returns the full list of contacts from Office 365. However, the Action code needs only the one the user selected to assign the lead. So, the list is then queried further to find the one with the correct ID.

During development of this application, the first attempt included using the contact.Id property in the initial query against the Exchange service, through the ExchangeClient. The code was similar to the following:

```
var contactResults = await (from i in client.Me.Contacts
                            where i.Id == vm.selectedLeadID
                            select i).ExecuteAsync();
```

However, this resulted in error. The error message stated "The property 'Id' does not support filtering." A couple of different methods were attempted, but the error remained. It was deemed this might be a bug in the Preview version of the API or the Tools.

Once the proper contact is available, the plan is to forward the e-mail and delete it from the current Mailbox. Then, refresh the Messages from Outlook and display the same View to the user.

The HttpClient is used to accomplish the Forward and Delete methods, accessing the Office 365 REST APIs directly, rather than through the client libraries.

The HttpClient object is initialized and configured similar to the example earlier. The authorization process returns an access token, which becomes part of the Headers content. The previous example used the HttpClient to access a GET endpoint. The Forward endpoint expects a POST. Before sending the request, we must prepare the client. This is done through the following code section:

```
//prepare POST content for forward request
ForwardMessage forwardContent = new Models.ForwardMessage();
forwardContent.Comment = "This lead has been reassigned to you";
forwardContent.ToRecipients.Add(new Recipient() { Address = contact.EmailAddress1,
Name = contact.DisplayName });
```

```
//convert POST content to JSON
StringContent postContent = new StringContent(JsonConvert.SerializeObject(forwardContent));
postContent.Headers.ContentType = new MediaTypeHeaderValue("application/json");
```

First, a C# object (ForwardMessage) is populated from the contact information. The code for this object is found in Listing 10-9. This object is then converted to JSON using the JsonConvert.SerializeObject method. This is then used to create a StringContent object. This content object is required by the PostAsync method, used in the following section to send the request to the Office 365 service.

```
//send forward request
var forwardResponse = httpClient.PostAsync("/ews/odata/Me/Inbox/Messages('" +
vm.selectedLeadID + "')/Forward", postContent).Result;
```

This line calls the HttpClient.PostAsync() method, specifying the Forward endpoint and passing the JSON content.

Once the message has been forwarded, it needs to be deleted from the current Inbox. This is achieved through the following line of code:

```
//send delete request
var deleteResponse = httpClient.DeleteAsync("/ews/odata/Me/Inbox/Messages('" +
vm.selectedLeadID + "')").Result;
```

This line calls the HttpClient.DeleteAsync method. This sends a HTTP DELETE request to the specified URL. For this request, it is the URL of the specific message.

The remaining section of the Action method repeats the code from the previous example to query the ExchangeService to receive the list of Sales Leads messages and add them to the ViewModel class. This ViewModel class is then passed to the same View and returned to the user.

Listing 10-9. ForwardMessage Class

```
public class ForwardMessage
{
    public ForwardMessage()
    {
        ToRecipients = new List<Recipient>();
    }
    public string Comment { get; set; }
    public List<Recipient> ToRecipients { get; set; }
}
```

At this point, the View Leads Use Case has been implemented. The Assign Lead Use Case has also been implemented. That leaves the Set Appointment and Check Appointments Use Cases remaining. Begin with the Set Appointment, which is called when the Submit button is clicked on the Sales Lead page.

27.   Add the LeadAppointment action to the SalesLead Controller. The code is in Listing 10-10.

Listing 10-10. LeadAppointment Action

```
[HttpGet]
public async Task<ActionResult> LeadAppointment(string leadID)
{
    var client = await GetExchangeClient();
    LeadAppointmentViewModel vm = new LeadAppointmentViewModel();

    vm.leadID = leadID;

    //look up lead information

    //get authorization token
    Authenticator authenticator = new Authenticator();
    var authInfo = await authenticator.AuthenticateAsync(ExchangeResourceId);

    HttpClient httpClient = new HttpClient();
    httpClient.BaseAddress = new Uri(ExchangeResourceId);
    httpClient.DefaultRequestHeaders.Authorization = new AuthenticationHeaderValue("Bearer", await
    authInfo.GetAccessToken());

    var response = httpClient.GetAsync("/ews/odata/Me/Inbox/Messages('" + leadID + "')").Result;

    if (response.StatusCode == HttpStatusCode.OK)
    {
        var responseContent = await response.Content.ReadAsStringAsync();
        var message = JObject.Parse(responseContent).ToObject<Message>();

        vm.appointmentMessage = message.BodyPreview;
    }

    return View(vm);
}
```

This Action uses the HttpClient object to access the Office 365 REST APIs directly. This action results in displaying information only, so the message is retrieved from the Exchange service and used to populate the LeadAppointmentViewModel class.

■ **Note**   The examples using the HttpClient contain similar, even repetitive, code used to create and configure the object. These steps were purposefully left within the method to aid in demonstration. For a production-level application, this functionality would likely be moved to libraries, similar to the client libraries included in the Visual Studio Office 365 API Tools.

---

28. Add a new class to the Models folder called LeadAppointmentViewModel. The ViewModel code is in Listing 10-11.

Listing 10-11. LeadAppointmentViewModel

```
public class LeadAppointmentViewModel
{
    public LeadAppointmentViewModel()
    {
        appointmentDate = DateTime.Now;
        currentAppointments = new List<Event>();
    }

    public string leadID { get; set; }
    public DateTime appointmentDate { get; set; }
    public string appointmentMessage { get; set; }
    public string appointmentTitle { get; set; }

    public List<Event> currentAppointments { get; set; }
}
```

The LeadAppointment Action requires a new View for displaying the form for setting the appointment.

29. Add a new View to the Views\SalesLead folder called LeadAppointment. Set the Template to Empty and the Model class to the LeadAppointmentModelView class. The code for this view is Listing 10-12.

Listing 10-12. LeadAppointment View

```
@model SalesLeadMVC.Models.LeadAppointmentViewModel

<h2>Lead Appointment</h2>

@using (Html.BeginForm("LeadAppointment"))
{
    @Html.HiddenFor(x => x.leadID)
    @Html.HiddenFor(x => x.appointmentMessage)
    <div class="well">
        <h3>Lead Information</h3>
        <div style="white-space: pre-line;">
            @Model.appointmentMessage
        </div>
    </div>

    <fieldset>
        <legend>Set Appointment</legend>
        <label>Appointment Date:</label><br />
        @Html.TextBoxFor(x => x.appointmentDate)
        <input type="button" value="Check Appointments" onclick="checkAppointments();" /><br />

        <input type="submit" value="Set Appointment" style="margin-top:40px;" />
    </fieldset>
}
<div id="currentAppointments" style="margin-top:40px;"></div>
```

```
@section scripts
{
    <script>
        function checkAppointments() {
            var currDate = $('#appointmentDate').val();
            var url = '/SalesLead/CheckAppointments?appointmentDate=' + currDate.split(' ')[0];

            $.get(url, function (data) {
                $('#currentAppointments').html(data);
            });
            return false;
        }
    </script>
}
```

HOW THE CODE WORKS

This View creates the form for setting the appointment. This essentially consists of a text box for the date/time for the appointment. This page also allows the user to check their current appointments for the given date, in order to ensure they set the new appointment for a time when they are free.

The JavaScript function checkAppointments()calls the CheckAppointments Action on the SalesLead Controller.

```
function checkAppointments() {
var currDate = $('#appointmentDate').val();
var url = '/SalesLead/CheckAppointments?appointmentDate=' + currDate.split(' ')[0];

$.get(url, function (data) {
    $('#currentAppointments').html(data);
});
return false;
}
```

The script uses jQuery to access the form elements on the page. The current date is retrieved from the "appointmentDate" field. The date is then used to create the URL. The jQuery method get() is used to make an AJAX call back to the application. The results from that HTTP call are used to populate a DIV on the screen. The user can enter a date and click the "Check Appointments" button and view the current appointments for the given date.

To complete the application, we must implement an Action to accept the POST from the LeadAppointment form.

30.   Add the POST Action LeadAppointment to the SalesLead Controller. The code is in Listing 10-13.

Listing 10-13. POST LeadAppointment

```
[HttpPost]
public async Task<ActionResult> LeadAppointment(LeadAppointmentViewModel vm)
{
    var client = await GetExchangeClient();

    Event appointment = new Event();
    appointment.Subject = "Sales Lead Meeting";
    appointment.Start = new DateTimeOffset(vm.appointmentDate);
    appointment.End = new DateTimeOffset(vm.appointmentDate.AddMinutes(30));
    appointment.BodyPreview = vm.appointmentMessage;

    await client.Me.Events.AddEventAsync(appointment);

    return RedirectToAction("Index");
}
```

This Action uses the Office 365 client libraries to create a new calendar event for the chosen date. The message content from the chosen lead is used as the content of the Event. A new Event object is instantiated and populated from the POST data. The AddEventAsync() method is called and passed to the populated Event object.

Once the method completes, the user is redirected back to the Index action. The final implementation is the CheckAppointment Action and View.

31.   Add the CheckAppointment Action to the SalesLead Controller. The code is in Listing 10-14.

Listing 10-14. CheckAppointment Action

```
[HttpGet]
public async Task<ActionResult> CheckAppointments(DateTime appointmentDate)
{
    CheckAppointmentsViewModel vm = new CheckAppointmentsViewModel();

    var client = await GetExchangeClient();
    var appointmentResults = await (from i in client.Me.Calendar.Events
                         where i.Start >=new DateTimeOffset(appointmentDate)
                         select i).ExecuteAsync();

    foreach (Event appointment in appointmentResults.CurrentPage)
    {
        vm.appointments.Add(appointment);
    }

     return PartialView("_CheckAppointments", vm);
}
```

This action uses the Office 365 client libraries to access the ExchangeClient and query the events for the given date. The CheckAppointmentViewModel is populated and passed to the View. It is important that this returns a PartialView. This means only the rendered HTML from the View is returned and not any additional markup from Layouts or other processing. This action is called from an already rendered page. The returned markup is inserted into a DIV in the browser. Only the View code is wanted, not any added scripts, CSS references, or any additional markup.

32. Add a new class to the Models folder called CheckAppointmentViewModel. The code for the ViewModel is Listing 10-15.

Listing 10-15. CheckAppointmentViewModel

```
public class CheckAppointmentsViewModel
{
    public CheckAppointmentsViewModel()
    {
        appointments = new List<Event>();
    }

    public List<Event> appointments { get; set; }
}
```

33. Add a new View to the Views/SalesLead folder called _CheckAppointments.cshtml. Set the Template to Empty, the Model class to CheckAppointmentsViewModel, and check the PartialView check box. The underscore prefix in the name denotes this is a Partial View. The code for this view is in Listing 10-16.

Listing 10-16. _CheckAppointments View

```
@model SalesLeadMVC.Models.CheckAppointmentsViewModel

<fieldset>
    <legend>Current Appointments</legend>
    <table width="600">
        <thead>
            <tr>
                <th>
                    Date
                </th>
                <th>
                    Appointment
                </th>
            </tr>
        </thead>
        <tbody>
            @foreach (Microsoft.Office365.Exchange.Event appointment in Model.appointments)
            {
                <tr>
                    <td>
                        @appointment.Start.Value.DateTime
                    </td>
            }
```

```
            <td>
                @appointment.Subject
            </td>
        </tr>
    }
    </tbody>
</table>
</fieldset>
```

This completes all Use Cases for this application. Ensure the project builds successfully and runs the application. Confirm it performs as expected.

34. Assign a lead to another sales person. Run the application and navigate to the Sales Lead page. Choose a lead by clicking on the radio button. Select a contact from the droplist. Click the Submit button. You should return to the Sales Lead page, only the selected lead should not appear on your screen.

35. Log into your Outlook online account to confirm the lead was sent to the chosen contact. Look in the Sent Items folder and you should see the forwarded leads. Figure 10-26 shows a similar situation.

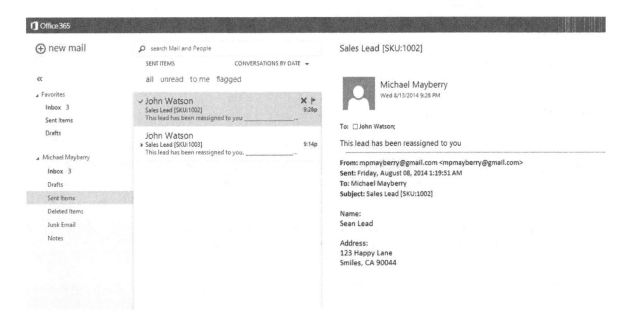

Figure 10-26. *Message Items Forwarded Through MVC Application*

36.   Click the "Set Appointment" link on one of the leads displayed on the screen. You should see a screen similar to Figure 10-27.

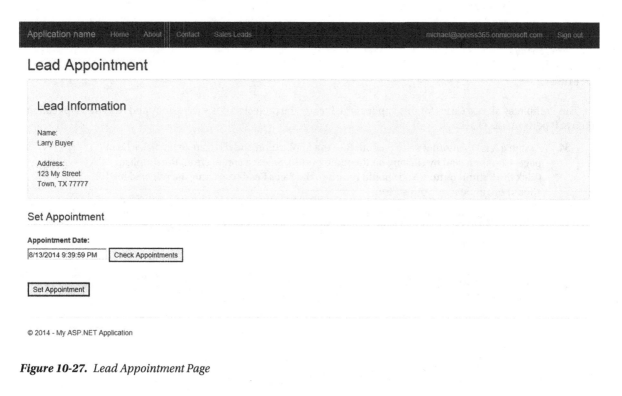

Figure 10-27. Lead Appointment Page

■ **Note**   The Check Appointments functionality relies on existing Events in the user's calendar. Before testing this section of the application, access your online calendar and create some Events manually.

---

37.   Enter a date you know has some events on your calendar and click the Check Appointments button. You should see events appear, similar to Figure 10-28.

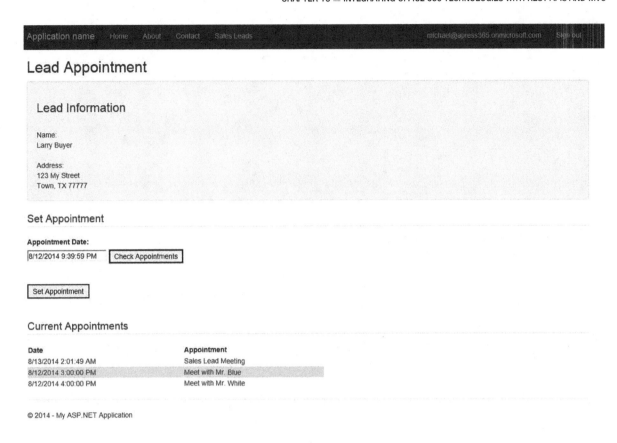

Figure 10-28. *Check Appointments Results*

38. Enter a date and time and click the Set Appointment button. Log into your online calendar to ensure the event was added. You should see items similar to Figure 10-29.

August 2014

◄ jan feb mar apr may jun jul aug sep oct nov dec ► go to today

SUNDAY	MONDAY	TUESDAY	WEDNESDAY	THURSDAY	
27	28	29	30	31	/
3	4	5	6	7	8
10	11	12 10a Meet with Mr. Blue 11a Meet with Mr. White 9:01p Sales Lead Meeting 9:39p Sales Lead Meeting	13	14	1
17	18	19	20	21	2
24	25	26	27	28	2

Figure 10-29. *Online Events with Added Appointments from MVC Application*

Summary

In this chapter, you build an ASP.NET MVC application that consumes the Office 365 APIs. This application demonstrates how easy it can be to incorporate Office 365 data into a custom application. The methodologies in this chapter can be used for any type of application development, not only ASP.NET MVC.

The Visual Studio Office 365 Tools were installed and configured to aid in authentication and application registration. This is not required for application development, but it does help. The functions performed by these tools can be done manually as well.

The Office 365 client libraries were used to demonstrate how to access Office 365 services through familiar .NET coding and methodologies, such as LINQ. These libraries aid in the communication between the application and the services, handling the common, but necessary, "plumbing" required for consuming the Office 365 APIs.

This chapter also demonstrated how to consume the Office 365 APIs directly, using the HttpClient object. JSON content was both consumed from the services and passed into the APIs to achieve desired functionality.

The primary purpose of this section was to introduce the Office 356 APIs and demonstrate how developers could integrate them into custom applications. The current functionality of the APIs is limited, as they have only been released as Preview services. However, Microsoft is dedicated to this direction of service and the ability of developers to extend the Office 365 experience through custom applications will only improve with time.

■ ■ ■

SharePoint Primer

This appendix is intended for anyone who is fairly new to the SharePoint technology. I'll give you a brief description of the various types of objects that are used to implement a SharePoint solution. In a very loose sense, SharePoint can be thought of as a database where the "tables" are the lists and the "rows" are the items you put in the lists. Because SharePoint also provides the visualization of this data, presentation aspects are considered at every level in the "database" design.

■ **Note**   Most of the figures included here were taken from the SharePoint Designer, a client application that is used to customize a SharePoint site. You can also modify these same objects using web pages within SharePoint itself. The user interface is a little different but the concepts are the same.

Columns

The basic building block is the column, which holds a single piece of information.

■ **Note**   Columns are also referred to as fields. In the SharePoint object model, columns are accessed through the SPField class. SharePoint Designer calls them columns. So you will see the terms column and field used interchangeably.

Each column definition must include the column type, which specifies both storage and presentation details. Figure A-1 lists the available column types.

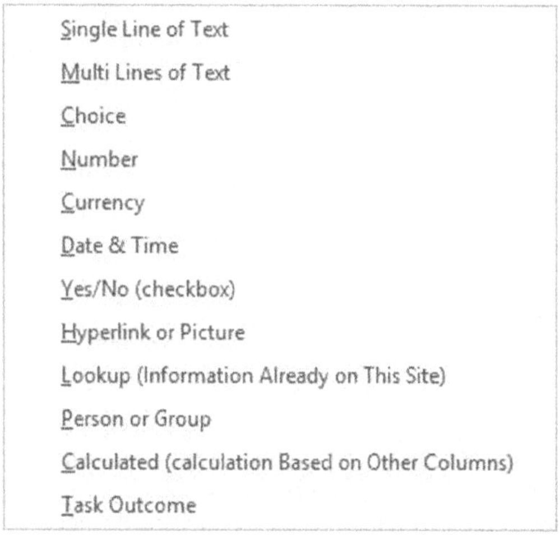

Single Line of Text

Multi Lines of Text

Choice

Number

Currency

Date & Time

Yes/No (checkbox)

Hyperlink or Picture

Lookup (Information Already on This Site)

Person or Group

Calculated (calculation Based on Other Columns)

Task Outcome

Figure A-1. *Column types*

Text Columns

Notice that there are two text types: one for a Single Line of Text and another for Multi Lines of Text. A single line text field is used for shorter fields, like Name. A multi-line text field will take up more space on the form (you can specify the default size) and has additional display options. Figure A-2 shows the column editor for a Multi Line of Text column.

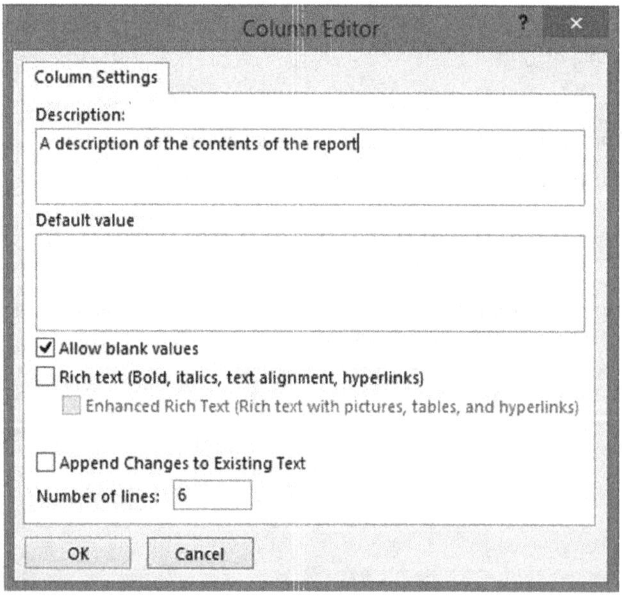

Column Editor   ?   ×

Column Settings

Description:

A description of the contents of the report

Default value

☑ Allow blank values

☐ Rich text (Bold, italics, text alignment, hyperlinks)

☐ Enhanced Rich Text (Rich text with pictures, tables, and hyperlinks)

☐ Append Changes to Existing Text

Number of lines: 6

    OK   Cancel

Figure A-2. *Multi-line text field settings*

One of the particularly interesting features of the multi-line column is the append option. If you select the Append Changes to Existing Text checkbox, the text entered in that field is appended to the existing contents. This is often used on a comments field. If the item is edited multiple times, the comments are appended at the end of the previous comment, giving you a running history of all the comments.

A multi-line column can also support rich text formatting and even pictures. Contrast this to the settings for a Single Line Text column shown in Figure A-3.

Figure A-3. *Single-line text field settings*

Date & Time Columns

When defining a column you can also specify a default value. For example, when creating a Date & Time column you have an option to default to the current date and time or a fixed date, as shown in Figure A-4.

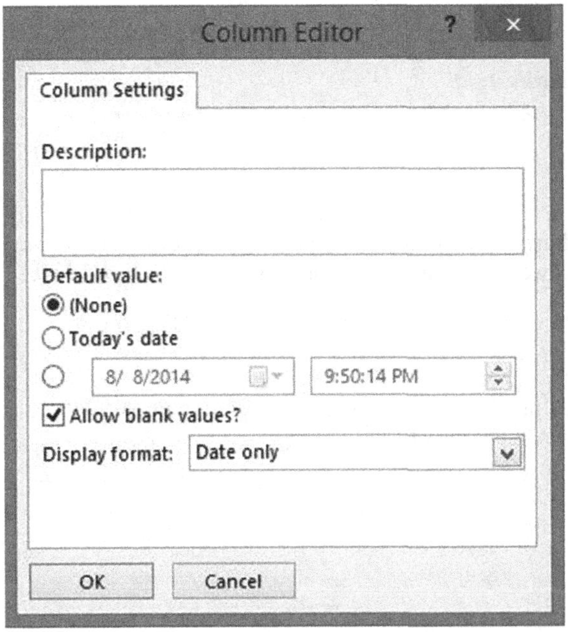

Figure A-4. *The date & time column settings*

Notice also that you can choose to display the value as a date only or as both date and time. This only affects how the data is displayed, not how the data is actually stored.

Person or Group Columns

If you use a column type of Person or Group, the edit form will use a PeoplePicker control. You'll use this control a lot and it's a very useful way to select users, ensuring only valid choices are allowed. The column editor shown in Figure A-5 illustrates the settings you can use to configure how this control works.

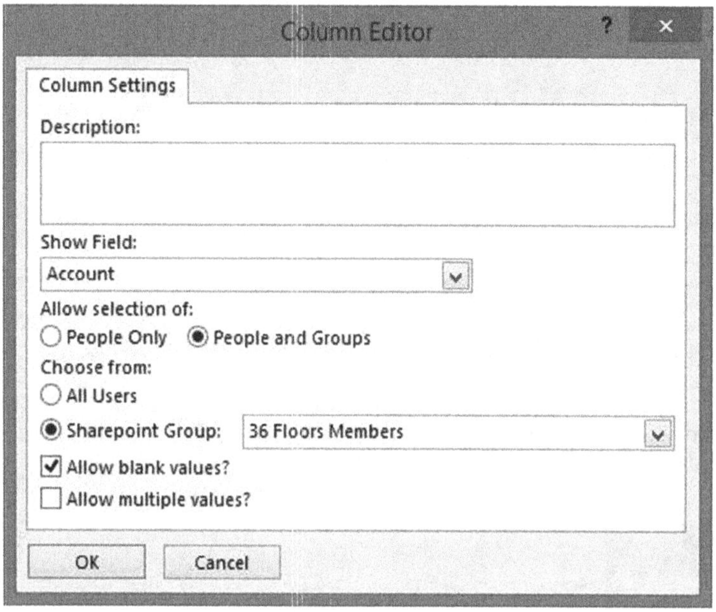

Figure A-5. Person or Group column editor

You can also use these settings to determine what attribute of the user to display. By default this is the account or login name. However, you could display the name, e-mail address, phone number, or whatever is appropriate for your application. You can also control which users or groups are allowed and if multiple people or groups can be selected.

Choice Columns

The Choice type is another interesting column type. You'll use this when you want to provide fixed values for the allowable options. The column editor for a Choice field is shown in Figure A-6.

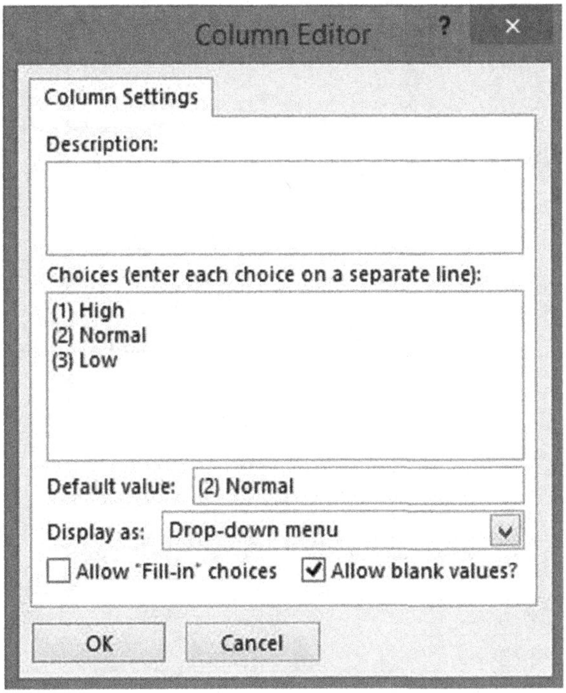

Figure A-6. *Choice column type editor*

When defining the column, you'll specify the available options in the Choices list. You can decide how the choices are presented. There are three options.

- Drop-down list

- Radio button

- Check boxes

Select the Allow Fill-in choices check box if you want the users to enter a value other than one of the pre-defined choices.

Lookup Columns

The Choice type should not be confused with the Lookup type. A Choice column has a fixed set of allowable values. Often, however, you'll want to restrict values to a dynamic list. The Lookup type allows you to do this by specifying another list as the source of the allowable values.

For example, the Parent Request column, shown in Figure A-7, references the ID column of the Request list. This means that this column, if not empty, must contain an ID that exists in the Request table. If the Allow blank values? check box is not selected, this column cannot be empty.

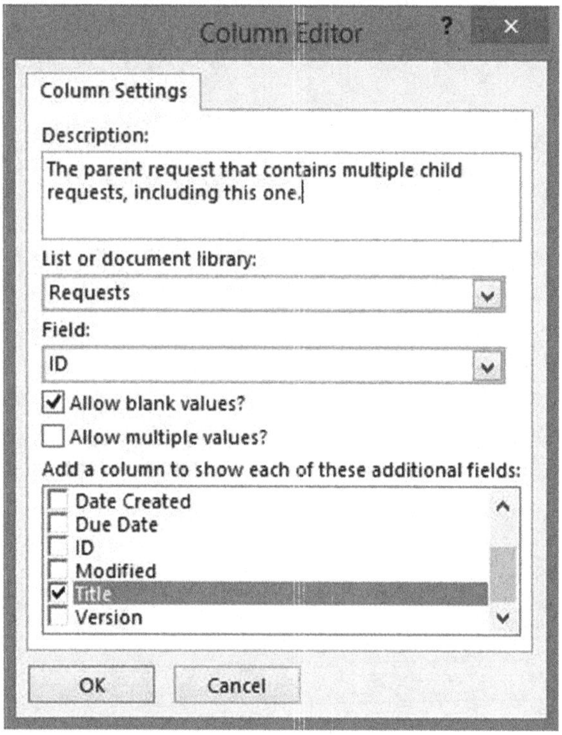

Figure A-7. Lookup column type settings

You must first choose the list to be used for the lookup. You'll then select the field that will be stored in the new column. This is typically an ID field or some other unique identifier. You can also select additional fields that will be displayed on the form.

Lookup columns are the mechanism that you'll use to ensure referential integrity. In database terms, this is equivalent to a foreign key relationship. By defining a Lookup column, you ensure that selected values are valid. This also improves the user interface. The user can search for the record using any of the additional fields that you specify.

Calculated Columns

A Calculated column allows you to define a column with a formula that includes the values of other columns. A sample is shown in Figure A-8.

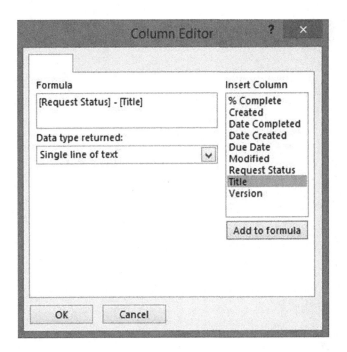

Figure A-8. *A calculated column*

In this example, the Request Status and Title columns are concatenated to form a new column.

Task Outcome Columns

We demonstrated the use of a Task Outcome column in Chapter 4. This is used by workflow forms to influence the subsequent processing when a task is completed. In the example column shown in Figure A-9, the possible outcomes are defined as:

- Completed - the request is completed and can be closed

- On Hold - the request is not completed and follow-up work is still required

- Need Info - the request must be sent back to the user that requested it, in order to provide more information

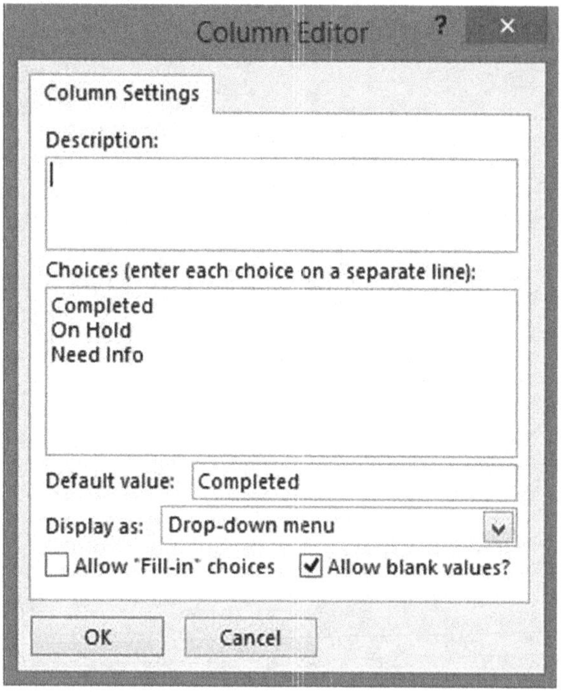

Figure A-9. *A task outcome column*

A Task Outcome column is configured just like a Choice column but has special meaning for the workflow process.

Site Columns Collection

SharePoint provides a set of column definitions referred to as Site Columns. These are defined as independent pieces of information that you can assemble into your own custom lists. You can use any of these existing columns when creating a list. Site columns are organized into groups. You can also define new site columns and new groups to help organize them.

When creating a list you also have the option of creating a new column that is only used by that list. The difference is in how the column is created. In the first case, the column is created, added to the Site Columns collection, and then added to the list. In the second case, the column is created and added to the list. It requires an extra step to create reusable column definitions.

In SharePoint, the mantra is "Build once, use often." A column definition should be reused wherever appropriate. This means taking the extra step to define the column first and then add it to the list. But it also means carefully considering the design of the column and how you expect it to be used. Keep in mind that if you change an existing site column, every place that it is used will change. This can be a good thing if used properly. Give your columns meaningful names and descriptions that explain the intended use. When choosing an existing column, don't just look for one with the correct column type. Make sure the description matches how you're planning to use it.

Content Types

Content types define a reusable collection of properties and are used throughout SharePoint. One use of content types is to define the items (rows) that are contained in a list or document library. A content type specifies a collection of columns. To control how the field is displayed in the form, columns can be specified as either Required, Optional, or Hidden. For example, the columns included in the Task content type are shown in Figure A-10.

Column Name	Type	Property
Task Name	Single line of text	Required
Start Date	Date and Time	Optional
Due Date	Date and Time	Optional
Assigned To	Person or Group	Optional
% Complete	Number (1, 1.0, 100)	Optional
Body	Multiple lines of text	Optional
Predecessors	Lookup (information already on this site)	Optional
Priority	Choice (menu to choose from)	Optional
Task Status	Choice (menu to choose from)	Optional
Related Items	Related Items	Optional

Task | Apress 365 Team Site ▶ Content Types ▶ Task ▶ Editor

Figure A-10. *The columns included in the Task content type*

For each content type, you can specify a custom form to be used. SharePoint uses the following three forms for each content type:

- New: Used when creating a new item.
- Display: View-only form used to display an item.
- Edit: Used to modify an item.

Content types support inheritance, which means you can derive a new content type from an existing one. The new content type will inherit the columns and properties of its parent content type. The base content type is Item and all other contents are derived (directly or indirectly) from Item. The Document content type, which is derived from Item, is the root type for all document libraries.

Lists and Libraries

If content types represent the things in a SharePoint site, lists are the containers they are stored in.

■ **Tip** A document library is just a special type of list, so we will often use the term "list" to refer to both.

Supporting Content Types

One thing that is somewhat unique about SharePoint and different from traditional databases is that a list can contain items of different types. For example, the standard Workflow Tasks list that was created in Chapter 4 allows the content types shown in Figure A-11.

Content Types			Add... ^
A content type is a reusable collection of columns and settings that you can apply to your list.			
Name ▲ ▼	Show on New Menu ▼	Default	▼
▦ Request Approval	Yes		
▦ Request Fulfillment	Yes		
▦ Task	Yes	Yes	
▦ Workflow Task (SharePoint 2013)	Yes		

Figure A-11. *Content types supported by the Tasks list*

This is a really handy feature. For instance, a document library can contain different types of documents. The Tasks list is another good example. This allows you to have a single Tasks list that contains different types of tasks. This was demonstrated in Chapter 4.

You can also create a new list and add columns to it without using content types. In this case, a content type definition is inferred from the list definition. This is a quick way to create a custom list.

Views

You can define any number of views for each list. A view usually includes a filter to define a subset of the items in the list. The Tasks list, for example, provides views to show only active tasks or only tasks assigned to the current user. Views can also define a subset of columns that are to be displayed. The views that have been defined for the Workflow Tasks list are enumerated in Figure A-12.

Views			New... ^
Views display list data in prescribed orders and selections.			
Name ▲ ▼	Type ▼	Default	▼
▣ All Tasks	HTML	Yes	
▣ Calendar	CALENDAR		
▣ Completed	HTML		
▣ Gantt Chart	GANTT		
▣ Late Tasks	HTML		
▣ My Tasks	HTML		
▣ Upcoming	HTML		

Figure A-12. *The views defined for the Workflow Tasks list*

View options are best defined using the SharePoint UI, not in SharePoint Designer. A collapsed version of a view definition page in SharePoint is shown in Figure A-13.

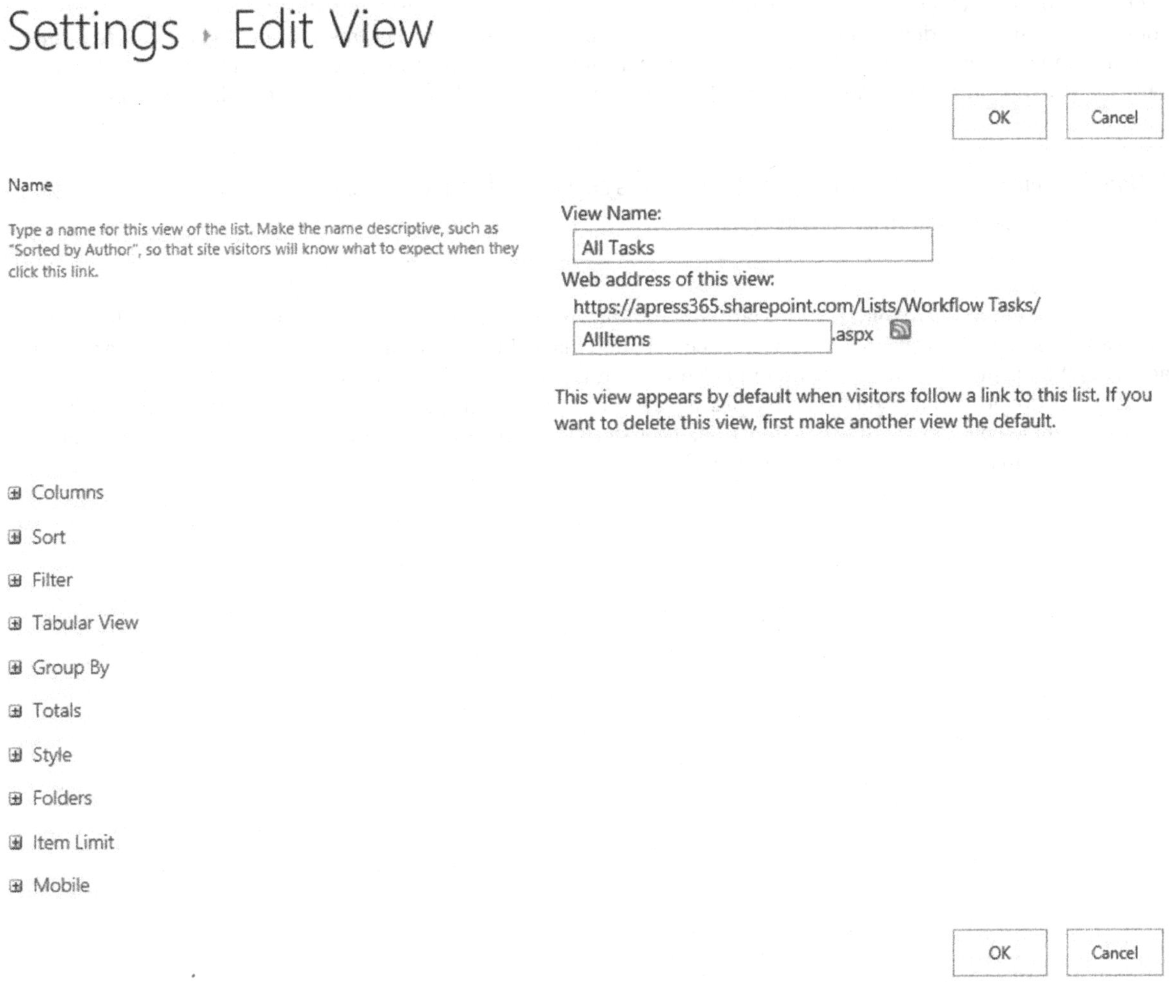

Settings ▸ Edit View

OK   Cancel

Name

Type a name for this view of the list. Make the name descriptive, such as "Sorted by Author", so that site visitors will know what to expect when they click this link.

View Name:

All Tasks

Web address of this view:

https://apress365.sharepoint.com/Lists/Workflow Tasks/

AllItems   .aspx 🔊

This view appears by default when visitors follow a link to this list. If you want to delete this view, first make another view the default.

⊞ Columns

⊞ Sort

⊞ Filter

⊞ Tabular View

⊞ Group By

⊞ Totals

⊞ Style

⊞ Folders

⊞ Item Limit

⊞ Mobile

OK   Cancel

Figure A-13. *Edit View page*

As you can see from the Edit View page, there are a lot of options that you can configure using a view, including sorting, grouping, and subtotals.

Subsites

You can create subsites on a SharePoint server. Site columns and content types are inherited by all subsites. All the columns and content types that are defined by the home site are also available to any subsite. However, any custom column or content type defined on a subsite is not available on the home site. For this reason, it is best to define site columns and content types at the home (or root) site. Subsites can have their own subsites, creating a hierarchy of sites. Lists are not inherited, however. A Tasks list on one site, for example, is not available to child (or sibling) sites.

■ **Note**   Columns, content types, forms, and permissions are inherited from the parent site. Lists and content are not inherited. Reusable workflows are also inherited.

When creating a SharePoint site for a large organization, each department will often have their own subsite so they can manage their own lists and libraries. Keep in mind that column and content type definitions are shared across all the subsites. This is why you should give some thought when defining them.

You can create columns and content types at each subsite as well. If a need is unique to a particular department, you may want to consider creating it at that level. If you do, it will not be available to other subsites. If you think other sites may want to use it, create it in the home site.

APPENDIX B

■ ■ ■

SharePoint Designer's Text-Based Workflow Editor

In Chapter 4, you created a workflow in SharePoint Designer using the Visual Designer view. We showed a brief glimpse of the Text-Based Designer view. Once you get used to the Text-Based view, you may find it to be a more efficient tool for authoring the workflow details. In this appendix, we'll provide a basic overview of the Text-Based editor.

Creating the Workflow Editor Components

The basic building blocks of a declarative workflow are actions and conditions. Actions are the things a workflow does and conditions define the rules that determine when certain actions are performed. These are often combined into stages and steps that help organize the workflow in logical blocks. There are also some special components such as loops and parallel blocks that you can use to control the program.

- Actions – the things a workflow does such as update a list or send an e-mail.

- Conditions – these allow you to perform different processing based on the data or previous outcomes.

- Stages and steps – these enable you to organize a workflow into smaller blocks.

- Special components – provide advanced execution such as loops and parallel processing.

■ **Note** The workflow platform has been completely redesigned in SharePoint 2013. Both 2010 and 2013 workflows are supported but they cannot work together. The actions shown here are for 2013 workflow. If you create a 2010 workflow, the list of actions and conditions will be different.

Actions

Actions are the things your workflow will do, such as create a task, send an e-mail, or update a variable. Figure B-1 shows a partial list of the actions that are available to you.

Figure B-1. *Available actions*

■ **Note**   This figure shows only a partial list of the actions available to you. Refer to Chapter 4 for more information about workflow elements.

These actions correlate with the stencil shapes that you used in Visio. The actions are grouped into categories to help you find the one you need. The first group, called Recent Actions, contains the actions you have used recently. These same actions are also listed in their normal groups. Listing them here makes it easier for you to find actions that you use frequently.

Conditions

Conditions give you the ability to execute actions based on the outcome of previous actions or input parameters. For example, if an item was approved, you may want to perform different actions than if it was rejected. Figure B-2 shows the list of conditions that you can use.

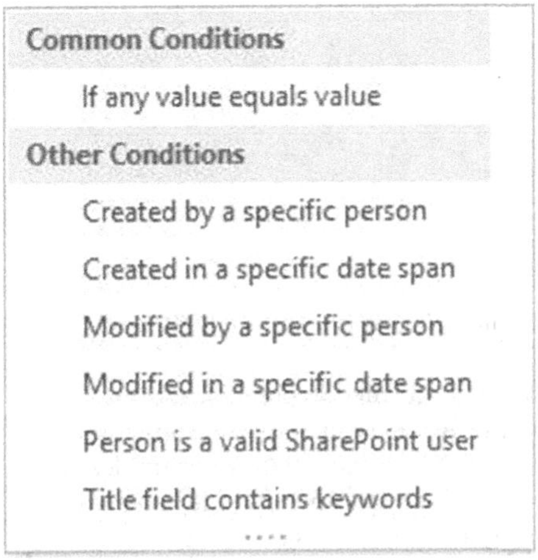

Figure B-2. *Available conditions*

When you insert a condition, the designer creates a line in the workflow starting with If and followed by the condition. Subsequent actions are indented to show that they are performed only if the condition is true. You can also add an Else block, which will be executed if the condition is false.

Stages and Steps

We explained stages in Chapter 4. Within a stage, steps are used to further divide your workflow into smaller blocks that are easy to visualize. When you create a new workflow, the initial implementation contains Stage 1. You can add all of your actions and conditions into this stage. However, for longer workflows, creating additional stages and steps will make your workflow easier to read. Steps can also be nested so a single step can contain other substeps. However, stages cannot be nested.

Special Components

Figure B-3 shows the buttons available on the ribbon for inserting elements.

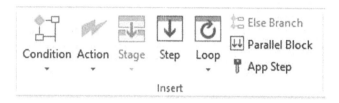

Figure B-3. *Insert section in the Workflows ribbon*

We've explained the Condition, Action, Stage, and Step buttons, but there are a few more buttons that provide some interesting features. A Loop action allows you to execute one or more actions repeatedly. You can either repeat a fixed number of iterations or until a specified condition is true. A sample action is shown in Figure B-4.

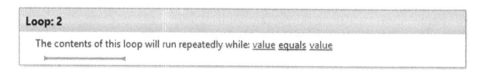

Figure B-4. *A Loop action with condition*

The Else Branch button will create an Else block for an existing condition. Clicking this button while on a condition will create the corresponding Else block.

The Parallel Block button allows you to create a group of actions that are performed in parallel, although not necessarily simultaneously. The default logic is to perform actions sequentially (one at a time). As you start entering actions, you'll notice that the wording on the workflow will indicate how the actions are executed. For example, the second action will be prefixed with the word "then", implying that the second action is started after the first action is completed. However, in parallel blocks, the word "and" is used, indicating they are being started at the same time.

The App Step button creates a new step, just like the Step button, with one important difference. The actions performed in this step are run using the privileges of the registered app. Normally, a workflow is run with the permissions of the user that initiated the workflow. The App Step is used when the workflow must update a list that some users may not have access to to avoid getting access denied errors.

To create an App Step action, you must first enable this feature. Go to the Site Settings page and then click the Manage Site Features link. Scroll to the bottom of this list and find the Workflow can use app permissions feature, shown in Figure B-5. Click the Activate button to enable the feature. You will also need to register the app and configure its privileges. For more information, check out the article at http://msdn.microsoft.com/en-us/library/office/jj822159(v=office.15).aspx.

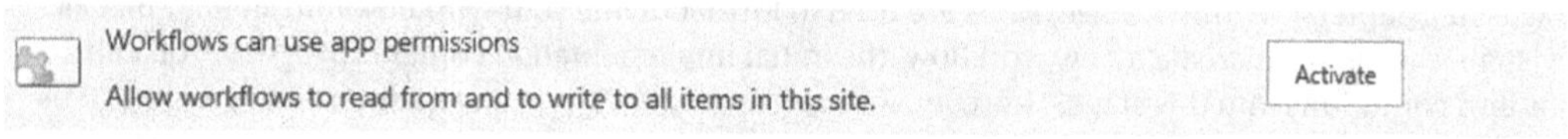

Workflows can use app permissions
Allow workflows to read from and to write to all items in this site.

Activate

Figure B-5. *Enabling the App Step feature*

Using the Editor Features

When you design a workflow, you'll add actions, conditions, and steps to your workflow and then configure them. The workflow editor provides some nice features to help you add the necessary components and then to specify how they are to function.

Using the Insertion Point

You will quickly notice the flashing orange bar, which indicates the insertion point. This indicates where actions, conditions, or steps will be inserted when you click one of the buttons in the ribbon. The flashing orange bar indicates the current insertion point. You can move the insertion point by hovering the mouse pointer over where you want to insert an action, condition, or step. If this is a suitable location, a solid faint orange bar will appear where the mouse pointer is, as demonstrated in Figure B-6.

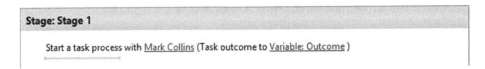

Figure B-6. *Moving the insertion point*

The flashing orange bar (insertion point) is inside Stage 1. If you hover the mouse just below Stage 1, a faint orange bar will appear. If you click it, it will start flashing, indicating that this is now the current insertion point. You can generally move the insertion point to any of the following:

- Between existing actions (to insert a new action or condition).

- After the actions for a condition (to create an Else branch).

- After the last action in a step (to add an action or condition).

- Between existing steps (to insert a new step).

- After the last step (to add a new step).

- Before, after, or between stages to add a new stage.

When you click the insertion point, it will open a search box where you can search for the desired action or condition. For example, click the insertion point, and enter **email**. The designer should look like the one shown in Figure B-7.

> **Stage: Stage 1**
>
> email | ✓ Press Enter to insert Send an Email.

Figure B-7. *Searching for the e-mail action*

■ **Tip** You don't have to click the current insertion point. If you just start typing, it will automatically open up the search box.

This is a really handy feature! As you started typing and entered **em**, it would show that it found 12 actions or conditions. If you press Enter at that point, it would list them for you to select one. By the time you typed **ema**, the search was narrowed down to a single result, and it told you to press Enter to select the matching action. So, by only typing **ema** and pressing Enter, you can add an action to send an e-mail.

Defining Parameters

Most actions and conditions have parameters that you can specify to control its execution. In the Send an Email action, for example, you'll need to specify who the e-mail will go to as well as the subject and body of the e-mail. Parameters in an action or condition are underlined and are displayed as links, as shown in Figure B-8.

Figure B-8. *The Send an Email action with an undefined parameter*

When you click one of these parameter links, the display will change to allow you to specify a value for the parameter. The controls that are made available to you will vary depending on the type of parameter. For most simple parameters, the display will look like Figure B-9.

Figure B-9. *Editor changed to accept input*

The link has changed into a text box and two buttons. This provides three ways for this information to be entered. For fixed text, you can simply type it in the text box. If you want to use a column, parameter, or variable defined in SharePoint, use the lookup (fx) button to provide a Lookup dialog box, as shown in Figure B-10.

Figure B-10. *The Lookup dialog box*

This third option is to click the button with the ellipses. Click this button, and the String Builder dialog box will appear. This allows you to combine static text along with dynamic data stored in SharePoint. To add dynamic data, put the cursor where you want the data inserted and click the Add or Change Lookup button. This will display the same Lookup dialog, as shown in Figure B-11.

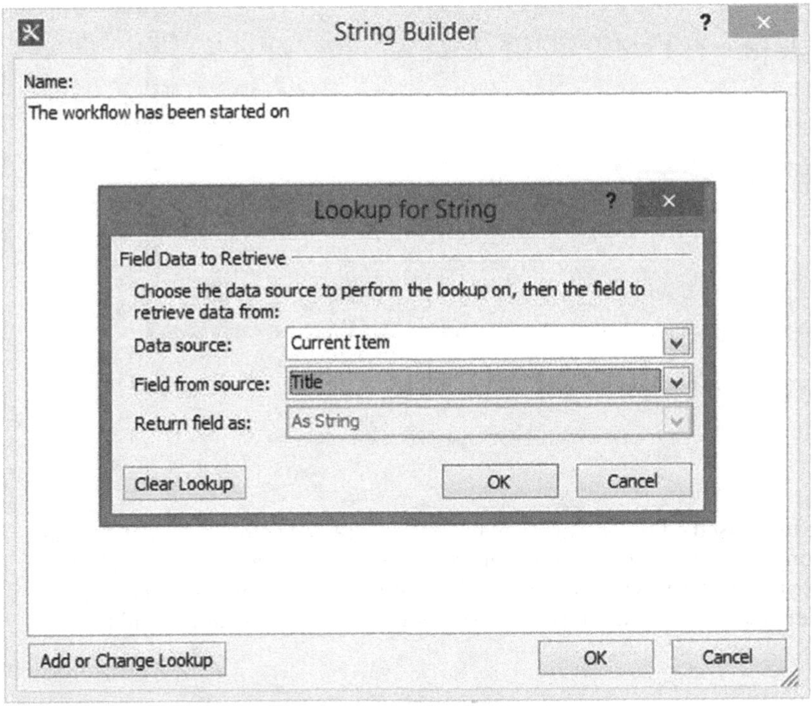

Figure B-11. *Using the String Builder dialog box*

Complex parameters will display a dialog box that allows you to define multiple values. The these users link in the Send an Email action, for example, will display the Define E-mail Message dialog box shown in Figure B-12. This is used to specify the recipients as well as the subject and body of the e-mail.

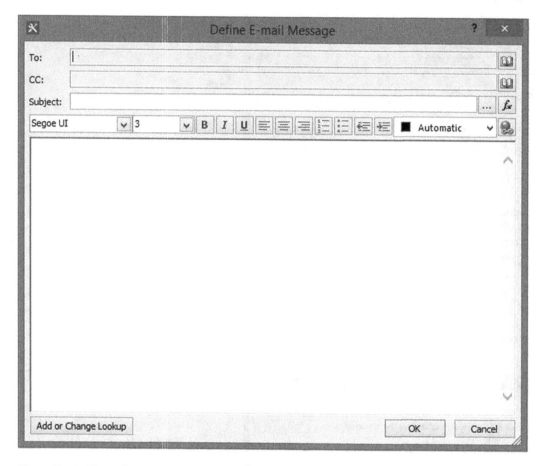

Figure B-12. *The Define E-mail Message dialog box*

Summary

Workflows that are created with the text-based editor are identical to the ones created using the visual designer. You have the same actions, conditions, and other components available to you. You can also switch back and forth between editors. For example, you can start a workflow using Visio, edit it with the text-based editor, and then finish up with Visio. The text-based editor may take a little getting used to but you might find it more efficient to work in.

Index

Get the eBook for only $10!

Now you can take the weightless companion with you anywhere, anytime. Your purchase of this book entitles you to 3 electronic versions for only $10.

This Apress title will prove so indispensible that you'll want to carry it with you everywhere, which is why we are offering the eBook in 3 formats for only $10 if you have already purchased the print book.

Convenient and fully searchable, the PDF version enables you to easily find and copy code—or perform examples by quickly toggling between instructions and applications. The MOBI format is ideal for your Kindle, while the ePUB can be utilized on a variety of mobile devices.

Go to www.apress.com/promo/tendollars to purchase your companion eBook.

Apress®
THE EXPERT'S VOICE™